Advancing Science Education: the first fifty years of the Association for Science Education

Editors: Edgar Jenkins and Valerie Wood-Robinson

The **Association**
for **Science Education**
Promoting excellence in science teaching and learning

Published by the Association for Science Education,
College Lane, Hatfield, Herts AL10 9AA

ISBN: 978 0 86357 433 7

Design and page layout: Commercial Campaigns

Printed by: Ashford Colour Press, Gosport, Hampshire

Contents

It was largely due to the achievements of Britain's scientists and engineers during, what has become known as, the Industrial Revolution that Britain did so well as the workshop of the world.

Times have changed, but our national prosperity remains in the hands of our scientists and engineers. Their potential can only be discovered and nurtured within an inspiring and challenging system of science education.

It therefore gives me the greatest pleasure to offer my congratulations to all members of The Association for Science Education on the occasion of its 50th anniversary celebrations. It can certainly look back in satisfaction on what has been achieved under difficult circumstances. The challenge is to keep up the momentum over the next fifty years.

Notes on Contributors

Derek Bell has been both Chair of ASE and Chief Executive. He has extensive experience of teaching and learning in science, having taught in schools and higher education institutions and undertaken science education research and curriculum development. He was a member of the SPACE (Science Processes and Concept Exploration) Project team based at the University of Liverpool and co-ordinated the Nuffield Primary Science Project. He recently stepped down as Head of Education at The Wellcome Trust. Derek remains active in science education, across the United Kingdom and internationally, through his education consultancy, committee and advisory work. He was awarded his professorship by the College of Teachers in July 2007 and an Honorary Doctorate of Education by Manchester Metropolitan University in July 2012.

Peter Borrows has an MA from Cambridge University and later did a PhD, part-time, whilst teaching. He taught in various secondary schools in London, becoming Head of Science and Senior Teacher, then becoming Science Adviser in Waltham Forest. Subsequently he was Director of CLEAPSS, until 'retiring' in 2007. Peter joined the ASE in 1963 whilst doing a PGCE at King's College London. He has been Chair of three different ASE Region Committees. He was Honorary Treasurer of the Association and a member of ASE Council and a trustee from 2007 to 2012. He has been a member of Safeguards in Science Committee since 1966, serving as its Chair for 21 years, and has been actively involved in all its publications. He was also a member of the Chemical Nomenclature Working Party and involved with a number of other groups and projects. Peter went to his first Annual Meeting in 1968 and has attended all but a handful since then, running activities at many of them.

Jane Hanrott has the dubious distinction of being the first non-scientist to hold a senior position at ASE Headquarters, having graduated with a Master's degree in Linguistics. She joined Headquarters staff first in 1977 as an assistant to the Journals Manager, re-joined after her degree in 1984 and, following several years in charge of the ASE's publishing arm, went part-time after starting a family. Jane now holds the post of Journals Co-ordinator and Executive Editor of *Education in Science*. In her extensive time as a member of HQ staff, Jane has worked with four Chief Executives and has seen many developments. She appreciated the opportunity to collaborate with John Lawrence, as the two longest-serving members of HQ staff, to look back over the years and reflect on what ASE has achieved, 'from the inside'.

Wynne Harlen has a physics degree from Oxford, and an MA(Ed) and PhD from Bristol University. She was ASE President in 2009 and is an Honorary Member. Wynne took a leading role in several influential primary science projects, became a Professor of Science Education at Liverpool University and then Director of the Scottish Council for Research in Education. She acts as a consultant to various UK and international science projects. She was Chair of the PISA expert group for science and now chairs a major international committee on the development of inquiry-based science education. Wynne was a member of the Secretary of State's original working group on the creation of the national curriculum in science. She has been awarded honours for her distinguished services to science education: the OBE in 1991, a special award by ASE in 2001, and in 2008 the Purkwa prize for science, with which she funded an international seminar and the resulting *Principles and Big Ideas of Science Education* (ASE, 2010). She is the author of several books on primary science and on assessment and edited two editions of the *ASE Guide to Primary Science Education* (2006, 2011).

Martin Hollins has a first class degree from Birmingham University and a PhD from Imperial College, London. He has a PGCE and has taught in schools and colleges in Malawi, Surrey and London, and at Roehampton University. He was Director of the North London Science Centre for teachers and has directed school science curriculum projects at Bath University and at the BBC. He was a science adviser, then science team leader, at the Qualifications and Curriculum Authority from 1997–2005. Martin now works as an independent education consultant on a range of projects across the STEM spectrum including evaluations of the Science Learning Centre Network, and is a trustee of AstraZeneca Science Teaching Trust. He has authored and edited many publications, including the ASE journal *Primary Science* and the *ASE Guide to Secondary Science Education* (2011). Martin has been a member of ASE for 40 years and was created an Honorary Member in 2006.

Edgar Jenkins taught chemistry in secondary schools in Leeds and the former West Riding of Yorkshire before joining the University of Leeds where he became Professor of Science Education Policy, Head of the School of Education and Director of the Centre for Studies in Science and Mathematics Education. He is the author of numerous articles and books concerned with the social and political history of school science education. Edgar joined the SMA as a PGCE student in 1961 and has been a member of ASE since its inception. He is particularly supportive of his Region. Recently he authored *75 Years and More:*

The Association for Science Education in Yorkshire and was presented with Honorary Membership of the Yorkshire and Humberside Region.

John Lawrence went to Salford University for his BSc, then to Cambridge for his PGCE (where he was persuaded to become a student member of the ASE), then to Chelsea College in London to take an MPhil. John taught chemistry in Essex and in Redbridge, during which time he was an active member and officer of Region 18. He joined ASE Headquarters staff as Assistant Secretary in 1989, becoming Deputy General Secretary in 1991. John's current responsibilities include 'Corporate Operations' and he is Director of Finance. In addition, he is Registrar for Chartered Science Teacher, Registered Scientist and Registered Science Technician status. He is married to the Chair of the Association 2013.

Liz Lawrence was a medical student in Cardiff before transferring to a BEd course for primary and middle school science and maths. She taught in NE London and Essex for 14 years before becoming an advisory teacher for primary science and technology. For most of her career she has been active in ASE, holding various section and region officer posts and chairing Primary Science Committee before becoming Chair-elect. She presents at local and national conferences and has contributed to several ASE projects and publications including *Be safe!, It's not fair – or is it?* and Getting Practical. She was one of the first ASE members to be awarded CSciTeach.

Katie Mackenzie Stuart read Zoology at Exeter University. She went with VSO to teach Maths and Physics in Kenya, then English as well. In 1982, she joined the African and Caribbean Division of Longman Publishers, as a desk editor on English, Maths and Science textbooks. She moved to Collins Educational in 1984, to commission books for international markets and then science titles for UK schools. Following her move to John Murray, Katie was the Science Publisher for 14 years, continuing when the company was acquired by Hodder Education. In 2011, at Hodder, she took up the newly created role of Teacher Event Manager, running workshops for teachers around the world.

David Moore joined ASE in 1966 on the recommendation of his head of department, and never regretted it. While progressing through his school teaching career, he became a member of the Education (Research) committee in 1981, and became the Honorary Annual Meeting Secretary in 1982. David has not missed an Annual Meeting since then. In 1988, while he was a secondary school Deputy Head and Chair-Elect of the Association, David was appointed to the position of General Secretary. His achievements in this post are detailed in Chapter 2. David was awarded the OBE in 2002 for 'services to science education' and feels it is for the whole Association in recognition of the work we do.

Malcolm Oakes created and directed ASE INSET Services from 1991–2006, bringing a wide range of experience. Graduating from Birmingham University, he taught in four Birmingham schools and was active in the West Midlands Region. He became Head of Biology at the Birmingham Science Centre moving on to become a Project Officer for the Secondary Science Curriculum Review and then joining the science team of the Consortium for Assessment and Testing at King's College London writing the first SATS. He helped create the Midland Examining Group's (MEG) first biology GCSE syllabuses and was Chief Examiner for MEG GCSE Science in Society. From 1989–1994 he was Honorary Annual Meetings Secretary and for five years was ASE Field Officer for the Midlands.

Phil Ramsden graduated and took a PGCE at Leeds University before teaching chemistry and science in comprehensive schools in Derbyshire and Leeds. He returned to his alma mater to take an MA in Science Education and subsequently became Advisory Teacher and then Adviser for Science in Sheffield. He has been active in ASE throughout his career and was Chair of the Association in 1993/4, and is now an Honorary Member. He was for 15 years the ASE Field Officer for Yorkshire and Humberside and has also served for five years as Honorary Annual Conference Secretary. Phil has been involved with various science education projects such as the Royal Society Partnership Scheme. Currently he tutors ITT students for the University of Leeds.

Annette Smith took up the post of Chief Executive at the Association for Science Education in March 2009. Prior to this she was Director of Regions with the British Association for the Advancement of Science, with responsibilities relating to young people. She has a Physics degree from the University of Liverpool, a PGCE and a Masters in Science Education. Annette has wide experience of science education and public engagement, with teaching experience in adult and further education as well as in secondary school science. She has been a lecturer in primary science education, a laboratory technician and has worked in environmental health physics and safety in industry. Recently, she was President of the European Science Events Association (EUSCEA) and she is a Fellow of the Institute of Physics.

Valerie Wood-Robinson took her degree and her PGCE at Cambridge University, then taught in Nigeria, Canterbury and London. Subsequently, in Leeds, she taught, and trained teachers, in various schools, colleges and Universities. At the University of Leeds she took her MA Education and worked at CLIS on the project that became Making Sense of Secondary Science. Following a spell as Science Adviser in Sunderland, she undertook consultancy and curriculum development, including the AKSIS Project at King's College London. As a student, Valerie attended AWST/SMA meetings, and she has been an ASE member since 1964, with committee and officer roles in Regions 4 and 1. Serving on Publications Committee for 12 years, she is currently the Chair. She has co-authored or edited several books including the *ASE Guide to Secondary Science Education* (2011).

Acknowledgements

We are grateful to Stuart Farmer for information about science curriculum developments in Scotland and the contribution made by members in the Scottish Region/ASE Scotland.

We thank the following people for their time and patience as they were interviewed by the authors and Editors, or as they contributed information in response to our enquiries. People named as authors or contributors in 'Notes on Contributors' are not acknowledged again below, although several made inputs into a number of chapters other than those attributed to them.

Duncan Alexander
Geoff Auty
David Barlex
Paul Black
Jenifer Burden
Marianne Cutler
Suzanne Dickinson
Rebecca Dixon-Watmough
Colin DuQueno
Mark Ellis
Bob Fairbrother
Rosemary Feasey
Don Foster
Alastair Gittner
Anne Goldsworthy
John Holman
Sue Howarth
Pauline Hoyle
Andrew Hunt
Roger McCune

Edith McLean
Caroline McGrath
Peter Merriman
Dick Orton
Claire Pearson
Andy Piggott
Daniel Sandford Smith
Miranda Simond
Steve Smyth
Dennis Sutton
David Tawney
Jeff Thomson
John Tranter
Anthony Tomei
Catherine Wilson
The Technicians' Committee
Staff in the Special Collections
    part of the Brotherton Library,
    University of Leeds

We thank the following photographers, and are grateful to all the unidentified photographers whose anonymous work has been retrieved from ASE archives and *Interpreters of Science: A History of the Association for Science Education* by Layton, D.

Michelle McGaughey (Figure 6.2), Siobhan Tolson (Figure 4.1), Ralph Whitcher (Figure 7.2), Valerie Wood-Robinson (Figure 5.8).

Introduction

In 1984, the ASE and John Murray published David Layton's magisterial history of the Association since its origins in two separate organisations, the Association of Public School Science Masters and the Association of Women Science Teachers. This remains the first port of call for anyone who wishes to acquire a scholarly understanding of how ASE came into being and of the first 20 or so years of its history. The present volume takes the story of the Association beyond 1984 but it differs in several important respects from this earlier work, most obviously as a multi-authored volume. Each of the authors is not only a long-standing member of the Association but can call upon experience of close involvement with a particular aspect of its work, often over many years.

Multiple authorship, however, presents a number of problems if the final outcome is to have some coherence as a book, rather than offer the reader a series of disconnected articles. This is especially the case when, as here, each author was invited to write about a particular aspect of the work of the Association and each, inevitably, has written about matters that he or she judges significant and likely to be of interest to the reader. This approach is not without risks. Inevitably certain events and initiatives are so significant as to have implications for all aspects of the Association's activities, with the potential for overlap in the contents of individual chapters or even discrepant details recalled about the same events. In addition, some important events or issues may be overlooked because they fall outside the chapter boundaries and the reader may fail to gain a sense of the work of the organisation as a whole, while the differences in authors' writing styles may detract from a coherent understanding.

An important part of our work as Editors has been to address these and other problems, whether actual or potential. Our task has been made easier than we might have anticipated by the courtesy with which authors have greeted our suggested changes, emendations or additions. It is neither an easy nor a welcome prospect to abandon or substantially revise text that has been carefully and painstakingly constructed, the more so when the author has been much more intimately involved with the topic under discussion than either of the Editors. We therefore thank most warmly all those whose work appears here, both for that courtesy and for their willingness to devote time and effort to preparing and revising the chapters that appear in this volume. We also wish to emphasise that this is very much a collaborative project, with all the authors commenting on their colleagues' work, and with many other people contributing, as acknowledged on page xiii. How far we have succeeded in overcoming the problems of editing a multi-authored account of the first 50 years of the Association for Science Education, only the reader can decide.

Unlike David Layton's study, the invitation from the Council of the Association to prepare this book was prompted by a particular landmark in the history of ASE, namely its 50th 'birthday' in 2013. This may appear anomalous to those readers who recall the Centenary celebrations in 2001, but that anniversary commemorated the inauguration, in 1901, of the older of the two main science teachers' organisations that eventually merged to form ASE. Chapter 1 of this book reviews the forerunners of the Association and the events that led to its formation in 1963. Each of the subsequent Chapters 2–7, charts the 50 years of the ASE through a particular context and perspective. Chapter 8, in profiling the partnerships and projects with which the Association has been involved, inevitably refers to some items from previous chapters but serves to provide a coherent overview of the influence of the ASE. In the Postscript, the editors, CEO and Chair offer some brief personal comments about some of the future challenges facing the Association.

The half-century of achievements of the Association as set out in the following pages rightly have something of a celebratory quality. The contributions that ASE has made to science education, particularly but not exclusively in the UK, are impossible to over-estimate and there is much to be proud of. We hope that anyone reading this book will share in that sense of pride, as well as the understanding that no organisation can survive and flourish for half a century amid massive changes both in schools and their curricula, without encountering problems and challenges. Inevitably, not all of these problems and challenges have been overcome as successfully or as quickly as might have been desired, and we have made no attempt to disguise this fact.

Throughout the text, readers will find reference to many of the publications (books, journals, and, recently, web-based resources) produced by ASE, solely or in partnership, which the writers find significant in the context of their chapters. These items are only a sample of the output of hundreds of ASE publications over the period of 50 years. Limitations of space prevent listing them all, or their authors, most of whom contributed their writing and editing work for no financial recompense.

Naming or picturing individuals in the text may be seen as invidious and the reader may feel that the authors and editors have omitted the names and photographs of many worthy of mention. There are many hundreds, if not thousands, whose names do not appear in this book but whose commitment to the Association and to science education have made possible all that ASE has been able to do over the past 50 years. These are the members of the Association who serve as Officers of the Association or as members of committees and working parties, and those who give their scarce time to prepare ASE publications and organise or attend local, sectional, regional or national meetings. Many of these meetings are held in the evenings after school, at locations that require travel and at times of the year when the weather is often more conducive to remaining at home. Yet the overall level of voluntary attendance by science teachers and their technician colleagues has remained high throughout the history of the Association. It is a powerful indication of the level of their dedication that is perhaps not always as appreciated as it might be. In a very real sense, therefore, this book is a tribute to all these often unnamed individuals, without whom ASE could not function. Their true legacy, however, lies not in the chapters of this book but in the contributions they have made, in various ways, to the professional development of science teachers and to the advancement of science education.

We are also aware that limitations of space have allowed us to do less than justice to the role of the Branch, Section and Regional structure of the Association upon which much of the work of the ASE is based. This applies especially in the case of Scotland and Northern Ireland where the history and structure of schooling differ markedly from the rest of the UK. It is a limitation that deserves to be overcome by a number of more localised studies.

Throughout that half-century of remarkable change, the ASE has been extremely fortunate to have as its Patron, HRH The Duke of Edinburgh. The long-standing commitment of The Duke of Edinburgh to the advancement of science, technology and engineering is well-known and, as some of the following chapters indicate, he has maintained a close interest in the work of the Association and been a strong supporter of many of its activities. It is therefore entirely appropriate that this account of the history of the ASE gratefully acknowledges the contribution he has made to the work of the Association and, more generally, to the promotion of scientific and technological education.

ASE has, of course, changed, profoundly in many ways since it was formed in 1963. In particular, its governance and management have become much more professional, with salaried officials undertaking work that was once done, at least in part, by working school teachers. Even so, it remains the case that much of the help and advice that is available at ASE meetings is provided by fellow members of the Association. It is equally true that the history of ASE mirrors the history of school science education in the United Kingdom, a history that it has helped to shape. As an organisation now open to all with an interest in science education, the Association is well-placed to continue to fulfil that role, although is likely to have to do so as the school systems and science curricula of the constituent parts of the UK become increasingly diverse.

Finally, we wish to express our thanks to the Council of ASE for the invitation to prepare this volume to mark the 50th anniversay of ASE and to those authors who, in turn, agreed to contribute. We also warmly thank the professional publications staff of ASE who co-operated with us so agreeably: Jane Hanrott who acted as copy-editor and Donna Evans the Publications Manager, who has patiently and carefully managed the project to bring the text to fruition in the form of this volume.

Edgar Jenkins
Valerie Wood-Robinson

November 2012

Figure 1.1: *A group of former Officers of the Association. From left to right: Frances Eastwood, Chairman 1964; Ernest Coulson, Chairman 1969; John McGeachin, Chairman of the SMA 1961; Helen Ward, Chairman 1970; Bertie Broad, Chairman 1966 and Don Harlow, Annual Meeting Secretary 1961–67. (From* Education in Science, *January 1985).*

1 Creating an Association for Science Education

Edgar Jenkins

'The question is always being asked, especially by visitors from abroad, "Why do you have two Associations?"
The answer is very simple – it's just a historical fact.'

J.S.G. McGeachin 1962

'Inevitable' is a word that historians normally use with caution when seeking to account for the events of the past: 'likely', 'predictable' and 'understandable' are among the adjectives more commonly deployed. Nonetheless, this is how David Layton described the formation of the Association for Science Education (ASE) in 1963 in his account of the merger of the Science Masters' Association (SMA) and the Association of Women Science Teachers (AWST) that took place in that year (Layton, 1984: 104). Who were the individuals involved and what were the circumstances that led Layton to this judgement?

The two organisations from which ASE was formed differed in a number of important respects, not least in their history. The SMA owed its origins to the Association of Public School Science Masters (APSSM), set up as the result of an initiative taken by four science masters at Eton College at the beginning of the twentieth century. On 14th May 1900, T.C. Porter, W.D. Eggar, M.D. Hill and H. de Haviland were the joint signatories to a letter sent to the science staff of 57 schools, suggesting that a conference of public school science masters be arranged to consider several aspects of science teaching in public schools, including the way in which science should be taught. Following a planning meeting in November 1900, details of the conference programme were sent to all schools in *The Public Schools Yearbook* and the conference was duly held in London in January 1901. It concluded with the passing of a resolution, proposed by M.D. Hill, which led to the formal creation a year later of the APSSM. Those who attended this 1901 meeting became the core of the new organisation which, a further year on, had 68 members, drawn from 44 public schools.

The origins of the AWST were very different and lie in the Association of Assistant Mistresses in Public Secondary Schools (AAM), established in 1884. In the early years of the twentieth century, the AAM increasingly turned its attention to the science education of girls, generally regarded as presenting a number of issues that did not arise in the case of boys. Unlike the APSSM, the AAM was organised on a regional basis and, in 1909, the London Branch formed a special Science Section with its membership open to any member of the Branch. Two years later, sufficient interest had been shown in the work of the Science Section to consider the establishment of a larger science teachers' association. An inaugural meeting, held in November 1912 and addressed by H.E. Armstrong, led to the formation of The Association of Science Teachers (AST) and to the subsequent separation of the new Association from the parent AAM. The six objectives of the Association were agreed at this meeting and they remained unchanged throughout the life of the AST and the AWST, into which, for reasons given below, it metamorphosed in 1922.

These objectives differed in several significant ways from those of the APSSM, although both associations acknowledged the need to improve communication between science teachers in schools and their counterparts in the universities. For the APSSM, the principal concern was the promotion of natural science in the curriculum of the public schools from which its members were drawn, along with the establishment of links between them and the examining

Figure 1.2: Two future Presidents of the AST, on the staff of Newnham College in 1896. Miss M. Greenwood (circled, seated), later as Mrs Bidder, President 1915 and Miss E.R. Saunders (circled, standing), President 1917 and 1918.

bodies. The AST, in contrast, could afford to be less concerned with promoting science in the school curriculum, since the practical teaching of science in the grant-aided secondary schools, in which many of its members taught, was guaranteed by the annual Regulations issued by the Board of Education created in 1899. Its objectives therefore were drawn much more widely. They included *'affording opportunities for intercourse and co-operation among those interested in the teaching of science'*, providing *'an authoritative medium through which the opinions of science teachers may be expressed on educational questions'*, discussing *'methods of teaching science'*, and co-operation with *'other Associations for special correlation of subjects'* (quoted in Layton, *op.cit.* 38). There was, however, no reference to 'links with examining bodies' and the Association took no significant interest in this field until the establishment of the system of School Certificate examinations at the end of the First World War. The category 'others interested in the teaching of science' was capable of broad interpretation and the AST actively sought co-operation with organisations representing the teaching of other subjects. Unlike the APSSM, therefore, the AST readily accepted invitations to hold its annual meeting in conjunction with the Conference of Educational Associations, first held in 1913. For the AST, the 'correlation of subjects' involved more than the mathematics and science of particular concern to the APSSM: of more immediate concern was the relation of science to the domestic subjects, which constituted a significant component of the curriculum in girls' schools. The AST also differed from the APSSM in giving more attention to the initial professional training and continued professional development of science teachers, one of its earliest initiatives being the setting up of a sub-committee to investigate and report on the training of women science graduates for teaching.

The different origins and objectives of the two associations were mirrored in their membership. Whereas membership of the APSSM was restricted to men teaching science in public schools or others who had *'contributed to the advancement of science in such schools'*, the AST placed no restriction on either gender or type of educational institution. The APSSM was particularly strict in enforcing its membership rules: an application in 1908 for membership from a science teacher at King Edward VII School, Lytham, was refused on the grounds that more time was needed to see how the school might develop. By 1918, 82.1% of the 308 members of the APSSM were teaching in public schools and, for much of the rest of the twentieth century, public school science teachers were to play a dominant role in the work of its successor organisation, the SMA. Although the governing committee of the AST was likewise drawn from a small number of leading girls' secondary schools, men were allowed to become members of the Association and, although always in a minority, they played a significant role in its work, especially at Branch level. Many members of the AST taught in teacher training colleges and, when the Articles of the Association were revised in 1916, membership became open to any science teacher in any type of school, including public elementary schools. By 1918, the AST had 200 members, a figure which, along with the 308 APSSM members (above), needs to be placed in the context of the 1500 members of the Classical Association and the 1100 of the Modern Language Association. The APSSM was unique in being the only subject teaching association open purely to men.

Exploring co-operation

In August 1916, partly in response to the lobbying of a self-appointed 'Neglect of Science Committee', the Prime Minister appointed a committee to *'enquire into the position occupied by natural science in the educational system of Great Britain'* (Jenkins, 1973). The APSSM and the AST were both official witnesses before this committee, each being represented by four members of their respective Associations. This 'Prime Ministerial committee', chaired by Sir J.J. Thomson, PRS, was followed by three others appointed to enquire into the position of other subjects, including classics, where the two science Associations were once again invited to express their views. In offering evidence to these committees about school science on behalf of their members, it was obviously important to avoid expressing opinions that were in conflict, a fact that clearly suggested that closer collaboration between the two Associations would be desirable.

Collaboration was also encouraged by the growth of advanced, i.e. sixth form, courses in science prompted by the availability of grants from the Board of Education. Although controversial at first, the number of such courses increased rapidly after the First World War. In the year 1918–19, 140 advanced courses were recognised in science and mathematics, 26 in classics and 76 in modern studies. By 1924–25, the numbers had increased to 212, 36 and 177 respectively, the increase in science and mathematics being mostly in boys' schools. The development of these courses focused attention on the relationship of such advanced work with the first year of undergraduate study, which became an ongoing concern to members of both the APSSM and the AST. The AST took the initiative in establishing a Consultative Council of University and School Teachers to consider the relationship between the advanced work increasingly being done at school and that offered in higher education. In the event, this achieved little, principally because of a lack of interest and support from the university side.

Collaboration, however, was not at this stage the main concern of the APSSM. As it became increasingly clear that the Association was simply one of several organisations invited by government to express an opinion about the form, content and assessment of school science, the APSSM sought to broaden its own membership to become more representative of school science teachers. Accordingly, the Business Meeting of the Association in January 1918 considered a recommendation to replace the rule requiring applicants for membership to work in public schools by a requirement that the aim and interests of the applicant be similar to those of members of the Association. A further recommendation sought to seek power from the next General Meeting to offer membership to a maximum of 20 science masters from schools *'different from our own'*. These recommendations were strenuously opposed by some members of the APSSM, an amendment in favour of the *status quo* being defeated by only one vote. The Business Meeting eventually voted to allow up to ten members from 'different' schools. Nonetheless, almost a year later on 31st December 1918 and no doubt increasingly aware that men were eligible to join the AST, the General Meeting of the Association changed its membership rules to admit any science master in a secondary school who had either a university degree or its equivalent, or was registered with the Teachers' Registration Council. At a committee meeting the following day, the birth of The Science Masters' Association was formally noted and recorded in red ink at the top of a page in the Minute Book.

It was, however, as the APSSM that a decision was made in July 1918 to publish a journal, *The School Science Review*[1], in order to keep its growing membership in touch with advances in science and with recent developments in science teaching. The cost implications of such a venture for a small organisation were considerable and strenuous efforts were made by the Editor, G.H.J. Adlam, to build up an economically viable circulation when the journal was launched in 1919. An offer was thus made to the AST to provide its members with copies of the journal at a cost of six shillings (c.30p.) per annum, the AST itself bearing the cost of distributing *SSR* to its members, collecting the subscriptions and transmitting the income to the Treasurer of the SMA. A year later, when Adlam was asked by the AST if the journal could be sent directly to AST members, he responded by offering a direct distribution at a cost of seven shillings per annum, or five shillings if all the members of the AST would agree to receive the journal. As the latter would have required an increase in the annual subscription, the matter was considered at the General Meeting of the AST in January 1922. The response of the meeting was cautious, partly because it was felt that the contents of *SSR* were almost exclusively concerned with physics and chemistry, to the neglect of the biological sciences that featured prominently in the

---

[1]*The School Science Review* is now known as *School Science Review*. The two terms and the abbreviation *SSR* are used interchangeably throughout this book.

curricula of girls' schools. Further necessary discussions took place at a meeting in March of the same year. At that meeting, Adlam and C.L. Bryant (Harrow School) suggested that the name of the AST should appear alongside that of the SMA on the cover of *SSR* and that the AST might have a representative on the advisory committee of the journal. Moreover, each issue would carry a full-page advertisement giving information about the AST, including the names of its officers and committee members, as well as details of its meetings and publications.

The offer from the SMA, however, carried two stipulations. First, the appointment of the Editor of the journal was to remain the exclusive right of the SMA. Secondly, and arguably of even greater importance, the rules and title of the AST were to be changed to exclude men from membership. The benefits of such an arrangement to the SMA are perhaps more immediately obvious than those to the AST. However, the latter had no journal of its own and it was less well-known than the SMA with its strong connections with the leading universities, public schools and examination authorities. It is thus perhaps not too surprising that when a recommendation embodying the terms offered by the SMA was considered by the General Meeting of the AST in July 1922 it was carried unanimously. As a gesture of goodwill, a further resolution allowed that members of the SMA, which had no Branch structure at this time, would be eligible for Branch membership of the organisation henceforth to be known as the Association of Women Science Teachers (AWST).

The inter-war years

1922 marked the beginning of 40 years of collaborative but separate existence on the part of the two principal science teaching organisations, the SMA and the AWST. Unfortunately, it is somewhat easier to identify aspects of the separate existence rather than the co-operation, except for a small number of major issues of common concern. This is partly because of the limited availability of documentary and other sources, partly because the two organisations operated in significantly different ways and partly because, where collaboration occurred, much of it was at the local level and often unrecorded save in Branch Minutes, many of which have not survived. It is also the case that, when the admission of men to the Branch membership of the AWST was agreed in 1922, neither Association seems to have wanted to move towards establishing a genuinely mixed organisation. According to the SMA Annual Report of that year, *'The admission of women to the SMA has been suggested but never pressed'*. Interestingly, the SMA concluded that, if the question had been put to a full meeting of its membership, *'it might have been carried, but only in the face of strong opposition'* (SMA, 1922: 51). Not surprisingly, the SMA Committee took the view that two separate associations, working amicably together, were better than one. Such a view no doubt reflected the opinion, expressed by Adlam when the merger was under discussion, that *'a weak association'* wanted to *'tack itself onto a stronger'* (quoted in Layton, *op.cit.*: 47). It would be easy but unjust to dismiss Adlam's opinion as mere sexism, since it was widely accepted at the time that the scientific education and career aspirations of boys and girls differed in important ways. His opinion also needs to be set alongside the comments made many years later by Miss M.W. Sutton, the retiring President of the AWST. Having joined the AWST in 1925, she used her Presidential Address in 1949 to tell members that: *'Some people have thought and may still feel that we ought to have amalgamated with the Science Masters...I think many would agree with me that that would not be to our best advantage. I personally feel that the aims of the women teaching science to girls is [sic] so different from that of men teaching boys, that we could not do ourselves much good by joining with them. We should be in a very small minority and our own interests would not be furthered'.* (AWST, 1950: 14).

Nonetheless, it is difficult to avoid the suggestion that Adlam, along with at least some members of the SMA Committee, regarded the AWST as a somewhat inferior organisation to his own Association.

Whether inferior or simply different, both the SMA and the AWST increased their membership substantially during the inter-war years. In 1921,

Figure 1.3: *SMA Annual Meeting group, Oxford 1926.*

the SMA had 600 members. By 1938, this number had increased to 2664. The corresponding numbers for the AST/AWST are 360 and 900, although in the case of both organisations the precise numbers need to be treated with caution because of the ongoing difficulties that each faced in maintaining accurate records. The difference in the size of the two organisations had financial implications. As early as 1925, the SMA committee was obliged to consider how best to invest part of a large annual surplus of income over expenditure. Two years later, it was able to pay an honorarium to the Editor of *SSR* and subsequently to do so for the other officers of the Association. The financial resources of the AWST were much more limited and it struggled to provide the secretarial assistance needed as its own activities increased, despite not having to bear the cost of producing *SSR*. It was not until 1944 that the four elected honorary secretaries of the AWST were replaced by a salaried appointed official.

The different perspectives of the AWST and the SMA on school science education are clearly evident in the responses of the two organisations to the development of general science as a component of the secondary school curriculum. The origins of this curriculum initiative lay in a discussion in the General Committee of the APSSM as far back as May 1916. Prompted by the fact that not all the students to whom they taught science went on to more advanced scientific studies, members of the Committee drew a distinction between 'formal' science and 'general' science. The precise nature of the latter was unclear save that it would be broader in its scope than the specialised courses currently taught and would attempt to *'awaken interest in and an appreciation of the possibilities of natural science'* (APSSM, 1916). Although the Committee was divided over the merits of such a general course, some members regarding it as having no educational value and constituting a poor subject for examination, the need to develop a clear statement of fact, policy and principle became pressing with the setting up of the Thomson Committee (see above) a few months later. On 7th October, the General Committee approved a text to guide the four members of the APSSM when they appeared before the government committee. It also set up a sub-committee to provide the details of the kind of science course that should be available to all pupils in public schools, whose work culminated in a report entitled *Science for All*. Published as a separate pamphlet, it also appeared, in part, in the report of a committee appointed by the British Association for the Advancement of Science (BAAS) charged with investigating *'the method and substance of science teaching in secondary schools, with particular reference to its essential place in general education'* (BAAS, 1917: 1 ix). Published in 1917, this report accepted the distinction between 'formal' and 'general' science, an acceptance that reflected the fact that, unlike the Thomson Committee, almost all the members of this committee were science teachers and that, among them, were three members of the APSSM and two members of the AST. In addition, its chairman, Sir R.A. Gregory, the Editor of *Nature*, had been elected a member of the APSSM in May 1916, and another of its members, Professor H.H. Turner, was both General Secretary of BAAS and President-elect of the APSSM.

Although there was fierce opposition from some quarters to establishing science as a component of general education (Jenkins, 1979; Layton, 1984), the tide was clearly running strongly in favour of school science as *'science for all and not for embryonic engineers, chemists...or biologists'* (BAAS, 1923: 207). Henceforth, school science was to concern itself with *'furnishing the mind and giving some knowledge of the world in which we live...without intruding the notions of discipline and training in method'* (Tilden, 1919: 12). In short, school science was to be humanised.

In 1920, *SSR* published a plea by Adlam for the teaching of General Science (Adlam, 1920: 197–202) and in the following year the Oxford and Cambridge Examination Board added this new subject to those already included in the list of Group III subjects for the School Certificate Examination. By 1930, six of the eight Boards conducting School Certificate examinations offered a syllabus and examination in General Science, thereby making the subject available to candidates in all types of secondary school. However, controversy and dispute about the form, content and value of General Science were ever present and matters came to a head when the Secondary School Examinations Council (SSEC), the body responsible for overseeing School Certificate examinations, published a highly critical report of the existing syllabuses and examinations in General Science. After some unproductive deliberations about a possible compulsory paper in Elementary Science, the SMA decided to establish a new General Science sub-committee to undertake a fundamental and detailed review of the Association's stance on General Science. The result was the publication in 1936 of an interim report entitled *The Teaching of General Science Part 1* and a second part published two years later. According to the latter, the proposals seem to have been *'well received by various branches of the Association, by the Association of Women Science Teachers and by the Science Panel of the Association of Assistant Mistresses (AAM)'* (SMA, 1938: 3).

Matters, however, were not quite so straightforward. Whereas in boys' schools, the introduction of General Science led to the inclusion of some hitherto neglected biological topics in the school science curriculum, the position in girls' school was very different. Here the dominant science was botany and the frequently neglected subject was physics and, to a lesser extent, chemistry. The diverse membership of the AWST also made it more difficult than in the case of the SMA to formulate a clear policy for the school science curriculum. The result was that the AWST favoured a degree of diversity that met the different needs of its members. Thus, unlike the SMA, it was very strongly opposed to the idea that there should be a compulsory School Certificate examination paper in Elementary Science. When in 1934 the University of London Examination Board considered introducing a General Science syllabus along the lines of the SMA proposals, the AWST was also less than enthusiastic, with a strong minority of members at its summer meeting arguing for the retention of both botany and a paper in physics-with-chemistry.

When the SMA published its Interim Report on the Teaching of General Science in 1936, the AWST set up a sub-committee to prepare a response (SSR, 1937: 134–6). The response, which met with approval from the membership and the science panel of the AAM, judged the minimum syllabus proposed by the SMA too long. It recommended that much of the physics, notably aspects of mechanics and electricity, be deleted, along with some biological topics. The latter included the study of insects, the removal of which would leave more time for the study of genetics and heredity. The guiding principle of the response was the 'the needs of the average girl' and the claim that these needs had not been considered by the SMA. C.L. Bryant, the chairman of the SMA'S General Science sub-committee agreed, admitting that 'We were thinking of boys all the time' (SSR, 1937: 136).

It is clear that initial attempts by the AWST to collaborate with the SMA over the development of General Science were unlikely to meet with success. A letter in March 1935 from the AWST to the Chairman of the SMA asking him to consider the setting up of a joint SMA/AWST committee to discuss matters of common interest prompted the somewhat discouraging response that the officers were always prepared to act as such a committee. A year later, when the AWST Committee suggested a joint production of a General Science syllabus, it was told that the SMA was already committed to collaboration with the Incorporated Association of Assistant Masters (IAAM) and that further joint activity was not a realistic possibility at that moment (Layton op.cit: 216).

The logical response of the AWST to the position in which it thus found itself was to ask its own sub-committee to devise a General Science syllabus suitable for girls, along with an examination paper. The sub-committee countered by recommending its dissolution and the setting up of a joint committee with members of the science panel of the AAM to compile a suitable syllabus. This joint committee eventually produced a syllabus 'of School Certificate standard' involving two 2-hour papers covering the biological and the physical sciences. After minor amendments by the General Committee of the AWST in November 1938, the syllabus was printed and distributed to the Examination Boards and a variety of teachers' associations, including the SMA. The SMA, however, declined to publish the syllabus in *SSR*, much to the disappointment of the AWST. The content of the AAM/AWST syllabus was substantially less than that of the SMA's proposals and no attempt was made to integrate topics drawn from the three basic sciences. Only the biological section included content that was not in the SMA's proposals: more explicit attention was given to sexual reproduction and a reference made to the evolution of parental care.

As Layton has noted (*op.cit.* 218), the degree of congruence between the proposals of the SMA and those of AWST eventually allowed the latter to come to the view that a General Science course suitable for both boys and girls was feasible, provided that sufficient time was allowed for teachers to address the particular needs of those whom they taught. The reality, as always, was that the teaching of any examination syllabus was likely to occupy all the time made available to do so.

The outbreak of the Second World War brought an end to further developments by the AWST and the SMA, although both Associations responded when the Norwood Committee, inquiring into the curriculum and examinations of secondary schools, asked whether General Science was suitable as 'the science of the main school'. That Committee eventually commended General Science as an initiative of *'great promise'* that was *'much to be encouraged'* (Board of Education, 1943: 109). Although the AWST returned to the question of General Science for girls in the post-war years in connection with science teaching in secondary modern schools, and the SMA issued its own revised proposals in 1950, the demand for post-war specialisation meant that the days of General Science were numbered. Examination entries in General Science in the 1950s declined steadily, while those for physics, biology and chemistry greatly increased.

Whatever the procedural and substantial differences at the national level between the AWST and the SMA over General Science, evidence suggests that, at Branch level, members of the two organisations were well aware of each other's activities and were often invited to take part in them. Whereas the AWST had had Branches since its inception, it was not until 1926 that the Business Meeting of the SMA voted to allow the creation of Branches. The response to the necessary change in the Rules was prompt, a Branch being established in the North East later the same year. Two years later the example was followed by South Wales, with the North West, Yorkshire and the Eastern Counties all having

Branches by 1935. Any member of the SMA was free to belong to any Branch and non-members were able to attend by invitation. The centres of activity of these Branches were often different from those of the AWST, differences that stemmed from their individual histories and which were sometimes reflected in their titles. For example, the Yorkshire-based Branch of the AWST, established in 1926 and known as the North Eastern Branch to distinguish it from the North West Branch on the other side of the Pennines, owed its origins to initiatives centred upon girls' secondary schools in Sheffield and Chesterfield. The initial locus of the activities of the corresponding Branch of the SMA, named the Yorkshire Branch, centred upon Leeds.

In the case of both the SMA and the AWST, each Branch organised its own programme of events. A few of these events, especially in the case of the women, were mainly social but all Branches devoted time to the discussion of teaching methods, curriculum reform, examination syllabuses and laboratory management. Lectures by distinguished academics and visits to manufacturing industries were also a regular feature. When a Branch was new and/or membership small, co-operation between the SMA and AWST was sometimes the only way of trying to ensure the financial viability of an event. When the Yorkshire Branch of the SMA planned a conference on General Science to be held in Hull in the spring term of 1939, only three SMA members signed up to attend. There was rather more interest in the conference from the North East Branch of the AWST, nine of whose members indicated their wish to participate. Even so, the event made a financial loss, which the Yorkshire Branch was ill-equipped to bear. Sometimes Branches co-operated with one another. In 1936, members of the North East Branch of the AWST travelled across the Pennines to attend a meeting with the North West and Midland Branches to discuss the proposal for General Science put forward by the Northern Universities Joint Matriculation Board. In 1934, the Welsh Branch of the AWST spent a morning with members of the AAM discussing General Science, before holding a joint Annual Meeting with the South Wales Branch of the SMA in the afternoon.

Invitations from a local Branch of the SMA to a nearby Branch of the AWST to attend various events arranged by the men were usually acknowledged with courtesy and gratitude in the Annual Reports of the women's organisation. In 1927, for example, the Northern Branch of the AWST reported that its members 'have appreciated very much the close co-operation which exists between the two Associations in this area'. A decade later, co-operation between the two Associations in the North East of England had become even closer. It became the practice to hold the Annual Meeting of the AWST Branch in conjunction with that of the North Eastern Branch of the SMA, although Business Meetings remained separate, and members of the AWST were routinely invited to all the meetings and excursions arranged by the local Branch of the SMA. A year later in 1938 this joint meeting was described as having become a *'very popular and successful Annual event'*. Just before the outbreak of the Second World War, the Northern Branch of the AWST reported that there was *'every prospect'* that the co-operation with the corresponding Branch of the SMA would *'continue and develop'*. When a small meeting at the Leys School decided early in 1937 to set up a Cambridge and District Branch of the AWST, it resolved to have one meeting a term and expressed the hope that it would be possible *'to co-operate with the SMA'*. That hope was realised later in the year in the form of three joint meetings with the Eastern Branch of the SMA and a joint excursion to Wicken Fen. In some parts of the country, the two local organisations exchanged committee minutes and attempted to co-ordinate the programmes of events for the coming year.

Given the growing collaboration of the various Branches of the two organisations and the lengthy debate about the form and content of General Science, it was perhaps inevitable that the question of forming a single national organisation would eventually be raised, if not by the men then by the women. At the Business Meeting of the AWST in January 1936, Miss Lewis of Greycoat Hospital School in Manchester asked the Chairman whether there was *'any possibility whatever of amalgamating completely with the Science Masters' Association'*. A substantial discussion then followed the Chairman's reply that *'As far as I can say at the moment, it is not a question that is being discussed'*. Miss Wells of Abbeydale Secondary School in Sheffield then commented pointedly that *'I do not know if I speak accurately, but I should have said the Science Masters would not discuss it'*. The subsequent comment of Miss Hatfield of North London Collegiate School merits quoting in full: *'I happened to be discussing that question this week with Miss Drummond [also of North London Collegiate School]. She told me that when they founded the Association, they founded it because they had approached the men who would not have them in. They tried again about ten years later, but they still would not have them in.*

'Is it not time to try again? I think [this] question of biology gives us a very strong hand. I was very struck at a meeting in January when a man got up and said "Can you throw light on what the girls' schools wanted in the [General Science] syllabus? We wanted to put in the rabbit but were told that the girls would not stand it, so we had to put in the frog."' (AWST, 1936: 39).

Responding to Miss Hatfield, the Secretary attempted to deal with both the somewhat bizarre reference to the 'frog versus the rabbit' and the issue of renewing discussions with the SMA about amalgamation. She told the Business Meeting that: '*We have written and had a favourable answer to the question that we should have a joint committee on questions such as [the frog or the rabbit]. They are anxious to co-operate in that way, but we understand that that there are some diehards who do not wish to have us. If you speak to any of the Science Masters' Committee individually, they say they long to be amalgamated with us but so-and-so will not have it. I think we ought to [amalgamate] but they say the questions that arise are quite different, and they do not want us at their General Meeting. They do not see why we should not be able to run our Association our way and they in theirs. If they would meet us, it would be a step in the right direction.*' (idem.)

Reading the relevant reports and minutes of the two Associations over the three decades or so, it would be easy to assume that the initiative to extend invitations to attend meetings or encourage other forms of collaboration came predominantly from the men. This is almost certainly because the two organisations documented their activities in different ways, the AWST perhaps giving more attention to recording shared activities than the SMA. Where they have survived and are available for consultation, the attendance lists of various events organised by the local Branches of the two Associations reveal a rather different story. Branch meetings of the AWST and the SMA were often attended by both men and women, although the evidence suggests that women more commonly attended SMA meetings than the other way round. Again, this may reflect that more attendance lists relating to the SMA Branches have survived than in the case of the AWST Branches. It should also be noted that meetings of either Association were frequently attended by non-members, present as guests.

Towards a common policy

Although the activities of the Branches of the two Associations were suspended during the Second World War, the ending of the conflict was followed by a growth in the membership of both organisations and a rapid renewal of the pre-war forms of collaboration. Membership of the AWST increased from 900 in 1938 to 1226 in 1946 and 1437 by 1950. The SMA, with 2548 members in 1938, had 2870 members by 1946 and over 4000 four years later. Interestingly, and perhaps to some degree a reflection of the sense of the pre-war rejection by the SMA, the AWST Business Meeting in 1946 was asked whether the Association should seek to strengthen its contact with the Assistant Mistresses

Association, the organisation from which it had developed a generation earlier and with which relationships had always been cordial. However, at Branch level, the Annual Reports of the AWST continued to record joint events with the SMA, including excursions. In the North East of England, a visit in 1946 to the bird sanctuary on the Farne Islands involved members of both Associations, following an invitation from the local Branch of the SMA. In the same year, the ladies were invited to an exhibition of science teaching apparatus at Barnsley Grammar School, organised by the Yorkshire Branch of the SMA. In 1947, the Cambridge and District Branch of the AWST reported that it was *'doing its best to co-operate with local Branch of the SMA'*, although so far it had been possible *'to organise only one joint meeting'*. When the Scottish Branch of the AWST was inaugurated in 1947, its 60 members were invited to attend the Annual Conference of the Scottish Region of the SMA, itself set up a year earlier.

The post-war growth in membership of both Associations took place in a social, political, economic and educational climate that was profoundly different from that which had prevailed when the two organisations were created. The Education Act of 1944 introduced a tripartite system of free secondary education to which all pupils proceeded upon completion of their primary education, thereby sweeping away the social distinction between secondary and elementary schooling created in the nineteenth century. The school leaving age was raised to 15 in 1947 and four years later the group system of School Certificate examinations was replaced by a subject-based General Certificate of Education available at Ordinary and Advanced levels. The massive school building programme initiated by the post-war Labour government was eventually to lead to over three million extra places by 1961, but even this proved insufficient to accommodate the additional number of pupils produced by the raising of the school leaving age, the increased birth rate and the trend for pupils to remain longer at school. Difficulties soon arose in meeting the demands for teachers of mathematics and science. In 1955, teachers were allowed to continue for a maximum of five years beyond the normal retirement age of 65. A year later, science and mathematics graduates who chose to enter school teaching were granted exemption from National Service, a concession that had been available for some time to those with first or second class honours degrees in those subjects. A series of graded posts and Heads of Department allowances in schools was introduced and equal pay for women teachers was agreed in 1955, although not achieved until April 1961.

By the later 1950s, the austerity and hardship that had marked the decade or so after the war had begun to give way to more optimistic economic circumstances, although the wider political environment presented formidable challenges, notably in the form of the still unresolved Korean conflict and the wider Cold War between Communist states and the West. When, despite the embarrassment and humiliation of the Suez debacle three years earlier, the Conservative party won the General Election of 1959, the Prime Minister, Harold Macmillan, chose to tell the electorate that they had *'never had it so good'*. There was much to justify this claim, although the subsequent devaluation of sterling in 1967 later showed that the seemingly buoyant British economy owed too much to a level of imports that the balance of payments was eventually unable to sustain. Nonetheless, by 1959, the post-war austerity that had lasted for most of the 1950s was over, the *Economist* noting a year later that the economic *'recovery was turning into a boom'*. The full capacity of Britain's steelworks reflected rapid growth in car production, house building, white goods and much else.

The public standing of science was also high, reflecting, among much else, its contribution to the prosecution of the war and the underpinning of technological achievements such as the world's first commercial jet airliner and the first nuclear power station, opened at Calder Hall in 1956. Recommendations in a short White Paper on technical education in 1956 led to the rapid creation of area and regional technical colleges, some of which became Colleges of Advanced Technology and, later, polytechnics. The education of 15–18 year-olds was examined in detail in the Crowther Report (1959), which expressed concern about the intense specialisation of sixth form education and highlighted a number of issues, notably teacher shortage, in maintaining academic standards. Such specialisation was, in part, a consequence of the pressure on undergraduate places, especially in the sciences. The university system was not to expand significantly until after the publication of the Robbins Report in 1964, which also eventually brought the universities into closer collaboration with the teacher training colleges, later colleges of education. The education of those pupils not judged to have a university education in mind was the focus of the Newsom Report (1963), significantly entitled *Half our Future*. The tone of this report, however, was retrospective and conservative and much of what it had to say was soon overtaken by the growth of comprehensive secondary schooling, following the publication of Circular 10/65 only two years later.

For the most part, the post-war programmes of the SMA and the AWST followed a well-established pattern of events, although as the number of members increased so too did the numbers attending meetings, at both Branch and national level. There was much to command the interest of members of both organisations. One-day courses concerned with recent developments in science were always popular and both the SMA and the AWST continued to take a keen interest in examinations, including Scholarship examinations, and in the syllabuses associated with the new General Certificate in Education. The supply and training of laboratory technicians remained an important issue for the SMA although subsequent improvement was to be slow. Collaboration with other organisations with an interest in science education, such as the professional scientific institutions, museums and other more local science teaching organisations became more common, especially but not exclusively in large cities and towns. A series of publications entitled *Science Teaching Techniques* was the result of collaboration between the SMA, AWST, the Association of Teachers in Colleges and Departments of Education and the London Association of Science Teachers. The University Institutes of Education set up in 1948 often provided courses for members of the SMA and AWST as well as facilitating productive links between schools and universities. Both the SMA and AWST created new Branches in the immediate post-war years. Branches of the AWST were created in the Liverpool area (1948), the Manchester area (1949), in Sussex (1949) and in Scotland (1947). In the case of the SMA, Branches were established in North Wales (1946), Scotland (1946), South Midlands (1949) and Northern Ireland (1949). One new Branch created in Essex in 1954 was a portent of things to come and its creation is an important reminder of the existence of a variety of local science teacher organisations in different parts of the country.

Figure 1.4: An intent SMA group of the early 1960s.

The Essex Science Teachers' Association, open to men and women from all types of school, flourished for several years after the War. Its demise paved the way for a joint Branch of the AWST and SMA at a time when leading officials of both organisations came from schools in Essex. It is significant that it was this Branch that subsequently submitted the following resolution to the General Committee of the SMA in 1961: *'The members of the Essex Joint Branch of the AWST and the SMA, after six years of work at this Branch, would like to recommend as a result of their experience, the fusion of both parent associations, and would therefore ask the Committee to put this proposal before the next Annual General Meeting of both Associations, to start steps towards fusion of both Associations'* (SMA, 1961).

When the General Committee of the SMA met on 25th November 1961 to consider the Essex proposal, the General Secretary reported that he: *'...had not received any adverse comment since the publication of the proposal and there was a great deal of approval for fusion, but that under Rule 11(g), the resolution could not be carried'*.

The General Committee thus formulated, and agreed without dissent, the following resolution that could be put to the next Annual Business Meeting of the Association: *'That in view of the close and harmonious way in which Branches and members of the AWST and the SMA are working together for the improvement of science teaching, the Committee desires from this meeting a mandate to draw up, in collaboration with representatives of the AWST, detailed proposals for the formation of a single Association open to all teachers of science'*.

There was also some pressure for some kind of fusion from within the AWST itself. Officers of the Association were aware that the AWST *'was bound to, and must, expand'* and that this would mean *'more clerical help'* and perhaps even a *'permanent headquarters'*. Setting up such quarters in London would have presented the Association with insurmountable financial and other problems, so that the possibility of collaborating in some way with the SMA held an obvious attraction. It was also the case that the rising cost of producing *SSR* and therefore of membership presented more severe problems for the AWST than for the larger organisation consisting of more highly paid men. Closer collaboration over secretarial and administrative costs might make it possible to keep the cost of the journal at a level which members of the AWST would find acceptable. 1957–8 was the *'busiest and probably the most successful year'* for the AWST. It was collaborating not only with the SMA but also with a large number of other organisations interested in science education. The Annual Report for 1955–6 listed no fewer than fourteen such organisations, including the Association of Agriculture, the Universities Federation for Animal Welfare, the Field Studies Council, the Royal College of Nursing and the Royal College of Midwives. As the standing and influence of the AWST increased, so did the need for adequate clerical and administrative support for members who were giving their time on a voluntary basis.

As early as 1950, a member of the Executive Committee had asked *'Could we not collaborate with the Science Masters by getting in touch with their Committee?'*, prompting the chairman to comment that she had *'felt all along we should get in touch with them'* (AWST, 1950). Whether as result of this feeling or not, the affairs of the two Associations were becoming entangled in a variety of ways. The first booklet on *Science Teaching Techniques* was not a financial success and in 1952 the AWST agreed to share the loss, estimated at about a quarter (£250) of the overall loss (£1000). In addition to collaborating in the production of this booklet, the two Associations worked jointly on a number of other publications. One was concerned with the MKS system of units and another was a study of the shortage of science teachers, the latter being described in the annual report of the AWST for 1952–3 as the *'outstanding piece of work for the year'*.

In January 1961, the Executive Committee of the AWST considered a request from the North West Branch of the Association to act upon the *'strong, but not unanimous'* resolution of the Branch that the AWST should begin discussions about a merger with the SMA. As within the wider membership, opinion within the Executive Committee was divided. It was pointed out that no approach had been received from the SMA, although *'since their headquarters had been set up in Cambridge, it was possible they would like the AWST to share the expenses of the accommodation'*. For Miss Lloyd-Williams, amalgamation would lead the AWST to lose its *'particularly friendly atmosphere'*, a concern that many members of the Association undoubtedly shared. Dr Owen pointed out that men were now teaching science in many girls' schools and that mixed schools contained both men and women science teachers. The Executive Committee eventually agreed to inform the North West Branch that *'very careful thought was being given to the resolution'*. In addition, individual members of the Executive Committee were asked to send their views, *'for or against amalgamation'* to Miss Buckley or Miss Kemlo so that *'general opinion could be collated and discussed'* at the meeting of the Executive Committee in September. By that date, Miss Buckley felt able to tell the Committee that there was *'undoubtedly a desire [for amalgamation or federation] among members'* and asked whether *'the time had now come'* to seek the opinion of all members of the AWST. The Executive Committee resolved to seek a formal meeting with the Officers of the SMA and, depending upon the outcome of that meeting, to send a questionnaire to all members of the Association (see below).

By 1961, however, it was not simply increased collaboration and co-operation at Branch level that led the SMA and the AWST to give active consideration to some kind of amalgamation at the national level. External developments were now beginning to force the pace of events. Five years earlier, Henry Boulind, the General Secretary of the SMA, had attended a conference in Hamburg on Science Curricula in Primary and Secondary Schools organised by UNESCO as part of its ongoing initiative to promote co-operation between various science teaching organisations. The Hamburg conference highlighted the need to modernise school science syllabuses in a number of ways. In the case of the UK, the content of science syllabuses had changed little since the introduction of the School Certificate examinations in 1918: physics syllabuses, for example, made no reference to atomic energy and school chemistry courses retained their emphasis on the preparation and properties of materials and, at senior level, on systematic qualitative analysis. In addition, the Hamburg conference stressed the importance of school science as a vehicle of general education, rather than as a narrow form of pre-professional training. Giving effect to this change of emphasis would require not simply modernisation of school syllabuses, but also attention to aspects of the history of science and its social and technological applications. It gradually became clear, within the General Committee of the SMA, that school science education *needed to be thought out afresh from first principles*. A Science Teaching sub-committee, later renamed the Science and Education Committee, was therefore formed, charged with inquiring into *the aims, scope and content of science teaching in grammar schools, with special reference to the part that science can play in general education*' (SMA, 1957). This ambitious goal quickly led to the publication of a draft statement of SMA policy, copies of which were distributed via *SSR* to members of both the SMA and the AWST and made more widely available to other organisations with an interest in school science. The draft statement was generally well received, although its relevance to schools in Scotland and Northern Ireland was questioned, and the AWST felt obliged to produce an alternative statement in 1959 designed to reflect the problems facing those teaching science in girls' schools.

The favourable response to the draft policy statement led the Science and Education Committee to direct its work towards implementing its recommendations, while continuing to revise the policy statement with the object of achieving a version that would be acceptable to both the SMA and the AWST.

That version, entitled *Science and Education,* was published by John Murray in 1961 as *A policy statement issued by the Science Masters' Association and The Association of Women Science Teachers,* although finalising the document was not without problems. The Minutes of the AWST Executive Committee for 14th May 1960 record that a *'great deal of time was spent in correcting the English and in discussing the section dealing with the allocation of time on the principle of which the AWST and the SMA did not agree as their problems were different'.* Even the revised draft prompted further suggestions for improvement from the AWST, the Executive Committee finally agreeing in September 1960 that, subject to their acceptance by the SMA, the AWST would 'sign up'. Nonetheless, from the perspective of the early twenty-first century, the policy statement can be seen as a seminal attempt by both Associations to acquire recognition as an authoritative voice on matters to do with school science education. It can also be seen as a contribution to remedying the absence of any national body concerned with the form and content of the school curriculum, a lack that was to be addressed by legislation when the Schools Council for the Curriculum and Examinations was established in 1964.

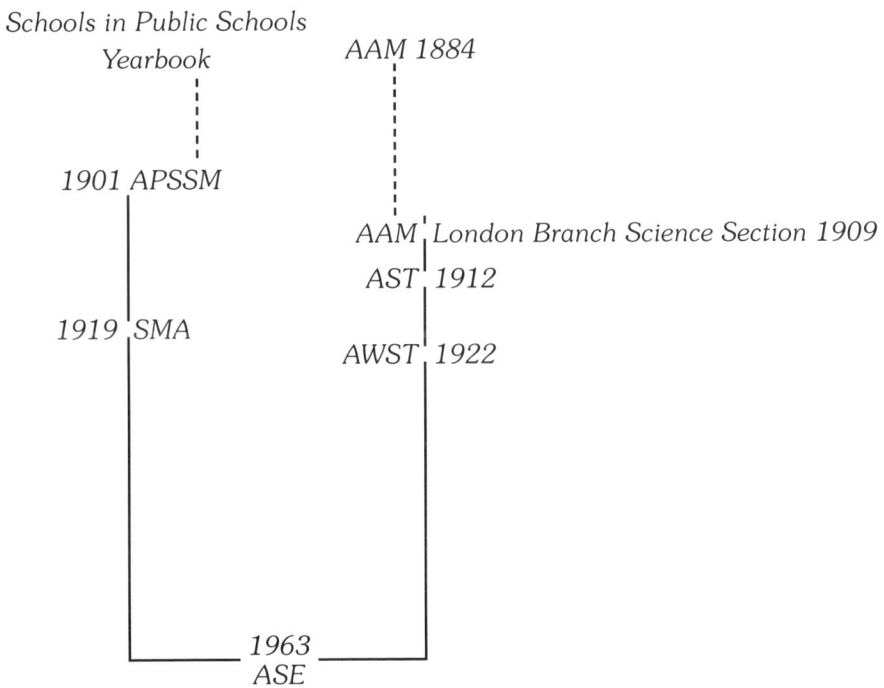

Figure 1.5: *The organisations that eventually joined to become the Association for Science Education.*

Fusion: amalgamation or federation?

On 5th January 1962, members of the Association of Women Science Teachers (AWST) met in London to celebrate the anniversary of the founding of an organisation that had begun life as an Association of Science Teachers (AST) half a century earlier. Staying at the University of London's Connaught Hall and enjoying the *'luxury of centrally heated bedrooms each with hot and cold water, a warm attractive Common Room, and good meals'*, over one hundred members of the AWST, together with ten guests from the SMA, attended the celebratory dinner that formed the highlight of the Jubilee Conference. At that dinner, they heard J.S.G. McGeachin, the Chairman of the SMA, propose a toast to what was referred to as the 'partner organisation'. Beginning his remarks with the question at the head of this chapter, McGeachin recalled that whereas his own organisation had been *'started by men from the more monastic type of public school'*, the AWST stemmed from an offshoot of the Association of Assistant Mistresses in Public Secondary Schools (AAM). As far as he personally was concerned, there was now *'no logical reason'* why there should be two associations.

In expressing this opinion, McGeachin was reflecting the view that had grown up within both the SMA and the AWST that the time was now right to establish some kind of more formal relationship between the two organisations, which went beyond the collaboration that had prevailed hitherto, particularly at Branch level. He went on to add the following:

'...As most of you will realise, [the question of some sort of joint organisation] was brought up at the Business Meeting of the Science Masters' Association yesterday and, in the company of about two hundred people present, I think six spoke against joining the women in a joint association and when a vote was taken, only eight voted against it. [Why did they so vote?]...They were frightened of being swamped by a swarm of women. Miss Going has just been telling me she is frightened of being swamped by a swarm of men! We have collaborated in many ways. I think the next step forward must be taken jointly.'

McGeachin told the members of the AWST that the SMA proposed to set up *'a sort of joint steering committee with your people to work out some details of how...amalgamation, if it is thought we should have it, can be brought about'*. Denying that there was any antagonism between the two Associations, he suggested that they were largely complementary: *'The men are very strong in physics and the women much stronger in biology, and perhaps we are pretty equal in chemistry'*.

Replying to McGeachin's address, Miss D.M. Scott, a former President of the AWST and a fellow Scot, chose to misquote Burns: '*the future, he could be guess and fear*'.

The day after the Jubilee Dinner, the members of the AWST held their Annual Business Meeting where they were told that their Officers had already held a number of informal discussions with Officers of the SMA about the advisability and possibility of forming a joint Association. These informal discussions had confirmed that many activities of the two Associations were already joint activities and that there were already three joint Branches. Both the AWST and the SMA were attracting members from preparatory and mixed schools where both men and women were teaching and there were now more married science teachers. This latter point had a bearing on the time that women with family responsibilities might be willing to devote to the administrative and secretarial burdens of an expanding, voluntary, Branch-based organisation. In addition, there was also a significant number of small joint local science teaching associations and the cause of school science would be better served if these smaller associations could be included within one joint organisation.

While no official decision could be made at the Business Meeting of the AWST in January 1962, Miss Buckley, the President, said that she would like '*to have the feeling of the Meeting*'. She advised that there was '*much to consider in regard to any fusion between the two Associations*', the word 'fusion' being carefully chosen as '*more relevant than amalgamation or federation*'. She noted that, although the finances of the AWST and the SMA were already run on similar lines with the same *per capita* allowance of four shillings, the two Associations differed greatly in size.

Only a handful of members spoke in response to their President's invitation. Miss Macwillie asked whether fusion meant one Association. She would support '*co-operation, working and meeting together but not that the AWST should lose its identity*', which she thought would '*cause many difficulties*'. Miss Jesson wanted reassurance that the membership as a whole would have an opportunity to express its views. Others wanted to know how many representatives there would be on the proposed joint committee to be set up to discuss possible fusion with the SMA, how they would be chosen and whether they would reflect the interests of those who taught science from primary school to university level. Although no formal vote was taken, a show of hands revealed that a 'vast majority' of those present favoured setting up the joint committee to take discussions forward.

The decision of the SMA Business Meeting to enter into formal negotiation with the AWST, to which McGeachin referred, stemmed from the passing of the resolution referred to above and prompted by the proposal from the Essex Branch. An attempt to add the words 'in secondary schools' to the resolution was overwhelmingly defeated. The AWST was represented on a Joint Steering Committee by its President (Miss E.L. Buckley), its Vice-president (Miss M. Going), two members of the Executive Committee (Miss F.M. Eastwood and Miss K.E. Parks) and Miss E. O'Shaughnessy, the Essex Branch representative. The SMA's representatives were W.H. Dowland (Chairman-elect), D.W. Harlow (Annual Meeting Secretary), F.C. Brown (Treasurer) and E.W. Tapper (the newly appointed full-time Secretary), with J.S.G. McGeachin (Chairman) being added later.

On 27th January 1962, the Joint Committee met at the SMA's new Headquarters at 52, Bateman Street in Cambridge. There was no dissent from the idea that the two Associations were 'so closely linked' that some form of amalgamation was desirable. Discussion therefore moved quickly to focus attention on the various issues involved and several presented themselves immediately. While the SMA was a Registered Charity, the AWST was not. There was also a big difference in the capital assets of the two Associations, although in proportion to the respective membership, the difference was perhaps not as great as it appeared. As for the form of any fusion, a number of options were considered. The 'simplest' involved the SMA changing its title and such rules as applied to enable women to become members. This could be achieved in one of two ways. The AWST could be wound up, its assets transferred to the SMA, and AWST members encouraged to join the new Association on an individual basis. Alternatively, the AWST as a body could join the new Association, bringing with it its assets, although this could make for possible legal difficulties over the disposal of such assets, should the SMA wind up its own affairs. It was agreed that legal advice would be necessary before deciding how best to proceed.

A number of possible names for any new Association were also considered. *The Association of Science Teachers: Joint Association of the Science Masters' Association and the Association of Women Science Teachers* found some favour, provided that the sub-title was dropped after five years. There was also some support for the *Association for the Advancement of Science Teaching*, although this was quickly discounted as being too cumbersome. The Joint Committee agreed to seek advice about Incorporation to give a full title of *Incorporated Association of Science Teachers*.

Later in the day, the Joint Committee discussed aspects of a possible new constitution and agreed that some means should be found to ensure that the opinions of women science teachers and of girls' schools would be expressed in committee. In addition, women should have equal status and eligibility for election to any office. The women members of the Joint Committee also pressed for a number of other 'safeguards' thought necessary to satisfy members of the AWST. There matters rested until the Joint Committee reconvened on Saturday 31st March 1962, by which time the advice of the SMA's solicitor had cleared the way for a new Constitution that would allow the new organisation to function as a Registered Charity. Further discussions, both formal and informal, throughout the year led to several further revisions of the draft Trust Deed and agreement on a timetable for implementing the changes that were planned.

At this first meeting of the Joint Committee, the AWST representatives made clear that, unlike their SMA counterparts, they were in favour of putting any proposals for fusion to a postal vote of their members. The AWST President, Miss Buckley, therefore sent a letter to some 1700 members seeking their views about a range of matters related to any form of fusion with the SMA. Of the 241 replies received, 227 were in favour of 'complete fusion', 12 for federation and 2 for keeping separate identities (AWST, 1962). Federation would have involved the continued existence of the two Associations, each with its own Executive Committee and a central committee consisting of representatives of the two organisations. While the letters also revealed a general disquiet among the women at the loss of identity and a fear of losing the intimacy and friendliness of meetings, there was also a feeling that these qualities need not be lost and would be outweighed by the benefits that a joint Association could bring. Inevitably there was concern that the 'problems of women's representation' and women's points of view should not be overlooked. The segregation of the sexes was regarded as 'archaic' and there was concern that any new organisation should be sufficiently broad in its remit to encompass all kinds of science teachers, from primary school to university and, in particular, to do more to meet the needs of those teaching science in secondary modern schools. AWST members offered their President yet more possible names for the proposed new organisation. These included *The Joint Association of Science Teachers, The Association for Science Teaching, The British Federation of Science Teachers, The Science Association, The National Science Teaching Association*, with the responses suggesting some preference for *The Association of Science Teachers* or *The Association for the Advancement of Science Teaching*.

As the work of the Steering Committee proceeded, the SMA chose to keep its members informed through joint meetings of its Officers and the Branch representatives, via *SSR* and, as events approached a resolution, a new publication, the *Bulletin* (the forerunner of *Education in Science*). The first issue of the *Bulletin* in April 1962, in addition to reporting the opening of the Association's Headquarters in Cambridge, had recorded the inaugural meeting of a joint South West Branch of the SMA and the AWST on 3rd December 1960, replacing the former Devon and Exeter Science Teachers' Association. It had also reported the appointment, referred to above, of E.W. Tapper as the first full-time Secretary of the SMA, an appointment that, as with the AWST, reflected the need to support the work of the increasing number of members and meet the demands arising from the increasing influence and standing of the Association. No fewer than 21 pages of the second *Bulletin* summarised the background to the proposed formation of 'The British Science Teachers' Association' and presented details of the new constitution, the qualifications for membership, the change in the system of elections, and the Trust Deed. Members were advised that *'no one will be required to join the Association against his or her will'*. The name of the new Association had been agreed in the Joint Steering Committee without any votes against, although two members abstained. The name was also the subject of considerable discussion at a meeting of the SMA General Committee and Branch representatives held on 22nd September 1962. Although this meeting eventually agreed on the name 'British Science Teachers' Association', a proposition from the Chairman that *'further discussion of the title be left until the [Annual*

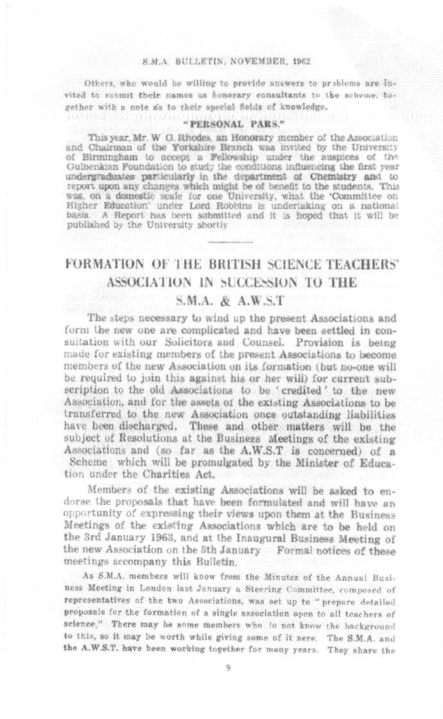

Figure 1.6: SMA Bulletin, November 1962 announcing proposed merger.

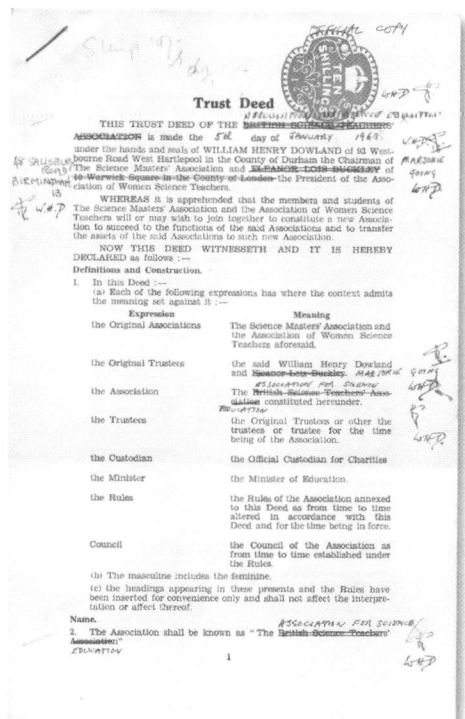

Figure 1.7: Redrafted Trust Deed, January 1963.

Business Meeting in] January 1963' was carried by a large majority. Unlike the AWST, the Rules of the SMA required that it was the Business Meeting that would need to resolve to bring about the change now being contemplated.

The few days before that Business Meeting of the SMA were occupied with a series of meetings called to settle a number of practical issues. The SMA General Committee met seventeen Branch officers at 7.30 p.m. on the evening of 1st January to secure agreement about the nomination of Officers for the new Association. There followed the Annual Business Meeting, which resolved to wind up the SMA's activities and transfer all property remaining after satisfaction of debts and liabilities to the Association to be known as the 'British Science Teachers' Association'.

The AWST also held its Annual General Meeting in Manchester, on the morning of 4th January, and agreed unanimously to a merger and to the necessary transfer of assets. The Executive Committee met on the following day, accorded Miss Buckley and Miss Eastwood 'plenipotentiary powers', resolved that no further business of the AWST would be conducted after 12 noon on 5th January, and that, as with SMA, all the Association's debts and liabilities be discharged and all surplus property and assets be transferred to the Association known as the 'British Science Teachers' Association'. In addition, *'pending settlement of the affairs and the transfer of surplus assets, not more than £1000'* would be paid to the new Association. On the same day, the SMA held the final meeting of its General Committee, which likewise agreed to transfer not more than £8000 to the 'British Science Teachers' Association' or its duly appointed Officers.

All therefore seemed in place for the inaugural Business Meeting of the British Science Teachers' Association on the morning of 5th January 1963, under the chairmanship of the retiring President of the SMA, Dr B.V. Bowden. A resolution relating to the transfer of assets was passed with three dissentients and seven abstentions. The Trust Deed and the Rules of the new Association were approved, but two resolutions proposed a different name for the new organisation. The first, proposed by the Honorary Treasurer and seconded by a former General Secretary of the SMA, was 'The Association of Science Teachers'. The second proposal, from the floor of the Meeting, came from a teacher at Loughborough Grammar School, D. Tomes, and W.H. Dowland, the retiring Chairman of the SMA. It was this second proposal that was carried and which gave the organisation the name by which it is known today, the Association for Science Education. By 12.05 p.m. on 5th January 1963, the formal business of the Meeting was over, a single organisation for all science teachers had been created and its Trustees and Officers appointed. The constitution provided for governing Council consisting of the Honorary Officers, six elected members and one representative of each Branch of the Association, along with those Trustees who were not already members in some other capacity. At least one of the Trustees, the Vice-chairmen and the Honorary Secretaries should be a man, and one a woman. Day-to-day management of the work of the Association was the responsibility of an Executive Committee of seven members and the Council was empowered to appoint other committees, the most important of which was the Education Committee, which replaced the SMA's Science and Education Committee and the Joint Education Committee of the AWST and the SMA.

A degree of continuity with the past of both the SMA and the AWST was ensured when the new Association followed the advice of the General Committee of the SMA to 'reappoint and combine the present Officers of the SMA and

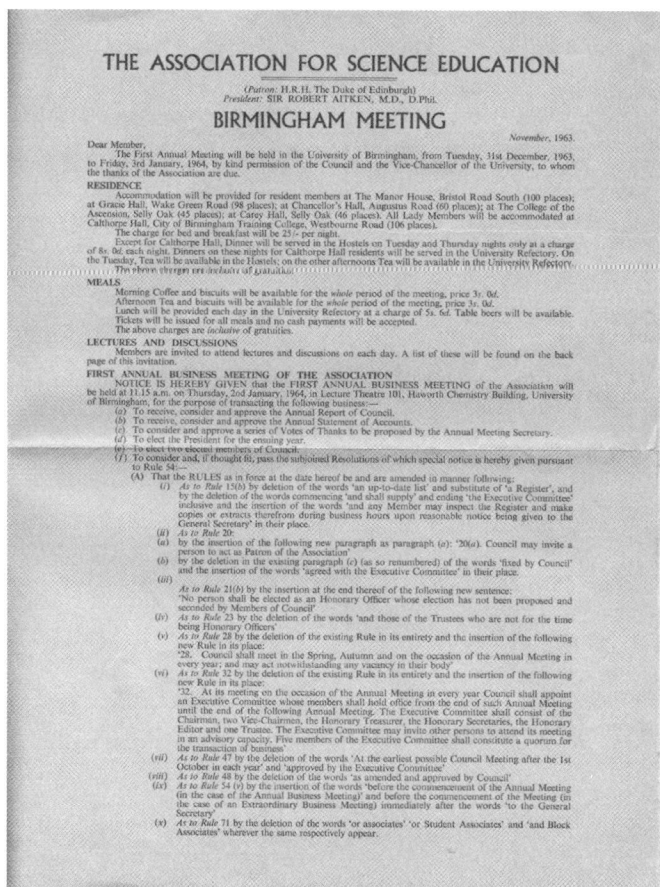

Figure 1.8: *Notification of the first Annual Meeting of ASE in Birmingham, 1964, with the Agenda of the first Annual Business Meeting.*

AWST'. R. Thurlow, a gifted experimenter and an employee of Leeds LEA, thus had the honour of becoming the first Chairman of the ASE. One of the three Vice-chairmen was Miss F.M. Eastwood, who had been Secretary of the London Branch of the AWST from 1951 to 1961. She had also served on the AWST Executive Committee and was to succeed Thurlow in 1964, thus becoming the first woman Chairman of the ASE. One of the four Honorary Secretaries of the ASE and one of the three Trustees were also women: Miss B.G. Ashton and Miss E.L. Buckley respectively. Editorship of *SSR* remained in the hands of R.H. Dyball . Those elected to the SMA General Committee and the AWST Executive Committee also became elected members of the consequently large Council of the new Association. As ASE developed, the safeguards thought necessary to protect the interests of both men and women in 1963 became less significant and, in 1977, the Annual Business Meeting resolved to delete from the Rules of ASE all clauses which required that at least one of the Officers or Elected Members be a male and one be a female. As in the Trust Deed, the masculine was taken to include the feminine.

Before concluding this chapter, it is important to acknowledge that the SMA and the AWST were not the only science teaching associations that offered professional support to science teachers. By the time ASE came into being, local science teaching associations had been established in many parts of the country. A Hertfordshire Science Teaching Association was set up in 1948: it produced a course for those teaching science in secondary modern schools, its own Bulletin and a number of key figures in the SMA played, or had played, an active role in its work. In 1949, the London Association of Science Teachers collaborated with the SMA in a sub-committee set up to consider how best to help teachers of science in secondary modern schools. The Leeds Science Teachers' Association, created in 1960, published its own journal, arranged meetings and visits for its members and continued to flourish until the 1980s. Some of these local science teaching associations eventually merged with a local Branch of the ASE: others preferred to maintain their independence, doing so satisfactorily for many years, sometimes with a degree of common membership and local collaboration with the ASE.

Figure 2.1: Chair 2001, Derek Bell and past Chairs at the Annual Meeting, 2001, at the University of Surrey.

Back row: Jeff Kirkham, Fred Archenhold, Andrew Bishop, Phil Ramsden, Peter Scott, Dick West, Alan Hall, David Standley

Next to back row: Roger McCune, Maurice Savory, John Nellist, Geoff Barroclough, Edwyn James, Jeff Thompson

Second row: Jane Wheatley, Rebecca Edwards, Mary Ratcliffe, Rosemary Feasey, Betty Preston, Ruth Schofield, Angela Dixon, Jean Glover

Front row: Brian Attwood, Derek Bell, Bertie Broad, David Moore.

2 Managing and directing ASE: some personal reflections

Annette Smith, Chief Executive

'Promoting excellence in science teaching and learning.'

The Association for Science Education is far from unique in its journey as a charitable organisation, having moved from a committed group of enthusiasts with a shared mission to a professionally-run membership body. In common with many organisations, the ASE now undertakes projects and takes part in programmes that supplement income while complementing its mission. This chapter charts that journey over the past 50 years and uses the period of office of each General Secretary and (later) Chief Executive as the staging posts along the way. I am indebted to David Moore and Derek Bell who contributed the main part of the text relating to their periods of office.

Introduction and context

Before the amalgamation of the SMA and the AWST, the organisation of the Annual Meeting and other activities, including the production of *The School Science Review,* were managed very well by the honorary officers and other volunteers. However, when the membership of the SMA grew from around 500 in 1919 to nearly 7000 in 1960, and of the AWST to nearly 1800 by 1963, concerns were evident over the management of both organisations. These mainly related to the keeping of membership records and to managing the increasingly substantial finances, and there were also opportunities for external collaboration that needed to be explored. As a result, it was decided to employ paid officials. In the case of the SMA this was achieved by paying honoraria to hitherto entirely voluntary officers of the Association whereas, in the case of the AWST, a salaried official was appointed. This chapter looks, amongst other issues, at the interaction between the salaried staff and the honorary officials, and at the ways in which this interaction has contributed to the progress of ASE.

It is clear that one of the factors encouraging the amalgamation of the SMA and the AWST was the possibility of increased collaboration between the two organisations, both in terms of activities organised for their members and a more efficient management of finance and membership.

Before amalgamation, the position of Membership Secretary for the SMA was a voluntary one. This changed with the appointment of SMA's first General Secretary, and responsibility for managing membership became part of his duties. The General Secretary also took over the previously honorary role of Publications Officer, another highly responsible and time-consuming task. At amalgamation, the membership of the ASE was close to 10,000 and rising, although an increase in subscriptions had trimmed the recent years' rapid growth.

The ASE at amalgamation

When the two Associations amalgamated in 1963, the management of the ASE was framed by the new governance structure, the General Secretary and other staff, and the location and condition of its Headquarters. Subsequently, the management and direction were also influenced by the projects and programmes with which ASE was involved.

The SMA was registered as a charity under the Ministry of Education, whereas the new Association for Science Education was constituted under a Trust Deed, in preference to being a company limited by guarantee (which would have protected the trustees from liability). It was decided that the new organisation would also be a Registered Charity set up by Trust Deed, and that the governance would be the responsibility of three trustees.

The first group of trustees comprised H.P. Ramage, Miss E.L. Buckley, and E.H. Coulson. Hugh Ramage had served as General Secretary of the SMA over the war years and was still involved as a trustee until the formation of ASE. Lois Buckley was a long-standing member of the London Branch of the AWST. She was AWST President in 1961–2, thus presiding over the AWST's activities in the years prior to amalgamation. Ernest Coulson (later Professor) was an influential figure in the SMA and ASE, and in the Nuffield O-level and A-level chemistry projects.

At amalgamation, E.W. (Bill) Tapper remained as General Secretary of the Association for Science Education, having been appointed the first full-time General Secretary of the SMA, taking up the post on 1st January 1962. He was supported by a newly-appointed Assistant Secretary of the ASE, Miss E.M. Taylor, who had joined the AWST as a member of staff in 1960.

The SMA had already taken the step of setting up a Headquarters to cope with the growth in its own membership and its publishing operation. In 1961, a large detached house at 52, Bateman Street in Cambridge had been secured on an 11-year lease. The building had previously been a preparatory school and still stands in 2012, housing the 'New School of English'. Hugh Ramage became Director of what he hoped would become the 'Science Education Centre' and was given the role of Warden of Headquarters. However, when it rapidly became clear that there was a need for a full-time General Secretary, Hugh and his wife left the Headquarters flat, making available much needed space. Thereafter, responsibility for supervising the work at ASE Headquarters fell to the General Secretary.

E.W. (Bill) Tapper – General Secretary (of SMA then ASE) 1961–1971

Bill Tapper had previously been senior physics master at Dulwich College, during which time he had received a grant from the Industrial Fund to modernise the laboratories at his school. Immediately prior to his appointment as General Secretary of the SMA he had been researching the teaching of physics at

Figure 2.2: E.W. Tapper of the SMA and ASE.

the University of Bristol as a Gulbenkian Fellow. The early days of the new Association were a busy and exciting time for the first General Secretary. In 1963 alone there were alterations to be made to the Headquarters building, including the stockroom; this was in the basement and required damp-proofing and new heating and lighting. A Science Education Conference was to be organised in April 1963, which would include a visit and dinner with ASE's Patron, HRH The Duke of Edinburgh. An alphabetical list of members was to be produced, and a membership brochure describing the new Association and communication with the Branches was to be regularised. During the year, a service agreement for the General Secretary was finalised, and he was awarded a richly-deserved pay rise. As the new ASE took shape, membership continued to increase and the attendance at the Annual Meeting and at Branch events was high – sometimes too high to be comfortably accommodated.

Governance

The General Secretary had a large governing Council with which to work – comprising the Chair of the Association, three Vice Chairs, four Honorary Secretaries, the Treasurer and the Editor, six elected members, 17 representatives of the Branches (of both AWST and SMA) and any of the (three) Trustees who were not members in some other capacity. The total number in 1963 was 36 and this had risen by 1971 with the inclusion of more Branch representation. Fortunately, a more manageable Executive Committee of only seven members worked alongside Bill Tapper to look after the day-to-day management. The Executive Committee had to work very hard in the first year of the ASE's existence, meeting no less than 11 times. This reduced to a more manageable six times in 1965. It was soon discovered that there would have to be rule changes to cope with the practicalities that arose after the merger, not least making provision for the position of Patron, already occupied by HRH The Duke of Edinburgh. The early structure of governance comprised only one standing committee – the Education Committee – but, perhaps inevitably, sub-committees and working groups proliferated. A diagram in *Education in Science* (no. 21) shows how, in 1973, the various task groups divided off from the Education Committee. In the first year of operation, the past Chairs of the SMA and the past Presidents of the AWST collectively supported the provision of a badge of office for the Chair. Two years later, the production of a past-Chair's badge was also approved.

In 1967, a major change to the committee structure took place when the Education Committee was split into the Education (Research) Committee and the Education (Co-ordinating) Committee. The title of the former indicates its role in future planning, whereas the latter, to which Bill Tapper was Honorary

Secretary, acquired responsibility for more immediate and day-to-day matters. In October 1966, Brian Atwood (of whom more later) chaired a committee to consider the structure of ASE Branches. At amalgamation, Branches from both the SMA and the AWST had been encouraged to continue, but they were of different sizes with huge variations in memberships. The work of Brian Atwood's committee led to a new National/Region/Section model, with 17 Regions divided into smaller Sections. At this time the Science Advisers group was also meeting regionally, and it was thought that other special interest groups might follow this model. The Rule Change to put this into action was placed before the Annual General Meeting in January 1968 and passed 'with four dissentient votes'. This resulted in the Council becoming even bigger, at 39. The boundaries of the new Regions had been drawn to create structures of similar sizes so that Regional representation on Council would be more aligned with the numbers of members. However, even then it was clear that, as the ASE continued to expand, further change would be necessary.

In 1970, taking over as Chair, Helen Ward remarked that there had been a proliferation of sub-committees, groups and working parties and that communication between these various bodies and with the Council was proving difficult. The number of sub-committees needed to be reduced. After much discussion and the delivery of an ultimatum, reorganisation led to the establishment of properly constituted committees, answerable to the membership by the production of regular reports.

Layton's account of a rift healed between ASE and 'Project Technology' in 1968 gives an insight into the role of the General Secretary at the time. He quotes Professor Harrison, who led 'Project Technology', as saying that *'Tapper's role as General Secretary is that of a very efficient administrator who does not have to, and is not expected to, make decisions committing the ASE to any new line of policy'*. This was written after Bill Tapper had been selectively quoted in the *Times Educational Supplement* and was engaged in restoring a damaged relationship – his role obviously included that of diplomat.

Staffing

In 1963, there were three members of staff – the General Secretary, the Assistant Secretary and the Publications Officer. In 1964, a working party was set up to look at the staffing situation at HQ, given the increased number of publications and the financial position of the ASE following amalgamation. The working party concluded that further administrative support was necessary and recommended the appointment of a Deputy General Secretary, with responsibility for publications and possibly for editing *SSR* if no Honorary Editor could be found. Following the appointment of a Deputy General Secretary, there were six full-time and three part-time staff, together with some occasional staff engaged to organise the distribution of notices and circulars. The report of this working party reveals that decisions on staffing were very much the responsibility of the Council committees at this time.

The workload imposed on staff by members sending incorrect subscriptions is referred to constantly during the early days in the *Bulletin* and in its successor publication, *Education in Science*. This was despite the use of automated equipment purchased with the aid of an Industrial Fund grant. There was a heavy burden of letter-writing and, although the membership data were handled using an Addressograph machine, this needed considerable manual attention in order to keep records up to date. The appointment of an Assistant to the General Secretary (J.H. Pleavin) in 1966 was prompted by the workload associated with a membership of nearly 12,000. When Pleavin left at the end of 1968, it was clear that the post of Assistant Secretary should be divided into two: one role being essentially administrative and the other fulfilling the role of deputy to the General Secretary. Mr Nesbitt-Larking was appointed as Executive Secretary in April 1969 and, in September, following the move of the ASE Headquarters to Hatfield (as described below), the General Secretary was empowered to engage staff as he judged necessary. This took some time and, until matters settled down, apologies had to be made to members for the late delivery of journals from the new building. The relocation served to sharpen the distinction between the administrative and the professional staff, many of whom were long-standing members of the Association. It was the professional staff largely who made the move from Cambridge to Hatfield. This was the cause of some anxiety for the Executive Committee as voiced in January 1970. At the Association Dinner at the University of Lancaster, Headquarters staff chose not to attend since *'they did not want to occupy places members could have had'*. Such sensitivity, while perhaps understandable, was soon overcome and Headquarters staff have attended all subsequent Association Dinners held at the Annual Meeting (later Conference). As the activities of ASE continued to grow, further staff appointments proved necessary. In 1971, with the move completed and all well settled in, there were eight full- and five part-time staff, again supported by a team of retired people employed on an occasional basis.

International

Although the Tapper era was very early in the life of ASE, international links were already developing, usually led by the General Secretary. The ASE

Executive approved the General Secretary's visit to Sri Lanka (then Ceylon) for the Commonwealth Conference in December of 1963, at which he presented a paper on 'The Work of the Association for Science Education'. The President and Secretary of the Dutch Science Teachers Association were invited to the ASE Annual Meeting in 1964, and large Dutch contingents continue to visit the ASE Annual Conference. In fact, from the very earliest days, the Annual Meeting attracted international visitors: for example, in 1966, seven different countries were represented. In 1965, the *Bulletin* listed five overseas science teachers' associations with which the ASE was affiliated and a further ten organisations with which it had contact, usually in the form of an exchange of journals. In 1966, Bill Tapper attended the World Friends International Youth Science Fortnight in Montreal, and the current relationship with the US National Science Teachers' Association started with attendance at their Annual Meeting in New York City in April 1966 by the General Secretary and the Annual Meeting Secretary. In April 1967, the first invitation was received to select students to be 'Five for Sydney' and attend the Harry Messel International Summer School, a project which is still continuing (See Chapter 8, Case Study 7).

Membership

In June 1967, for the first time, the editorial in *Education in Science* included *'from the General Secretary'* as the by-line. This was a direct communication between Bill Tapper and the membership at a point when the move to Hatfield was imminent, and there was a need to increase subscriptions for which the support of the membership was needed. Bill Tapper aimed to help members to understand the operation of Headquarters and the range of work that went on there. In September 1969, *Education in Science* was styled for the first time *'the official means of communication with members'*.

During the later 1960s, the importance of liability insurance for members was recognised, and arrangements were made to provide this within the membership subscription as a benefit to all members who might be reluctant to join a trade union but wanted the reassurance that this cover could provide. This remains an important member benefit in 2012. At this time, a membership questionnaire was introduced, looking principally at the qualifications of science teachers.

Towards the end of this period, the postal strike of early 1970 had a disastrous impact on management of the membership records, happening as it did alongside the move to the new Headquarters, and recovery took some time. At the end of 1971, as the General Secretary was about to retire, membership subscriptions were put up to £5 – an increase from £3 and justified by the fact that there had been no increase for the previous five years. This was a very substantial increase, however, and caused considerable debate amongst the membership.

Premises

Despite the settled situation in Bateman Street as the ASE started out in 1963, the Council and officers of the Association realised that a permanent, fit-for-purpose headquarters would eventually be needed, preferably closer to London, and a Building and Development Fund was set up. Meanwhile, other organisations were considering joining the ASE in 52, Bateman Street, although this came to nothing as they preferred to be in central London. The physics organiser on the Nuffield-funded Science Curriculum Development Project was based at Bateman Street for some time during 1963.

In January 1966, the Treasurer remarked that *'we are living very cheaply'* and cautioned that *'to move to other premises within the near future would constitute a major crisis'*. By the time the Annual Report was written the

Figure 2.3: 52, Bateman Street, Cambridge, the first Headquarters of ASE.

following year, however, it had become clear that a move was necessary and the search began. A number of alternatives were considered, including sharing offices with the College of Preceptors (now the College of Teachers) in London; bidding at auction for a property in Cambridge (turned down because of the financial uncertainty involved); and purchasing the lease of 52, Bateman Street. Eventually, because of a family connection between a past General Secretary of the SMA, H.F. Broad, and Hertfordshire County Council, which was responsible for the Technical College, a move to Hatfield was suggested. A site on the grounds of the (then) Technical College was identified in November 1966 and the plan went ahead to raise funds and build the building. The new location would allow the General Secretary ease of access to London, while keeping the costs of the Association low.

An appeal to members by the Chair of the Association to help fund the move was backed up (with a slight tone of panic!) by the Treasurer. The appeal asked for £1 from each member but, in the event, the cost of the relocation was met by a combination of the appeal, existing funds and a one-off grant from

Figure 2.4: The College Lane, Hatfield site, Headquarters from 1969.

the Department of Education. A Board of Trade office development permit for the new building was received in January 1968 and, following much planning and discussion, in November 1968, a drawing of the planned new building in Hatfield was proudly presented to members in *Education in Science*. The move took place in June of 1969, with the first meeting of the Executive taking place at the new Headquarters in September 1969, and the address was operational from October. The furnishing of Headquarters followed and, by January 1970, members were informed that *'steady progress'* was being made.

Retirement

Bill Tapper announced his intention to resign with effect from 31st December 1971. He had taken the Association from its formation to a new fit-for-purpose Headquarters and overseen the rationalisation of the membership data. As Tapper announced his intention to retire, Brian Atwood had just taken over as Chair of the Association and, to many, he appeared to be the ideal choice for the next General Secretary. He was reluctant to put himself forward, but was persuaded, and his appointment was announced in June of 1971. At the Association Dinner in Stirling in January 1972, a special presentation was made to the outgoing General Secretary, and both he and his wife were elected as Honorary Members at that Annual Meeting. Bill Tapper wrote his final notes as General Secretary in *Education in Science* in February 1972, maintaining his plea for subscriptions to be paid correctly and thanking everyone for his retirement gift. It is noticeable that in his final Annual Report there is a distinct air of his having been freed from constraint and *'able to blow the ASE trumpet'*. In the remarks made about him at the Annual Business Meeting after his retirement, it was said that *'The General Secretary has always in a quiet way been ready with sound advice, always found to be of value.'* He was remembered as an 'Edwardian gentleman', very large but gentle and polite. Following his retirement, he continued to help for a while on *Education in Science*. Bill Tapper died in August 1983.

Brian Atwood OBE – General Secretary 1972–1989

Having been Association Chair, Brian Atwood conformed to the tradition of appointing the General Secretary and other professional staff from within the membership. He had taught at Great Barr Comprehensive School in Birmingham. As the longest-serving General Secretary of the ASE, his care for the organisation and its people is remembered fondly by those who worked with him. The Association was still something of a cottage industry at this stage, with financial issues stemming from the move, and Brian's attention to quality control and his sound financial ability made him a good choice to lead the organisation into its next phase. His attitude towards the officers was that of the previous General Secretary: the General Secretary ran Headquarters and was the servant of the elected officers of the Association.

In April 1971, when Chair of the Association, Brian Atwood had called a meeting at Hatfield of as many subject teaching associations as he could contact. In the event, 20 such associations met and formed COSTA (the Council of Subject Teaching Associations), adopting a constitution in February 1972, by which time Brian had taken up the position of General Secretary of ASE. The ASE administered the new Council until 1977, when the Historical Association took over, and ASE continued to be involved thereafter. Indeed ASE, as the largest of the subject teaching associations, has played a central role in the groupings of various aspects of subject associations since that time.

There was an indication of the crossover between the roles of Chair and General Secretary when the Yorkshire Region decided to hold a Regional Conference to discuss science education issues, including the future role of ASE. This was in response to a paper written by Brian Atwood and the event was attended by Brian and by the then Chair of the Association, W.F. (Fred)

Figure 2.5: Fred Archenhold, left, (Association Chair 1973) and Brian Atwood, right, (General Secretary) with Mrs Joan Archenhold and Mrs Barbara Atwood at Hatfield HQ, 1973.

Archenhold. Following this, the view was expressed in the September 1973 issue of *Education in Science* that the ASE had not *'come to grips with comprehensive education'*, a comment taken up by *The Times* that prompted a response from the General Secretary. It is quite possible that this comment stung the General Secretary who had taught in a very large comprehensive school and he was hence enthusiastic about the participation of the Association in the LAMP (Least/Less Academically Motivated Pupils) project (see Chapter 3), which helped to change the perception of the ASE as being as a 'grammar school organisation'.

Staffing

Brian Atwood's style, according to those who knew him, was to be interested in and concerned for his staff; he checked everyone's welfare each morning and he recruited preferentially from the families of those already involved with ASE. Perhaps as a result, during his time in charge, there was a very long period of stability in staffing. He also liked to get involved, in particular with the bookselling operation where he would lend a hand with despatch if necessary. Brian recruited a small band of pensioners to work on the dispatch of *Education in Science* and was responsible, with his wife, for an annual party comprising a full Christmas dinner. This was cooked in the office kitchen for all the staff and is the subject of many fond memories of Brian.

In 1973, shortly after Brian Atwood took up his position, there were 3 'professional' and 13 'administrative' staff. This increased to 5 'professional' and 28 'administrative' by 1983. Part of the reason for this was the establishment of a book sales operation of considerable size at Headquarters. This operation worked very well, providing an excellent source of income for the Association, dealing in large numbers of school science textbooks with a turnover of around £800,000 per annum at its peak. This enterprise finally came to an end when the 'net book agreement' ended around 1990, allowing other suppliers to offer lower prices. It has to be remembered also that, at this time, books written by members were typed up from longhand copy, and that it was during this period that the move from manual to electric typewriters came about, and then to computers.

The other reason for the increase in staff was to extend the professional capabilities of Headquarters. This allowed the new staff to become engaged with science education policy while the General Secretary was content to run Headquarters and to interact with the top level governance of the Association. To this end Catherine Wilson joined the staff. She had been an active member of the Education (Research) Committee and in 1973 was appointed as Assistant

Secretary, to deal largely with science education and curriculum issues and the burgeoning range of important ASE publications. Catherine later became Deputy General Secretary. In 1975, she was joined by Richard Turner, who had responsibility for the Annual Meeting. Carol Abbott joined in 1980 to support the production of *School Science Review*. During a very busy time for the politics of education their efforts were augmented by a group of energetic enthusiasts from the membership, including Jeff Thompson, Dick West and John Nellist. There was a move to develop policy groups to respond to the raising of the school leaving age to 16 in 1973.

International

From its earliest days, ASE had links with other science teachers' associations across the world as can be seen from the early Annual Reports. Collaboration with the National Science Teachers Association (NSTA) in the USA in the person of Professor David Lockhard, and with UNESCO, led to the formation of a formal group – the International Council of Associations of Science Education (ICASE). Brian Atwood served as ICASE President from 1981 to 1985.

Membership

At the end of 1971, membership passed the 14,000 mark. During the period from 1971 to 1988, membership increased to nearly 20,000, reflecting the changes that were taking place with the greater politicisation of education and the forthcoming introduction of a national curriculum.

Premises

Having been perfectly suitable for the small staff immediately following the move from Cambridge, as the membership and the scale of the bookselling operation increased, the Headquarters building once again proved to be too small. Also, it was a prefabricated structure, which was so inadequately heated in the winter that the staff brought in their own electric heaters. A large extension was therefore built in 1978, following careful planning and gathering of funds, which effectively doubled the size of the building.

In 1988, Brian Atwood indicated that he wished to retire. He had been persuaded to take up the post of General Secretary, a little reluctantly, when the Honorary Officers had been unable to find an alternative suitable candidate and had presided over what were generally held to be happy times for ASE staff and successful times for the Association generally. He was given a splendid send-off at the Annual Meeting in January 1989 in Birmingham, with a spectacular firework display. He retired to Ludlow and died in 2001 at the age of 72.

David Moore OBE – General Secretary, then Chief Executive 1989–2002

David Moore was appointed to the position of General Secretary in March 1988 and took up his post in 1989. He was at the time Chair-elect of ASE and was Deputy Head at Caludon Castle School in Coventry. The features of his time leading ASE are in his own words, below.

I felt very honoured to be appointed as General Secretary of the Association in 1988, and looked forward to the challenge of transforming it from what was in many ways a learned society to a more professional support organisation. I became a member of ASE in 1966 and, as Honorary Annual Meeting Secretary, had been a member of Council and the Executive Committee since 1982, so already I was familiar with the processes and practices of the Association.

On taking up my post, I wanted to hear what was going on from the people who sustained the Association at grassroots level, and managed to attend Regional committee meetings in almost every region. It was evident that the arrival of the new National Curriculum was going to have a significant impact, and that both help and guidance together with a national voice on this development would be needed. I also tried to visit as many teacher training departments as I could to seek their help in creating a more positive approach to recruiting student members, as they would be responsible for carrying the Association forward in the years ahead.

Figure 2.6: Brian Atwood (left) at an ASE Annual Meeting.

Figure 2.7: David Moore (General Secretary, then Chief Executive).

Governance

There had been growing concern amongst the officers that the ASE Council, which met three times a year and comprised over thirty members, was doing little more than rubber stamping the decisions of the various standing committees. Many of those attending rarely, if ever, felt able to join in discussion. After considerable debate, and a very valuable weekend at the British Gas Management College, the Chair, Edwyn James, proposed that the Education (Co-ordinating) and Education (Research) Committees be disbanded. It was then proposed that Council be divided into three sections, or Divisions, called 'Communications', 'Curriculum' and 'Guidance'. The new Council would meet six times a year with a brief opening session to set the business for the day and then carry on to deal with current issues in the appropriate Divisions. The meeting would close with feedback on debates and decisions from each Division in full Council. Each Division would be supported by a specific member of the Headquarters team to ensure that the Division was fully briefed, and decisions implemented. The Executive Committee would be reduced to five or six members and meet between Council meetings to review progress and decide where further action might be needed. These changes were approved unanimously, and enabled all Council members to contribute to the work of the Association in a way which had not been possible previously. It also helped to bridge the gap between the centre and the Regions.

Staffing

In 1988, the Secondary Science Curriculum Review, under the Directorship of Professor Dick West, which had been set up with funding from the Department for Education and Science (DfES) was coming to an end. It had been designed to be a 'bottom up' rather than a centrally-managed process and its activities were co-ordinated by a number of full-time regional project officers (see Chapter 3). This seemed to be a successful approach, but quite beyond the resources of the Association to maintain beyond the project's lifetime. However, the 1988 Annual Meeting at the University of Nottingham had been the most successful in the ASE's history, attracting over 5000 delegates, no doubt due to a general need to find out how to cope with the science National Curriculum. This Meeting generated a surplus of around £70,000 and I proposed to Council that this be used to create a number of Field Officers who would support the activities of the Association locally.

I recommended that five Field Officers should be appointed, each working for one day a week and supporting two or three Regions. Their principal task was to support local committees in arranging meetings and other events, in order to take some of the burden off committee members. They were also to be a source of up-to-date information in times of rapid change. It was essential that these would be self-funded in some way, and it was agreed that each Field Officer would manage an 'Area Meeting' as a more easily reached local Annual Meeting during the summer months, to generate an income. After a couple of years, due to popular demand, a sixth meeting especially for technicians was added to the programme. Although these meetings were reasonably successful, the difficulty that teachers had in being released from their schools worked against them in the long term.

Another prompt in the move towards modernisation arose when, one morning, a member of the Headquarters team, Iris Sinfield, Assistant Secretary [Annual Meeting] came for a word. She told me that someone had asked in a telephone conversation what her role was and she had replied that she was an Assistant Secretary. He replied 'That's no good; I want to speak to a proper secretary'! When I reported this to Council, it was subsequently agreed that the titles of the Association officers should be updated to Chief Executive, Deputy Chief Executive and Director of Curriculum Support, Director of Publications and Director for the Annual Meeting.

International

There has always been a significant number of science teachers from countries around the world attending the Annual Meeting, many of whom would arrive in the UK ahead of the Meeting. Under the leadership of Mary Ratcliffe as ASE Chair, an extra day was added at the beginning of the Annual Meeting as the 'International Day' with a planned international programme. Over time this has attracted science educators from more than 50 countries, and inspired the establishment of the International Committee to assist with the management of ASE's international links.

Headquarters

A decade on from the start of Brian Atwood's successful booksales operation, most publishers had established their own direct sales departments, undercutting ASE prices, and sales via ASE were dwindling. With support from the Publications Committee, and encouraged by significant sales of the SATIS resources, a concerted drive was made to encourage new authors to publish and market their books through the Association. There was also, for good or ill, a steadily rising demand for Health and Safety advice and the Safeguards Committee responded with several advisory publications. Each of these required updating every couple of years, thereby producing a steady demand. The speed of turnaround from initial drafts to finished book helped to provide ideas and suggestions to the membership about the most recent concerns.

Policy and projects

In the original structure of the National Curriculum, English, mathematics and science were designated as core subjects. At an initial meeting of representatives of the core subject associations in September 1989, it was agreed that teachers would best be supported by offering advice relating to Key Stages 1 and 2 (ages 5–7 and 7–11). ASE hosted a writing weekend at which a booklet entitled *The National Curriculum – making it work for the Primary School* was put together. The Association took on the production and marketing of this booklet, which eventually sold over 70,000 copies. The initial meeting was the start of a termly gathering of seven subject associations under the leadership of ASE (see Chapter 8).

Throughout the life of ASE, the officers of the Association held regular but discreet meetings with science HMIs to exchange views on how well science education was evolving, looking at the successes or failures of the various new initiatives. It was partly through these meetings that the Secretary of State was persuaded to fund what was probably the only curriculum initiative on a national scale ever to happen prior to the arrival of the National Curriculum, namely the Secondary Science Curriculum Review (SSCR), set up in 1981 (see Chapters 3 and 5). It was no surprise that the science team who wrote the original science component of the National Curriculum were all active members of the Association. This reflects the fact that through regular debate and discussion a broad consensus existed amongst all parties regarding the nature of effective science education.

Once the National Curriculum had been adopted, the practice of regular meetings between ASE officers and HMI continued to take place. As the new agencies were set up, initially the NCC (National Curriculum Council) and SEAC (Schools Examination and Assessment Council), termly meetings with these organisations also took place where ASE views were represented. Interestingly, when the meetings were held at the NCC, officers of the ASE were joined by their counterparts from the English and mathematics subject associations, which gave the discussions a wider perspective.

The Association regularly invited the Secretary of State to attend the Annual Meeting and, from time to time, one of the Education Ministers came along. At the 1998 Meeting in Reading, Junior Minister Charles Clarke, having had some time to walk around and take in the scale of the event, said 'I really must make time to hear what you have to say'. A few months later he held the first of a series of meetings with representatives of all the major subject associations. This provided an opportunity to raise issues of general concern. Prominent among these was a need to recognise and support the professional development of teachers, especially those of the science community.

Curriculum development had begun to play an increasingly significant part in the work of the Association. In 1984, the Education (Research) Committee had held discussions with John Lewis, a past Chair of the Association and Head of Science at Malvern College, regarding a new venture that he had been piloting called 'Science in Society'. This was a resource to support A-level science courses, which used a series of units to illustrate how new discoveries were being applied and to examine their social implications. The Committee agreed to take on the management and production of these resources and to extend them into a wide range of teaching materials for use in GCSE teaching. The new resource was named 'Science and Technology in Society', usually abbreviated to SATIS, and is detailed elsewhere in this work (see Chapter 8, Case Study 2).

The SATIS materials attracted widespread interest in many European countries, so I asked John Holman (then at Watford Grammar School) to hold a session at the 1991 Annual Meeting to find out how this resource was being used abroad, and where it fitted into the many different curricula. The BP Education Manager was in the audience and offered funding to develop this further; hence 'Science Across Europe', later to become 'Science Across the World', was born

Figure 2.8: *Kenneth Clarke (centre) Education Secretary 1990–1992 visiting the ASE Annual Meeting*

(see Chapter 8). The scale of this project necessitated full-time leadership from the Headquarters team and led to the appointment of Marianne Cutler as Project Director. In time, the resources were made available electronically and reached some 2000 schools in nearly 50 countries.

As intervention by government in the processes of education increased in scope and frequency, the successes of ASE in the fields of curriculum development and in providing leadership and guidance inspired the Association to bid for contracts to provide a range of different products to support both members and non-members. One example was the bid, in collaboration with King's College London, to develop the new assessment tests to go alongside the National Curriculum for science. This was won and ASE appointed several members of the development team, who helped to manage the trials. However, this work, together with the English and mathematics developments, was terminated in mid-flight by the Secretary of State as being too cumbersome. Another example was a successful bid, in collaboration with CLEAPSS, to provide the text for a DfES publication Safety in Science Education and subsequently to market it after publication in 1996. This was just one of many examples of a situation where everyone knew that sound advice was already freely available, but government required its own approved and definitive reference work (see Chapter 7).

Another interesting development arose when, following the Year of Mathematics, the Association Chair, Rosemary Feasey, suggested to the Secretary of State that there be a Year of Science. After some debate this was approved and the Association, in collaboration with the British Association for the Advancement of Science (BA), put in a very creative, imaginative and well-managed bid to run this Year. Although the civil servants involved accepted our proposals, the Department appointed NESTA (National Endowment for Science, Technology and the Arts) to manage the Year, with the involvement of both ASE and the BA. This collaboration is detailed in Chapter 8, as is the development of ASE INSET Services.

David Moore decided to retire from the position of Chief Executive in the summer of 2002 and was succeeded by Derek Bell, another past Chair of the Association. Derek describes his experience below.

Derek Bell, Chief Executive 2002–2008

For me personally, David Moore's retirement could not have come at a more convenient time. I had had the privilege of being Chair of the Association in 2000–2001 and having oversight of the Centenary Annual Meeting in January 2001 at the University of Surrey. I therefore was deeply involved in the running of the

Association and felt that this was an opportunity I could not allow to pass by. Having joined ASE as a young science teacher and then over the years been involved with the organisation through contributions to local, regional and then national activities, I had come to see very clearly the value of the Association to me as an individual, as well as its ability and potential to influence the wider agenda of science education.

To be asked at interview to make a presentation addressing the question, *'Is there a future for subject associations?'* was a challenge. The answer had to be *'Yes'*, but it raised a whole series of issues which, as an incoming Chief Executive, one would have to address in order to ensure not simply the survival of the organisation but also to manage the change required for it to prosper in new and as yet unknown environments.

Inevitably, science education was again experiencing change with the introduction of revised versions of the statutory curricula in England, Wales and Northern Ireland. The profile of teaching and learning in science was very high as Science Year was coming to an end and its successor, Planet Science, was being considered (see Chapters 5 and 8). New organisations were beginning to appear, such as the transformation of the City Technology Colleges Association into The Specialist Schools Trust. In addition, there was the increasing influence of the National Strategy for Science in England and early discussions on the feasibility of a

Figure 2.9: *The Royal Charter displayed at the Annual Dinner 2006. Derek Bell, far left (Chief Executive), Alex Galloway (Clerk to the Privy Council), Bob Kibble (Association Chair) and Professor Sir Gareth Roberts.*

'Centre of Excellence for Science Teaching'. In short, the position of ASE, not for the first or the last time in its history, was being challenged.

It is interesting to note that a number of incidents in the first three months of my tenure in effect set the scene for much of what happened in the following six years. These included: the day I was presented with the plans for development of the University of Hertfordshire campus, which showed a new Senate Building on the site of the ASE Headquarters building; the announcement that the government and the Wellcome Trust were in discussions to establish a network of science learning centres; and the decision by ASE Council to proceed with a submission for a Royal Charter, including the powers to establish Chartered Science Teacher status; and finally, a very disturbing comment by a long-term member, who suggested that *'ASE might be part of the problem [in science education] and not part of the solution.'*

Governance

All organisations must frequently look at themselves in order to establish that they are 'fit for purpose'. This requires that they understand their purpose, are able to articulate it and then work towards achieving it. ASE is no different and, as it entered the 21st century, had started reflecting on this issue. For example, at a Council meeting in March 2001, members and invited guests met to explore what teaching and learning science might look like and how the Association should contribute to this future. A short report, published in *Education in Science* (September 2001), called on ASE to show, among other things, leadership in the teaching of science, the development of the science curriculum and the professional development of teachers. It went on to say that ASE must listen to its members, endeavour to meet their needs, work with government and other bodies and take advantage of external initiatives to further its own objectives. In many respects, this was a re-enforcement of the long-standing purposes of the Association, but it was also a recognition that the environment was changing, not simply in the field of science education, but also more widely.

Many discussions involving members, Regions, officers, Council and committees reaffirmed the overall purpose, which was then captured in a new logo and strapline: 'to promote excellence in science teaching and learning'. Importantly, this was supported by three further statements that reflected both the values that ASE espoused and the mechanisms by which it would work to achieve its objectives.

○ Encouraging participation emphasised that ASE was an inclusive organisation, which respected the individual and encouraged everyone to get involved, preferably by becoming a member, and share expertise.

○ Enhancing professionalism of, and for, teachers, technicians, members and staff through advocacy of chartered status, as well as the provision and promotion of high quality professional development and resources.

○ Working in partnership with others in order to strengthen its ability to influence policy and practice and to increase its reputation for innovation, delivering cutting edge initiatives and providing reliable advice and support for its members and the wider science education community.

These underpinning principles informed the strategic plans, the updating of the journals and other activities that followed, in order not only to communicate the messages but also to implement the many decisions that had to be made in running a complex organisation. At the same time, 'ASE', rather than 'the ASE' started to be used as the abbreviated name of the Association, as a more modern and less clumsy style, particularly for consistency in re-styling the Journals.[1]

Gaining the Royal Charter

The Association for Science Education became incorporated by Royal Charter in October 2004 and its legal status changed significantly thereby. The granting of the Charter underlined ASE's standing as a respected professional body. The instruments of governance, the By-laws and Rules had to be changed – a substantial task in itself. More importantly the process required Council to take on new responsibilities as the 'board and trustees' of the Association. It is to the credit of the Council members and staff working together that this transition went smoothly, but it also opened up discussions as to whether the governance arrangements were 'fit-for-purpose' in the new environment. Ultimately, these discussions led to the new arrangements that were introduced in 2011.

The significant addition to ASE's remit under the Royal Charter was the exclusive right, as a licensed body of the Science Council, to award Chartered Science Teacher status (CSciTeach) *'which recognises the unique combination of skills, knowledge, understanding and expertise that is required by individuals involved in the specific practice and advancement of science teaching and learning'.* The register of Chartered Science Teachers is a special section of the Science Council's register of Chartered Scientists (CSci), which underpins the quality and equivalence of the awards (see details in Chapter 8).

---

[1] In this book, the style 'ASE', rather than 'the ASE', is used (where grammatically appropriate) in referring to certain aspects of the Association, particularly to recent events or to publication matters.

Reaching this point involved extensive discussions with all the major professional bodies in science and related disciplines as well as with government and other subject teaching associations. This was crucial to ensure that there would be no objections to the granting of such authority by the Privy Council. Importantly, these extended negotiations provided a significant opportunity for the Association to engage with a wide range of science professionals and gain their support for promoting the status of science teachers and their importance in improving the quality of science education. ASE also took the opportunity to provide leadership in the educational arena by gaining the support of many of the other subject associations for chartered status for teachers. Schemes for geography and mathematics teachers are also available at the time of writing and the issue is being discussed again more widely.

Staffing and organisation

A major responsibility of the Chief Executive, besides providing leadership and championing the cause of science education, teachers and technicians (the public side of the job), is ensuring that the organisation is efficiently run, in other words managing the business. This involves maintaining, and where necessary improving, staff expertise and morale, using resources efficiently and effectively and ensuring that premises function to the benefit of the Association.

In an environment that has become ever more challenging in terms of regulations for businesses, competition for services and increasing expectations from potential members, a key consideration was the development of a stronger business-like approach, without losing the personal touch in working with members and other stakeholders. As my opposite number in the NSTA in the USA, Gerry Wheeler, used to say during our many conversations on running two similar organisations, 'I have to remind my Board [equivalent to ASE Council] that "not for profit" is a tax status – it doesn't mean we don't have to make money.' To aid the necessary developments, a new staffing structure was introduced at ASE to create a small senior management team consisting of the Chief Executive and three others, each with an area of responsibility that linked to the existing Divisions of Council, i.e. Curriculum Issues Division (CID), Communications and Public Image Division (CPID) and Guidance Division (GDiv). Not only did this provide a structure for day-to-day operations, but it also provided much more of a direct link between the governance structures of the Association and the management structures in Headquarters.

Changes in structure often demand changes in processes. A new website was needed and installed, following much hard work from John Lawrence (Deputy Chief Executive). Each website has been more sophisticated than its predecessor in an attempt to provide the range of services demanded by members and required as part of the public face of ASE. A new membership database and a new integrated financial system were also introduced – not without their teething problems. When developments go smoothly, there is rarely a complaint, but when there are problems it is the staff that have to deal with the reactions. It is their commitment that is so important to ASE and their professionalism that is needed to meet the demands put on the organisation. A signal of the Association's commitment to its staff was demonstrated when it gained Investors in People recognition in 2002, which was then renewed in 2007.

Premises

Perhaps one of the biggest barriers in 2002 to bringing about the changes needed to the organisation was the Headquarters building, known locally and affectionately as the 'scout hut'. It had served the ASE extremely well for nearly 40 years but was certainly showing its age. The need for planning ahead had already been acknowledged and, at the Centenary Annual Meeting in January 2001, an appeal had been launched to raise the funds needed to provide a replacement building. In the meantime, despite efforts to upgrade its condition, the layout, leaky roof, constant need for maintenance and the approaching end of the lease, meant that the current one was very much becoming a depreciating asset. However, as in the past with ASE premises, fate intervened.

Figure 2.10: *The Patron of ASE, HRH Prince Philip, The Duke of Edinburgh, at the opening of the new Headquarters building 17 March 2008.*

Being 'removed from the University plans' proved to be a turning point for the better in relationships with the University of Hertfordshire, which was crucial in the quest for new premises. Around 2005, the Director of Estates came to see me and outlined some new plans for the University campus, which required the ASE to move. This put the Association in quite a strong position, although nothing could be guaranteed. After various discussions and exploring options, agreement was reached on the new offices, which the University completely refurbished to ASE's requirements and which were secured on very favourable terms with a long lease.

Planning for such a move involved several levels of organisation and development. The most obvious were the physical changes to ensure that all works on the building were completed according to plan in terms of the design, layout and schedule. Then there was the fitting out with furniture, IT equipment and services as well as all the resources needed to run a business as well as meeting the needs of the organisation. For example, one of ASE's needs was a sufficient number of spaces for Council and committee meetings as well as other events.

Despite some moments of tension and some angst about what should be retained and what was surplus to requirements, the logistics of getting the building prepared and then making the actual move went quite well. This was down to the hard work of all the staff and in particular of Gerry Mears, who came out of retirement to act as site and project manager. Once we had vacated the old

Figure 2.11: *The new ASE Headquarters from 2007 – on the University of Hertfordshire (Hatfield) site.*

building, the university did not hesitate to do something they clearly had wanted to do for many years. The 'scout hut' was razed to the ground within a month of ASE moving out – a moment in history!

The official opening of the new offices was carried out by the Association's Patron, HRH Prince Philip, The Duke of Edinburgh, on 17th March 2008.

Relocation of an organisation involves much more than simply moving into nice new offices. It provides an opportunity to think about many of the fundamentals of the organisation because the offices are part of the public image – what messages do they give out? The decision to adopt an open-plan layout reflected the desire for more collaborative working and to improve communications both internally and externally. The provision of meeting rooms helped to increase the use of the space by members and others during the working day and the reception area provided a more welcoming introduction to ASE for visitors. Although it was only one factor, the advent of the new offices facilitated the move of ASE INSET Services to Hatfield. Planning ASE's move involved everyone on the staff as well as the committees and Council – it really was a team effort and those involved cannot be praised too highly for their contributions.

Managing external relationships

One of the strengths of ASE has always been its position as a rallying point for individuals and organisations with interests in science education. The Annual Conference, still held in the first week of January every year, is a clear manifestation of this role. As Chief Executive, walking around the Conference and exhibition is a strong reminder of the extent of ASE's reach both in the UK and worldwide. From a leadership point of view, the Conference is also a tangible reminder of the need for effective management of the many relationships that have been developed over many years with sponsors, project partners, government, science professional bodies, devolved administrations in the UK and international organisations (see chapter 8). The quality of these partnerships is a key element in enabling the Association to achieve its objectives, whether it is through direct collaboration in innovative projects, making joint approaches to governments to advocate changes in education policy or providing the best possible services for members.

There are many stories that could be told about the highs and lows of these relationships – shared achievements and moments of tension as a partnership comes under strain. Establishing CSciTeach, referred to above, is but one example of working with the science professional bodies: The Royal Society of Chemistry, The Institute of Physics, The Society of Biology, and the Science Council and the Royal Society. Another milestone in the development of ASE's relationship with these organisations occurred in 2006 when SCORE (Science Community Representing Education) was established, with the Association as a founder member. SCORE provides a key interface with government in the development of school science education policy. ASE's role in this group is important in ensuring that discussions remain grounded in improving practice and supporting teachers and technicians to the ultimate benefit of students.

In a similar fashion, the Association's relationships with other subject teaching associations – The Geographical Association, The National Association of Teachers of English, The Association of Teachers of Mathematics, The Mathematical Association, the Historical Association and the Design and Technology Association continued to mature. They include the setting up of a formal umbrella body, the Council for Subject Associations (see above and chapter 8), as the prominence to be given to subjects in education policy waxed and waned. This collaboration highlighted a key message that is too often forgotten in the ongoing debates about 'school league tables' and the 'overcrowded' National Curriculum in England: subjects do matter. It is not too big a step to say that subject associations are, in many respects, the guardians of their subjects in schools and the education system more widely. In part, this is through the associations' work, individually and collectively, at a national level but, of equal importance, it is also through the network of members in schools and colleges who are striving on a daily basis to provide a quality education for their students. Achieving the latter in and through science is the enduring core purpose of ASE.

Closer to home, as it were, one of the interesting relationships has been that between ASE and its landlord, the University of Hertfordshire. Although both organisations had 'rubbed along' for some years, publication of the development plan in October 2002 said a great deal. This was underlined by a subsequent comment from one of the University's senior management team that *'if they could have got rid of the Association from the campus, they would have done so on many occasions'*. However, things changed quite dramatically during this period due in part to a new Vice-Chancellor, who saw the value of having such a well-regarded organisation on the university site, but, more significantly, when the ASE agreed to partner the University in a bid, which was ultimately successful, to establish one of the regional science learning centres. During the development of the proposal and the subsequent setting up of the centre, the relationships improved considerably and in no small way contributed to the amicable arrangements that made possible the relocation of ASE Headquarters to its present site. The decision by the government in partnership with the Wellcome Trust to set up the network of science learning centres was a potential threat to the whole future of ASE. Some individuals felt that it would be the 'death knell' of the organisation. The challenge was to ensure that, to the contrary, the Association embraced the changing environment and ensured that its role was enhanced by working with these new organisations. Negotiations were not always smooth, nor was the way always clear, but ASE influenced the new developments both directly, via membership of the advisory boards of the National and the regional centres, and indirectly through courses provided by ASE INSET Services and the contributions of ASE members to the programmes.

Managing external relationships for an organisation such as ASE is a delicate balancing act, which presents two particular challenges that are interlinked. The first is avoiding the risk of becoming so subsumed in partnerships that the organisation starts to lose its identity. It is therefore important that the organisation retains some policy positions in its own right rather than as part of a consortium. The second is that of maintaining ASE's independence and its role as a unifying influence across its field of activity. As an organisation, ASE has to survive in the environment in which it happens to find itself and so it must remain viable, both intellectually and financially. This, however, does not mean that ASE should not have views or positions on particular issues or activities that it promotes strongly. Indeed, it might be argued that over the years ASE has been too conservative in expressing its views!

International

ASE's influence extends well beyond the UK – the increasing numbers of international delegates at the Annual Conference is but one indicator of the Association's standing with teachers from Europe and beyond. Much of this is built on the unstinting work of the International Committee, notably due to Lynne Symonds' service as Secretary then Chair for over 14 years, the success of the Science Across the World project and the Association's links with other organisations, including CASTME.

Working with other science teacher organisations from every continent is important but it varies in its nature and extent. There is always an openness to provide help and advice for international colleagues and much can be achieved. A major challenge is to establish and maintain lines of communication with other organisations to share good practice and resources where possible. The setting up of ICASE was a move to address this challenge and for many years it was able to meet the needs of all its members. Sadly, these needs became more and more diverse and, after much heart searching, ASE eventually decided to withdraw from membership of ICASE.

Membership

If there is one thing that runs through everything that ASE does, it has to be for its members and the way in which it supports them and acts as their champion. However, as a charity, the Association cannot act exclusively for its members if it is to meet the legal requirement to contribute to the 'public good'. Meeting the requirement imposed upon the Association as a Registered Charity is probably the biggest challenge for any Chief Executive of a membership-based organisation and it certainly was so during my term of office.

Gone are the heady days when the majority of science teachers joined ASE, but there is an imperative to enrol and retain a substantial body of members. Members are ASE's single most important resource, not merely because they provide income (although that helps), but because it is members who provide innovative ways of thinking and working; it is members who establish formal and informal networks; it is members who help run the organisation; it is members who give ASE status and credibility in the eyes of government and other bodies; and it is members who give ASE its independence to speak up for science education.

The rationale behind the increase in the number of Field Officers in 2003–04 and the enhancement of their role was in the first instance to provide a more robust interface between Headquarters and ASE regions and their committees. It also gave the Association a stronger presence throughout the UK, when it came to the regional development strategy of the government between 2002 and 2009, providing, for example, a one-to-one link between ASE and the nine regional science learning centres. Although not the only mechanism, the appointment of Field Officers for Wales and Northern Ireland in addition to that for Scotland helped to address the challenges that increasingly arose because of the devolution of powers to those countries. It is too easy to become too focused on England's education system and the presence of Field Officers in these nations was a tangible reminder that the Association serves the whole of the UK.

While Field Officers help to meet the needs of the membership in a geographical sense, the setting up of specialist committees and specific interest groups (SIG) are mechanisms for meeting the needs of particular sectors of the membership. The established committees, such as primary and secondary (which became 11 – 19), have fulfilled this role for many years. The formalisation of the Research Committee endeavoured to raise the profile of research and the importance of an evidence base on which to build our understanding of teaching and learning in science. Similarly, the incorporation of the Association of Tutors in Science Education (ATSE) as a special interest group of the ASE aimed to provide a stronger voice for those involved in teacher education in the way that NAIGS had done effectively, for many years, for advisers and inspectors in science.

Despite various initiatives and much thought, the conundrum of how to increase membership remains unsolved. It is no consolation that other subject associations – many to a greater extent – are having the same experience. We must not give up on this, otherwise ASE will no longer be the ASE in anything but name.

Annette Smith, Chief Executive 2009–

Derek Bell announced his decision to leave ASE to take up the post of Head of Education at the Wellcome Trust in the autumn of 2008. A selection process then took place and the author of this chapter was appointed in December 2008.

Figure 2.12: Annette Smith, Chief Executive (centre) in 2009 with ASE President, Wynne Harlen (left) and ASE Chair, Carolyn Yates (right).

I took up my position at the end of March 2009 following a period in which the Executive Directors had 'held the fort'. My background for the past 15 years was in a variety of roles with the British Science Association (formerly the British Association for the Advancement of Science) – a long term friend of ASE. I had managed their Festival of Science, been Director of the regional operation, looked after National Science and Engineering Week and run the Young People's Programmes. Way back, I had been a teacher and teacher educator and also worked in industry.

I celebrated my appointment to the post of Chief Executive of ASE just before Christmas 2008 with tepid champagne, as I was too excited to give it time to cool! As I worked through the interview process, I realised (and happily the panel concurred) that my spread of experience was useful for being Chief Executive of ASE and I was ready for the challenge.

Of course, the end of 2008 was not a propitious time for the UK economy, and as I write, there are no obvious signs of significant recovery, so the period about which I am writing has been tremendously difficult for subject associations, including ASE. I realised quickly when I took up my role that there was much to be done. There needed to be quick action on the functioning of Headquarters to build on the Investors in People work and to improve the financial systems. The governance systems put in place for the period following the granting of the Royal Charter had been reviewed, but now needed to be acted upon. In addition, there was the ongoing problem of falling membership. Amid the chorus of voices expressing views about science education, the need for a strong authoritative view from ASE was greater than ever.

My vision, then, on coming into the role was to create a tight, well-functioning Headquarters team with no wasted effort or resource. I knew that this had to be reflected in the workings of the governance of the Association, and for the thread of excellence to run through not just the science education that we sought for young people but through all of our work. This is of necessity a work in progress as I write, but the Association has come a long way towards being a 21st century organisation.

My appointment was a new departure for ASE. Although I can trace my first attendance at an Annual Meeting to 1995, unlike my predecessors I was not a member, let alone a previous Chair of the Association. I was very proud, when I lined up with the Chair, Carolyn Yates, and the President, Wynne Harlen, in July of 2009, to note that for the first time the ASE had females in all three leadership positions. I had always been concerned that charities and, to a certain extent schools, were typified by a largely female workforce with men in the positions of power and it was good to reverse that situation at ASE.

Governance

Following the award of the Royal Charter, a consultation on the structure and operations of the ASE was undertaken during 2007 by the Quality and Audit Committee, which reported to the Chair. At the Annual Business Meeting in January 2009, the Chair, Carolyn Yates, responded to the report and a working group was set up to consider a new structure that would separate the governance duties from the science education and membership issues, yet allow for the thorough and fruitful consideration of both. After much deliberation and consultation, a structure was proposed, which comprised a Council of up to 11 members to be the trustees of the Association, and the Assembly, numbering up to 29, which would be where issues in science education and about communication were discussed. The Quality and Audit Committee looked after the governance on behalf of the members and further committees were to be decided on by Council. The new structure allowed members to put themselves forward as individuals and/or as regional nominees. It also permitted appointments to both Council and the Assembly, which meant that an appropriate mix of talents could be created. This structure was agreed by the membership at the Annual General Meeting (AGM) in January 2011 and work then began to put it into practice. In August 2011, the incoming Chair, Lynne Horton, took responsibility for the Assembly and the past Chair of the Association, Richard Needham, was elected by Council to be the Chair of Trustees. It was then time to look in depth at the membership committees and at the specific interest committees and to make necessary changes. At the same time, the regional structure required attention. Patchy engagement across the UK and the advent of new forms of communication meant that a new look at the regions was needed, while retaining one of the most essential features of membership of ASE – the support of one's peers and the enjoyment of their company.

Following these major changes in the governance of the Association, it was important to look at the Strategic Plan. Various groups took part in exercises to look at the main purposes of ASE and, at the time of writing, the plan for 2012–2017 is in draft form. It was clear from the early work that there were three key features that we needed to focus on in order to take forward the vision of excellence in the teaching and learning of science – they are: the resources and services we provide for our members and for the science education community in general; the voice which we provide for our members' views; and, the management of the organisation which enables us to do these.

The change in the size of Council necessitated a change in the By-Laws in order to correct the composition of the Registration Board. This was passed at the AGM in January 2012 – just before ASE became able to offer, under the Science Council's new registers, the status of Registered Science Technician to our technician members and the status of Registered Scientist to members with a science degree and Qualified Teacher Status, thus championing the professional status of all science teachers and technicians.

Staffing
Staffing of the Association had grown over the years and the Investors in People status had been gained, although, in 2009, some of the recommendations had still to be implemented in full. The staff systems were therefore updated and regularised. Regular team and individual meetings were held, complemented by regular staff meetings and an improved appraisal system. In difficult financial times. limited opportunities to send staff on external courses were augmented by a system of 'surgeries' to share knowledge across the organisation. Investors in People was renewed in mid-2011, indicating the ASE's continued commitment to its staff. The financial situation could not be avoided however and, in 2011, a number of staff, including some Field Officers, had to be made redundant. This was a painful period, which coincided with a difficult personal time: for me the 2010/11 academic year truly was an 'annus horribilis'.

Projects and programmes
By the time I took up my appointment, the role of Chief Executive had changed enormously from the days of the management by Bill Tapper and Brian Atwood. My diary was crammed with meetings and panels as ASE's input was increasingly sought by other agencies. In 2009, one of the main concerns was the science diploma, the other being the proposed new Primary Curriculum. Neither of these came to fruition, however, as they were swept away by the incoming Coalition Government in 2010. Other large projects during this time included the Getting Practical project funded under the Labour Government's STEM Programme, and the Primary Science Quality Mark. (Both of these collaborative projects are described in more detail in Chapter 8.)

International
Despite some downturn in funded projects, relations with overseas organisations continued to flourish. Return visits to the NSTA conference took place and the ASE Honors Lecture continued to be held in the USA as part of that conference. A European project was completed, and relationships with individual organisations from overseas were kept up with interchanges where possible. Large numbers of overseas visitors came to the Annual Conference from a considerable number of different countries. ASE kept a watching eye on progress with ICASE, but was not sufficiently reassured about its progress to re-join despite very friendly interchanges with its new officers.

Membership

In the early days in my role, I was concerned to visit as many of the Region committees as possible. This was appreciated, as were my contacts with the national committees. The story of membership over this period has, unfortunately, been of rapid decline. The economic circumstances combined with the support for teachers from other quarters means that ASE membership is not now as valued by some as it once was. It is important to pay tribute here to two members who not only contributed their expertise to the Association while they were active, but also remembered ASE extremely generously in their wills. Their legacies helped considerably at a very difficult time. They were Margaret Collis and Bernard Dawson.

Premises

It was important to keep on friendly terms with the University of Hertfordshire, so one of my earliest visits was to the Vice Chancellor, Sir Tim Wilson. He, and his successor, Quintin McKellor, looked benignly on the presence of ASE on the campus and we felt secure with our lease, despite the new plans that we discovered going through the planning process, which put a large new engineering block on top of our existing building. The subsequent history of ASE will tell the tale of what happens to that.

Ensuring ASE's voice is heard

One of the major changes since the early days of ASE was the role of the Chief Executive as the face and voice of the organisation, operating politically on behalf of the Association. At the time of my appointment, changes were afoot to the Primary National Curriculum and the Key Stage 2 and 3 (age 7–11 and 11–14) SATs were being abolished. I had an early opportunity to be heard speaking up for the Association on these subjects. Soon after this, it became clear that a general election campaign was imminent so I engaged the services of a public affairs organisation to help me to meet politicians of all parties. Following the 2010 election, the face of education changed completely. Unlike the 1960s, when the ASE began, and when schools and teachers were largely left to get on with educational matters, the education environment had become highly political with governmental involvement in the finest detail of teaching and learning. Radical policies were introduced with little notice and funding withdrawn from the arms-length agencies. At the time of writing, future government policy remains unclear but the ASE is aiming to keep true to the principles of promoting excellent science education while navigating the policy turmoil.

Communication

By the time I arrived at the Association, the former ASE website was unattractive and difficult to use, lacking many of the features that were expected in 2009. I requested Council's approval for a complete re-design and the new website was inaugurated in September 2010 in time to receive online bookings for the Annual Conference in 2011. Alongside the website, appointment of a communications officer to replace the web editor meant that more staff and members could edit the site and the ASE could interact effectively with the social media.

One of the hugely interesting facets of being Chief Executive of ASE is the number of networks in which one can operate. Mention has been made of the groupings of subject associations, and despite the withdrawal of government funding, the CfSA (the Council for Subject Associations) continues as a 'self-help' group with one or two representatives doing an excellent job of lobbying on behalf of the rest. Another aspect is communication with other third sector organisations through their networks – such as the Association of Chief Executives of Voluntary Organisations (ACEVO) and the Cass Business School Centre for Charity Effectiveness. These organisations help ASE to measure its structure and performance against the most effective charities.

The ASE has been on an eventful journey in the last 50 years and the General Secretaries and Chief Executives who have had the privilege of leading the organisation have had a fascinating time. I hope that readers can detect from this chapter the enormous pride that leading the ASE brings. At a strategy workshop recently, I was asked what gave me joy about my current job. The answer was easy, as the previous Saturday had been spent at the second meeting of the Association's Assembly. I volunteered to be the first to speak and said this: *'The thing that gives me joy is the commitment of ASE's members – I never cease to be amazed that twenty-five of them will turn out on a cold Saturday, with snow forecast, from all over the UK because they want to have serious meaningful discussions about making science education better'.*

Figure 3.1: *Secondary school science students at the Norwich Science Olympiad, 2011 (from* Education in Science, *November 2011).*

3   The ASE and the secondary science curriculum

Martin Hollins

'The secret garden of the curriculum of 1963 has given way in 2011 to a crowded market place.'

The influences on the secondary science curriculum have changed significantly over 50 years, as have the nature of schools and the membership of ASE. The involvement of ASE and its constituent organisations in the reform of the school science curriculum has a long history. During the 1930s, the SMA and the AWST had developed new secondary school courses, intended to be 'science for all' as distinct from embryonic chemists, engineers or biologists. Although the courses, known as General Science, secured a place in the curricula of many grammar schools, the innovation was always controversial. By the mid-1950s, the greatly increased demand for science specialists meant that General Science fell out of favour and the attention of the two organisations was once again directed towards reform of a secondary school science curriculum that was widely regarded as seriously out of date. The General Secretary of the SMA, Henry Boulind, produced a memorandum arguing that the Association should take action to propose new aims, methods and syllabuses that would extend and revitalise science teaching (see Chapter 1). The following year, the SMA published a Policy Statement that proposed science should be a 'core' subject in the grammar school curriculum, alongside English and mathematics. Widely circulated, the statement met with an almost universally positive reaction. This encouraged the SMA to consider in detail how the policy recommendations could be translated into syllabuses, teaching methods and reformed approaches to assessment.

1960–1969: catalysing curriculum reform

In 1960, just prior to the time of ASE's creation, Sir David Eccles, Minister of Education, referred in the parliamentary debate on the Crowther Report (see Chapter 1) to the curriculum as a 'secret garden'. The SMA and AWST set about a collaboration to develop the science plot of this garden. By 1961, however, it had become clear that even the joint resources of the SMA and the AWST would be insufficient to carry the work forward on the scale required. A joint approach was therefore made to the Nuffield Foundation for financial and other support.

The Foundation's interest in the school curriculum had already been kindled by a number of earlier approaches for support, and the outcome of the initiative by the SMA and AWST eventually led to the programme of reform announced by Sir David Eccles in the House of Commons in April 1962. Within only a few months, the SMA and the AWST had amalgamated to form ASE and many members of the new Association found themselves heavily involved in the work of the first so-called Nuffield projects, concerned with O-level physics, chemistry and biology. Teams of biology, chemistry and physics teachers worked largely independently under a team leader to develop and trial teaching materials for use in teaching the three basic school sciences. The recruitment of leaders for the various projects did not involve ASE as an organisation, but many of them, such as John Lewis, W.H. Dowdeswell, Geoffrey Foxcroft and Paul Black, were prominent figures in the Association. Black's interest in school science education had grown out of his role as a university representative on the Northern Universities Joint Matriculation Board based in Manchester. His experience there had shown that there were substantial obstacles to effecting curriculum reform, not least in the field of assessment. With John Ogborn, he eventually became Director of the Nuffield A-level physics project (after the initial team was dismissed!) and, together, they set about designing a scheme that was radical in content (modern physics), in equipment and in teaching methods (to promote inquiry). As with the other Nuffield projects, these reforms entailed detailed negotiations with the universities as well as a complex trialling and dissemination programme. All the Nuffield projects sought to modernise the science curriculum and all shared a commitment to teaching for understanding through hands-on practical activities. Considerable effort was thus directed towards devising new practical activities, activities that often required the development and manufacture of new science teaching apparatus. Much of this work was mirrored by developments in Scotland of the Alternative Ordinary Grade syllabus. As with the curriculum itself, many members of ASE played a key role in these developments, as well as in reporting upon developments to fellow members of the Association.

Informing and involving ASE membership

That reporting to members took different forms. The Annual Meeting (now the Annual Conference) was, and remains, the highlight of ASE's year, providing members with an opportunity to learn of developments and ideas in both science and science education. It was, and continues to be, a major commitment both for the organisation (staff, officers and committee members) and for many individual members. The latter ventured out, often in inclement weather between Christmas and the start of the spring term, for several days of information, discussion and debate about all aspects of school science education and for lectures on recent developments in science itself. Those present were able to familiarise themselves with, and in some cases, try out, new science teaching apparatus as well as browse an always substantial publishers' exhibition. For those not present at the Annual Meeting, summaries and the Presidential Address were printed in the Association's journals, *School Science Review* and *Education in Science*. The professional development offered by the Annual Meeting and the journals was supported by the work of the various Branches, which, from 1968, became Regions as a result of a reorganisation of the governance of ASE. In Layton's words, these Branches and Regions were the *'solid foundation'* of the

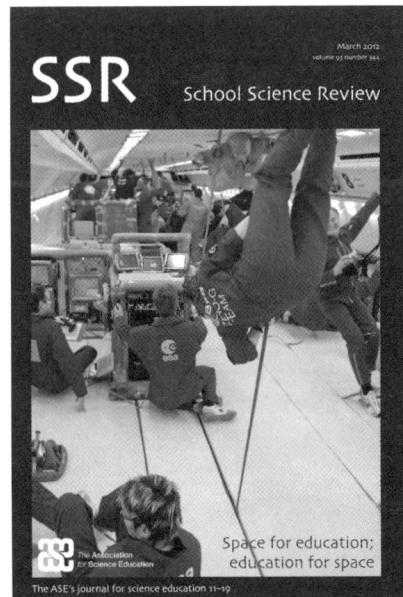

Figure 3.2: ASE journals: Education in Science, *November 2012 and* SSR, *March 2012.*

Association's work. They provided their own programmes for members, who were given an opportunity to familiarise themselves with the reforms proposed or under way and it is difficult to underestimate their importance in disseminating and promoting change. (See Chapter 5 for details of Annual Meetings and local CPD provision.)

The Nuffield projects also recognised the key role of assessment in determining what and how science is taught. Examination reform was therefore essential if the aims of the various Nuffield projects were to be achieved. In the absence of statutory or other official guidance about the school science curriculum, the examination syllabus, together with past examination papers, governed the work of those teaching in grammar and independent secondary schools. The projects therefore devised innovative approaches to assessment, including project work and multiple choice and other forms of objective testing. It can reasonably be argued that the development of new assessment methods, particularly for the practical and inquiry aspects of science, constitutes the most enduring legacy of the Nuffield-funded initiative in school science education. As with other aspects of the reform, members of ASE, such as Paul Black, Bob Fairbrother and Andrew Hunt, played seminal roles.

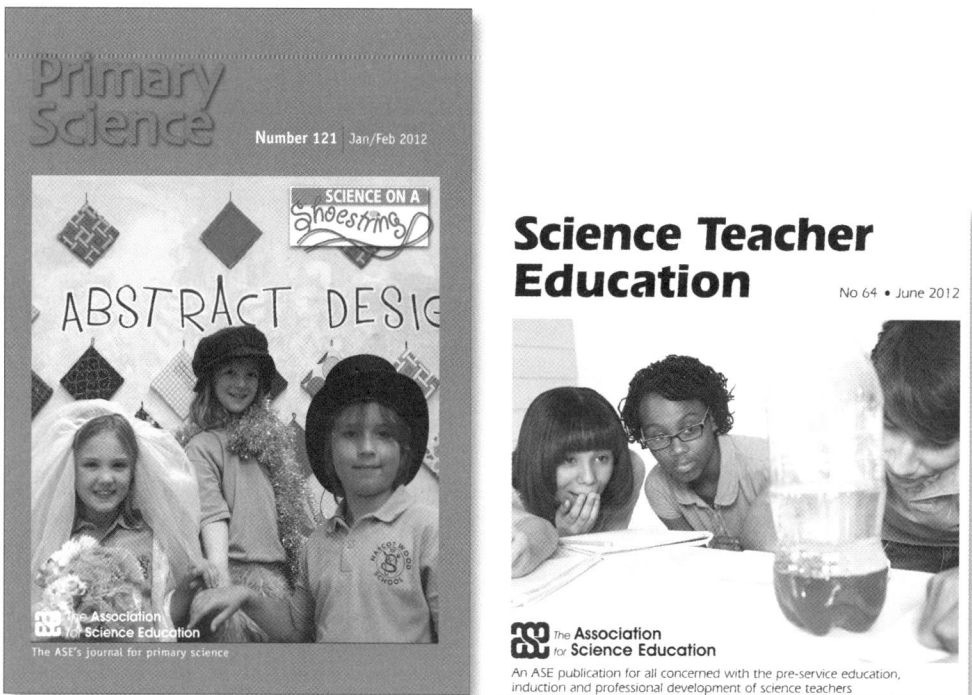

Figure 3.3: ASE journals: Primary Science, *January/February 2012 and* Science Teacher Education, *June 2012.*

The relationship between the Nuffield O-level Project and ASE has been described by Mary Waring as follows. Her judgement can be applied to the Nuffield science teaching projects as a whole.

'Having contributed in a major way to the establishment of the Project, the Association for Science Education was prepared to stand aside, though members were in constant contact at both group and individual levels. Projects were deliberately based on the Association's Policy Statement so there could be an assumption of consensus, at least in general terms. But the individual O-level projects' interpretation of the Policy was another matter, and here the Association maintained an independent platform for debate, both during and after development.' (Waring, 1979: 179)

The preceding paragraphs illustrate a number of significant features of the involvement of ASE and its predecessors in school science curriculum development. First, they reflect the fact that such involvement pre-dates the formation of ASE and is one that, for many years, was facilitated by the absence of any statutory body with responsibility for the school curriculum. The responsibility of the Secondary School Examinations Council lay with overseeing the work of the examination boards in England and Wales, controlled by the universities and offering syllabuses and examinations at the Ordinary and Advanced levels of the General Certificate of Education. As a former Minister of Education, George Tomlinson, had once remarked, 'Minister knows nowt about curriculum'. Secondly, although, as noted above, the pioneering work of the SMA and the AWST was of seminal importance to the projects funded by the Nuffield Foundation, the direction of the projects was not the responsibility of the newly formed ASE and the Association itself was free to determine its own position with respect to whatever was produced. The nature of this involvement is indicative of the way in which ASE played, and continues to play, an important role in shaping the form and content of the school science curriculum, namely through the involvement of its members in a variety of ways with the numerous and diverse organisations that have an interest in the school science curriculum.

In turn, such involvement reflects the fact that the Association included among its members some of the most able and innovative science teachers of their generation.

Challenges and opportunities
By the time ASE was formed, therefore, a major reform of the grammar school science curriculum had begun. However, wider and more profound changes were shortly to follow and these would present the ASE with new challenges

71

and opportunities. In 1964, the Secondary School Examinations Council was abolished and was replaced by the Schools Council for the Curriculum and Examinations. This was given responsibility for approving all syllabuses and examinations and for overseeing standards. A large body, the Schools Council represented almost everyone with an interest in the school curriculum. It operated through a number of subject committees, although ASE and other subject teaching associations were not formally represented until 1975. Perhaps inevitably, its relationship with the government Department for Education (DES), which had statutory authority for the work of schools, was often an uneasy one. It produced a number of important Working Papers, the first of which, *Science for the Young School Leaver*, addressed some of the concerns expressed in the Newsom Report, published in 1963. That report, entitled *Half Our Future*, served to draw attention to, among much else, the lack of science education offered to those pupils, the majority, who attended secondary modern schools. Such schools were gradually to be abolished after the publication of Circular 10/65, which required local education authorities to draw up plans for a system of non-selective comprehensive schooling (see Chapter 1).

It was not only the advent of comprehensive schools that influenced science teaching in the years following the formation of ASE. The Certificate of Secondary Education (CSE), conducted by no fewer than 14 regional examination boards, was introduced in 1965. This examination explored new forms of assessment, including oral examination, and involved many more teachers in syllabus design, examination and moderation, especially those opting for Mode 3, one of the three modes available. There was an emphasis upon coursework undertaken by pupils, ostensibly as an integral part of the teaching and learning process, and commonly assessed by teachers. Like the GCE, the entries for the examinations showed a familiar gender differential, with girls predominating in biology and boys in physics. However, in contrast to GCE, the CSE examination abandoned the concept of passing and failing in favour of grades recorded on five-point scale (plus 'U', ungraded).

Another area of reform was precipitated by the publication, in 1964, of the Robbins Report on Higher Education, which led to the creation of a number of new universities and presaged the closer involvement of higher education in the work of the teacher training colleges. The election in 1964 of a Labour government led by Harold Wilson promised reform in the the 'white heat of technological revolution' and led to the creation of polytechnics, with their degree-awarding powers resting with a Council for National Academic Awards. Yet, just at the time when the importance of science and technology were being acknowledged by government as never before, some aspects of science itself were being called into question. Rachel Carson's *Silent Spring*, published in 1962, highlighted environmental concerns and contributed to undermining the largely unalloyed enthusiasm for science that had prevailed since the Second World War: science was now coming to be seen by some more as a problem and less as a solution. By the later 1960s, government was sufficiently concerned at what was widely seen as a 'swing' from the physical sciences in schools to commission an investigation by Professor (later Lord) Dainton, which reported in 1968. (Professor Dainton had been ASE President in 1966.) Despite the enormous investment in science curriculum reform, it seemed that the future of science and technology was in some jeopardy.

As the decade closed, therefore, ASE and its members faced reform on an unprecedented scale: new curricula, new apparatus, new methods of assessment, new approaches to teaching science, two different systems of public examinations and the need to teach science to the many pupils whose interests and needs were often very different from those of the pupils familiar to the members of ASE. Both the SMA and the AWST had recognised the importance of addressing the needs of those teaching science in secondary modern schools. A number of relevant publications had been produced in the 1950s by both Associations, some in collaboration with other organisations, and 1959 saw the publication of a highly critical survey of the conditions and staffing, in *Science Teaching in Secondary Modern Schools*. The reality, however, was that relatively few secondary modern school science teachers, most of whom were non-graduates, were members of the SMA, AWST or ASE, and many chose to belong to smaller local science teaching organisations, which they felt better addressed their needs. A different group of teachers, those working in primary schools, also fell outside the historic remit of ASE, despite the fact that membership of the AWST had been more widely drawn than that of the SMA. Aware of this limitation, the ASE Primary Schools Science Committee produced a *Policy Statement* in 1963 and this was eventually incorporated in *School Science and General Education* published in 1965.

1970–1980: change and accommodation

In the years after 1970, ASE as an organisation continued to catalyse science curriculum reform, which many of its members worked to implement. Many ASE members were now also engaged in developing curriculum materials in response to reforms initiated by the Schools Council. In addition, the decade as a whole was marked by the need to accommodate the many changes in curriculum and assessment under way or already in place, including those introduced by the examination boards. The number of curriculum initiatives grew steadily. The Nuffield physics, chemistry and biology O- and A-level projects were complemented by a Nuffield-funded A-level course in *Physical Science*. A Nuffield-funded *Secondary Science* project developed materials for use in secondary modern schools. These were published in 1970 and constituted an important resource for teachers when the school leaving age was raised in 1973. The Schools Council funded a radical *Integrated Science Project* (SCISP), developed by a team based at the Centre for Science Education at Chelsea College (later incorporated into King's College London). Based on a 'patterns' approach, SCISP challenged the conventional boundaries between the three basic school sciences and broadened the scope of school science to include environmental science and aspects of the social and behavioural sciences. It offered a broad and balanced science course and, unusually for the time, led to an O-level examination with double-subject certification. There was, too, the *Schools Council Project in Technology* an initiative that required ASE to consider the complex relationships between science and technology and between science education and technology education. As Wynne Harlen makes clear in Chapter 4 of this volume, developments were also well under way in primary science, with initiatives such as the *Oxford Primary Science Research Project*, the *Nuffield Junior Science Project* and, later, *Science 5–13*.

The wider educational and political context was also continuing to change. Teacher training was re-organised, with many institutions closing or amalgamating. Science education became institutionalised as a field of teaching and research in universities. The number of Teachers Centres, working across all subject areas, not only science, grew very rapidly to over 600 by the mid-1970s. The number of comprehensive secondary schools, along with co-education, also grew rapidly throughout the decade and, as noted above, the school leaving age was raised to 16 in 1973. These developments presented teachers, including science teachers, with pedagogical challenges that many, given their background, training and experience, initially struggled to meet. Science teachers also had to respond to the requirements of the Health and Safety at Work etc. Act 1974, which brought schools within the remit of legislation that had been previously related to the industrial and manufacturing rather than to the educational environment. The passage of equal opportunities legislation in the following year also had implications for schools and for the science curriculum. Gender stereotyping was outlawed, whether in curriculum materials, pedagogy, assessment or timetabling; physics, for example, could no longer be timetabled against domestic science, or biology against mathematics.

Policies, projects and publications

Even before the end of the previous decade, the scale of innovation in the school curriculum and its assessment, allied with the roles played by the Schools Council and the Nuffield Foundation, prompted ASE to seek to reassert its position as the leading authority on school science. In 1971, the Association published a new policy statement entitled *Science and General Education*, followed by supporting statements on *Science for the Under-Thirteens* and *Science for the 13–16 Age Range*. Under the energetic chairmanship of Dick West, the Education (Research) Committee adopted a proactive role in encouraging curriculum innovation and development. This Committee which, along with the Education (Co-ordinating) Committee, had developed from the former Education Committee, was charged with (i) collecting and disseminating successful innovation in science curricula and examinations; (ii) serving as a 'link agency' putting teachers in touch with available support systems; and (iii) promoting future curriculum development and exploring alternative models to the centre-periphery approach adopted in the Nuffield projects.

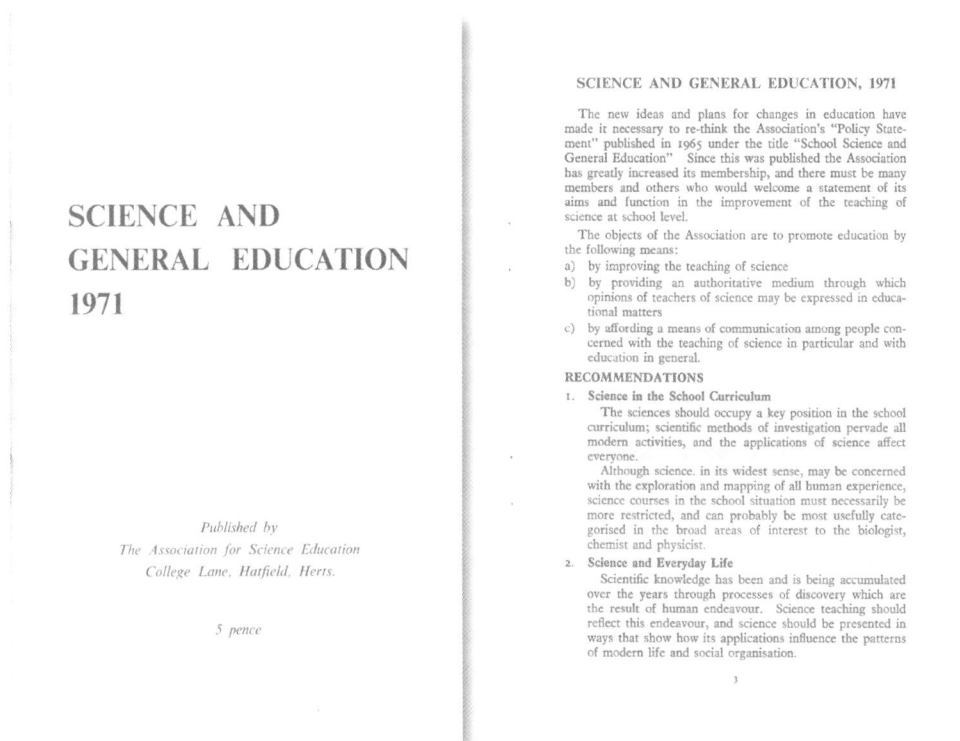

SCIENCE AND

GENERAL EDUCATION

1971

Published by
The Association for Science Education
College Lane, Hatfield, Herts.

5 pence

SCIENCE AND GENERAL EDUCATION, 1971

The new ideas and plans for changes in education have made it necessary to re-think the Association's "Policy Statement" published in 1965 under the title "School Science and General Education" Since this was published the Association has greatly increased its membership, and there must be many members and others who would welcome a statement of its aims and function in the improvement of the teaching of science at school level.

The objects of the Association are to promote education by the following means:

a) by improving the teaching of science
b) by providing an authoritative medium through which opinions of teachers of science may be expressed in educational matters
c) by affording a means of communication among people concerned with the teaching of science in particular and with education in general.

RECOMMENDATIONS

1. **Science in the School Curriculum**

    The sciences should occupy a key position in the school curriculum; scientific methods of investigation pervade all modern activities, and the applications of science affect everyone.

    Although science, in its widest sense, may be concerned with the exploration and mapping of all human experience, science courses in the school situation must necessarily be more restricted, and can probably be most usefully categorised in the broad areas of interest to the biologist, chemist and physicist.

2. **Science and Everyday Life**

    Scientific knowledge has been and is being accumulated over the years through processes of discovery which are the result of human endeavour. Science teaching should reflect this endeavour, and science should be presented in ways that show how its applications influence the patterns of modern life and social organisation.

3

Figure 3.4: ASE: Science and General Education, 1971.

One of the outcomes of the Education (Research) Committee's work was the Association's *Study Series* of publications, which continued throughout the 1970s to offer science teachers information and discussion material relating to issues of contemporary interest or concern. The titles reflect a range of coverage that would have been unthinkable a decade earlier. They included: *The Place of Science in Environmental Education* (1974), *Non-streamed Science: A Teacher's Guide* (1976), *Resource-based Learning* (1978), *What is Science?* (1979) and *Language in Science* (1980). The *Resource-based Learning* initiative reflected the contemporary interest in a more individualised, pupil-centred approach to school science education. This approach had been pioneered at a Resources for Learning Development Unit, funded by the Avon Local Education Authority and directed by Don Foster (later an MP and champion of ASE and of science education). He has recalled the value of ASE regional and national conferences for developing and disseminating the ideas and resources.

The Education (Research) Committee also undertook a number of research initiatives, one of which was subsequently funded by the Schools Council and later published as *Decisions in the Science Department* (Hull and Adams: 1981). This co-publication between ASE and the Schools Council was essentially

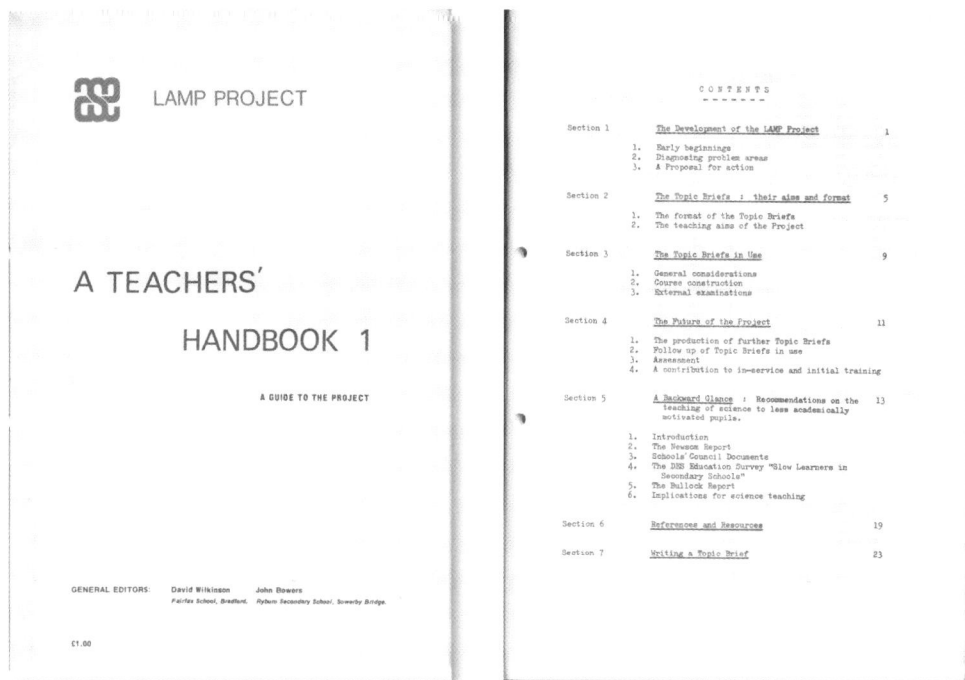

Figure 3.5: The LAMP Project, published in 1976, Teachers' Handbook.

a management training manual for heads of science departments and other senior staff in schools. It covered topics such as departmental management and organisation, curriculum policy, teaching methods and the management of change, and it was used, for example, by the Inner London Education Authority in its annual training course for new and prospective heads of science departments. This initiative, like several others on the part of ASE, reflected a number of factors that characterised the 1970s. Schools and science departments were becoming larger, the curriculum more varied, examinations more complex and diverse, and individual schools were having to teach pupils within a wider range of ability than many teachers, especially some ASE members, had hitherto experienced. In addition, there was a growing emphasis on accountability.

ASE members were, of course, kept informed of curriculum developments through *Education in Science* and *The School Science Review*. Each volume of the latter grew substantially in size during the later 1960s and a section devoted to curriculum development was introduced. The Association was also able to facilitate the work of science teachers by making the resources of other organisations, such as CLEAPSS (see Chapter 8, Case Study 8), available to its members. The flexibility offered by the CSE examination allowed schools, individually or in clusters, to develop a wide variety of courses, including some for pupils with learning difficulties, which led to the award of a limited grade. Many of these courses drew upon existing curriculum projects, especially *Nuffield Secondary Science*. The ASE made an important contribution through its *Least Academically Motivated Pupils* (LAMP) project[2]. This was developed by a network of local groups working on different aspects and topics and was co-ordinated by Rosalind Driver at the University of Leeds and John Nellist who was then Science Adviser at Sunderland. In 1976, ASE members were able to learn of another project initiated by John Lewis who became Chair of ASE in the following year. The ASE *Science and Society Project* was designed for more able students and sought to locate the teaching of science within the wider social context (see Chapter 8, Case Study 2). It eventually led to *A Teacher's Guide, Student Readers* and *Decision Making Simulation Exercises*, all co-published by the ASE and Heinemann Educational Books in 1981. Like all ASE publications, the focus was on helping teachers to engage not just with innovation, but also with problems and issues relating to pedagogy, the curriculum or assessment. The growing number of ASE publications meant that it was important not to undermine the traditional role of educational publishers in producing materials for use in schools. This was done partly by engaging in

[2]Originally the Least Academically Motivated Pupils project, LAMP gradually became the Less Academically Motivated Pupils project , which title appears on its publications.

co-publication where this seemed mutually beneficial and partly by ensuring that the Association never became involved in the publication of school textbooks.

Concerns and responses

By the latter half of the 1970s, the benefits of the rich diversity in curriculum and examinations, and the unparallelled degree of teacher freedom that had characterised the past ten or so years, were increasingly seen as outweighed by the disadvantages. There was concern about standards in examinations, especially at CSE level, and the relationship of CSE to GCE O-level remained a contentious issue. An added complication was the perceived need to provide for those pupils who wished to proceed from CSE to A-level in science. For many pupils, this was regarded as a bridge too far and various solutions were put forward for consideration. Among them was a reform of A-level into two levels, known as N and F. ASE had responsibility for developing this reform in the field of physics via a committee, chaired by Bob Fairbrother and including Catherine Wilson among its members.

In 1975, the government funded an Assessment of Performance Unit (APU), the necessary research to be undertaken jointly by King's College London and the University of Leeds and co-directed by Paul Black and David Layton respectively. The aim of APU was to identify and monitor standards over time in England, Wales and Northern Ireland. (Surveys of a similar nature, funded by the Scottish Education Department, took place in Scotland from 1984.) APU was viewed with suspicion by many teachers, including ASE members. Black has recalled the hostility with which he was received when presenting the project at an ASE Annual Meeting. Returning to the event the following year, with assessment questions to be shared with teachers, his reception was entirely different: teachers now had something with which they could engage. In due course, ASE was to publish the *APU Science Reports for Teachers*. Events in the next decade were to show the influence of the APU on the approach to practical assessment taken in the new GCSE examination.

In 1976, government concern over what was happening in schools to the curriculum and to standards found expression in a speech by Prime Minister James Callaghan at Ruskin College, Oxford, in which he called for a 'Great Debate'. That debate soon proved to be wide-ranging and of seminal importance to the relationship between government, the curriculum and the work of teachers in schools. In the following year, the senior HMI with responsibility for school science education urged ASE to *'speak for science teachers'*. To do so, the Association needed a policy that was clear and appropriate for the education system that had so rapidly evolved and was increasingly based on comprehensive secondary schooling. That need was underlined when ASE was asked by the Education, Arts and Home

Office Sub-committee of the House of Commons Expenditure Committee to give evidence on the attainments of school leavers. Recognising that the 1971 *Policy Statement* required revision, ASE set up a small working party under the auspices of the Education (Research) Committee and chaired by Jeff Thomson of the University of Bath. The dominant member of this working party was Dick West, Chair of ASE in 1978, and the consultative document published in 1979 owed much to his views. Entitled *Alternatives for Science Education,* the publication prompted a vigorous and acrimonious debate and much personal antagonism within the Association, which threatened a schism: some members referred to the document as *Alternatives to Science Education,* (Jenkins, 1998). The response to the consultative document was such that it was re-written under the direction of the Council of ASE. Highly contentious material was removed and, in a document entitled *Education through Science: a Policy Statement* (ASE, 1981), members were presented with a 'framework for policy decision' rather than a conventional policy statement as the title implied. Underpinning this attempt at policy formation was a commitment to 'science for all': a commitment that would inevitably present a challenge to an organisation that still owed much to its historical origins in a selective system of secondary schooling. Offered as the *'beginning of a further stage of development'*, the 1981 policy statement paved the way for the influential Secondary Science Curriculum Review (SSCR), discussed below. The revision, however, had led to the deletion of a section offering curriculum models that could be used to implement the policy outlined in *Alternatives for Science Education.* Regarded as 'too radical' an approach to school science education, ASE responded by setting up a Curriculum Models Working Party but, by the time this reported in the mid-1980s, it was too late. The long-awaited report was eventually published with the unimpressive status of an occasional paper and no more than a promise of eventual inclusion in the Directory of SSCR publications. As West had recognised, if ASE failed to translate its commitment to science for all into practical action, its position would be overtaken by external events.

1981–90: the government takes control

The SSCR and its impact

The SSCR was a joint undertaking by the Schools Council, the Department for Education and Science and ASE. It was headed by Dick West who, after the publication of *Education through Science: a Policy Statement*, resigned from the ASE's Executive Committee. The Review was focused on encouraging secondary schools to implement a broad and balanced science education for all. The conditions for effecting curriculum change were identified by Shayer and Adey in an influential book published at the start of the decade, in which the authors chose to contrast the centre-periphery model of curriculum reform associated with the Nuffield and Schools Council projects of the 1960s with what they saw as the emergent approach of the 1980s.

'The Sixties answer to [curriculum reform]…was the large headquarters team. The Eighties method does not yet have a recognisable face, but the signs are that it will be decentralised, even democratic in the sense that the experiences and imagination of many different workers in education will be utilised. Yet we do not believe that major change will come about unless some unifying body with power to act is there to direct effort.'

(Shayer and Adey 1981: 148)

Although a detailed history of the SSCR remains to be written, the development of the Review suggests that this is exactly what happened. Under West's leadership, the SSCR adopted a 'periphery-centre' model of curriculum development in which teachers and others formed groups throughout the country to review the science curriculum, make suggestions for improvement, and develop a series of guides intended to help teachers bring about change. At one stage the Review involved as many as 271 different working groups. Its approach to pedagogy reflected the growing body of evidence from the Children's Learning in Science Project (CLISP), which showed that pupils bring to their science lessons their own ideas about how the world works and that these ideas are highly resistant to change. A key figure in CLISP was Rosalind Driver. Although controversial, the 'constructivist' assumptions underpinning the Project were influential and they remain so to this day. The identification of children's 'alternative conceptions' or 'misconceptions' also served to draw attention to how scientific knowledge was established and verified. One outcome was the development by the Inner London Education Authority in the mid-1980s of a substantial scheme for the lower secondary school called Science in Process. The co-ordinating writers, Pauline Hoyle and Steve Smyth, have recalled the importance of ASE in the trialling and revision of the resources beyond London, through its regional and committee networks. They have also drawn attention to the value of ASE membership for someone in such a role, notably the sense of being part of a community in which dialogue and argument could prompt ideas, inspiration and encouragement. In doing so, they highlight the important role that ASE members, acting both as individuals and as members of that wider community, have played at a variety of levels and in diverse ways in shaping the school science curriculum.

The relationships between the Review and the Education (Research) Committee of ASE were not always harmonious and the nature and extent of the Association's involvement with the Review was discussed on a number of occasions within the Committee. As the work of the Review progressed and government and professional scientific bodies issued a number of statements relating to school science education, it gradually became clear that, by the middle of the decade, ASE had lost any claim to policy leadership in this field to which it might have aspired in the latter half of the preceding decade (Jenkins, 1998).

The SSCR produced a number of publications under the title of *Better Science*. Two important outcomes of the project were its commitment to a broad and balanced science for all and to the teaching of science in primary schools. Both of these commitments were mirrored in a statement of government policy, *Science 5–16: A Statement of Policy* published in 1985 (DES/WO, 1985). Not surprisingly, this was a statement that West was able to warmly welcome. Like many others, however, he was to be surprised at the speed with which events now moved.

Introduction of the National Curriculum

The re-election of a Conservative government in 1987 led to the passage of the beguilingly-named Education Reform Act 1988 and to the development and introduction of a National Curriculum in England and Wales. The twin notions underpinning the National Curriculum were entitlement and accountability, the latter soon to be reinforced by the demise of Her Majesty's Inspectorate in favour of the Office for Standards in Education (Ofsted). The task of developing that curriculum was given to a number of subject Working Parties. The first such Party to be set up was concerned with science. Its remit was to provide a general account of the contribution of science to the curriculum; identify Attainment Targets at the Key stages; and devise Programmes of Study.

The precise meaning of these requirements was unclear: the terms used were new and the whole process was without precedent. The Working Party was instructed to *'reflect current best practice'* and to leave space in its recommendations to *'accommodate the enterprise of teachers'*. Subsequent history has shown that the confusion surrounding the origins of the National Curriculum has by no means been resolved. In a study of the early years of the National Curriculum, Donnelly *et al.* (1996) have identified three issues that arose from the brief given to the Science Working Party.

○ To what extent was the Statutory Order intended to specify the substance of teachers' practice?

○ What is the relationship between 'best practice' and 'ordinary practice'?

○ Where does the authority of individual teachers lie?

It seems to the author of this chapter that, despite more than 20 years' work on successive versions of a National Curriculum, the answers to these questions remain unclear.

Although the political rhetoric surrounding the development of a National Curriculum was radical in tone, the Science Working Party was composed of what might be described as the 'science education establishment' of academics and senior managers in schools. Inevitably, therefore, ASE members played a prominent part in developing the curriculum recommendations that eventually found their way into the Statutory Order required by the 1988 Act. The Working Party was chaired by Jeff Thomson, Professor of Science Education at the University of Bath, and a former Chair of the Association and of the Steering Committee of the SSCR. In the latter role, he had shown his ability to relate to Dick West, a radical of a very different persuasion from the Conservative government under Margaret Thatcher and a strong opponent of the form eventually taken by the National Curriculum[1]. That relationship was important. Thomson has recalled that it was through ASE that Dick's contributions were accessed, in particular through the work of the then Deputy General Secretary of ASE, Catherine Wilson. Through a series of meetings and conferences, ASE provided opportunities for debate and dissemination, so much so that, according to Thomson, the Association had a *'massive influence'* on the development of the National Curriculum, not least through the regional groups involved in the work of the SSCR. Officially, ASE had no formal role in the developments taking place other than responding to documents made generally available for consultation. Members were, of course, free to comment and criticise. The Association, especially via its local and regional meetings, served as an important focus for their concerns. Many of those concerns related to the least familiar elements of the National Curriculum, especially to Attainment Targets (ATs) 1 and 17, *Exploration of Science* and *The Nature of Science* respectively. The criticisms were of different kinds. For some, AT17 was not 'real science'. For others, AT1, which addressed practical work and was thus central to science education, was 'wrongly formulated'.

The task facing the Science Working Party was complicated by another aspect of the 1988 Reform Act, a universal scheme of assessment, proposed

[1]A joke among the science education community at the time was that Dick West, Professor of Science Education at the Open University in a post funded by the Central Electricity Board occupied the electric chair, while Jeff Thomson, Professor of Science Education at Bath occupied the bath chair.

by the Task Group on Assessment and Testing (TGAT), chaired by Paul Black. These proposals derived, in part, from the work of the APU and involved a ten-point scale for assessing progression throughout compulsory schooling, from level 1 for the average child at five to level 10 for the most able at the age of sixteen. In setting out the proposed science curriculum, the Working Party was obliged to use this ten-point scale. This, as the report of the Working Party acknowledged, had presented particularly severe difficulties in the case of ATs1 and 17, where there was little *'current best practice'* to draw on. Not surprisingly, the subsequent history of these two Attainment Targets was to be a turbulent one (Donnelly *et al.,* 1996).

The close involvement of some prominent members of ASE in developing the science component of the National Curriculum and/or its assessment presented the Association with a potential problem. Although such involvement was on an individual, rather than a representative, basis, there can be little doubt that it owed much to the high profile that several individuals enjoyed within the Association and the various contributions they had made to its work. However, the clear obligation of the Association to help its members to implement the National Curriculum often conflicted with the need to ensure that their professional standards and judgements were given due consideration and accommodation. In the political climate of the time, a satisfactory resolution of such a conflict was all but impossible. The attempt to discharge that obligation led to a flurry of activity by ASE and its regions, sometimes in conjunction with other organisations.

Although the Minister responsible, Kenneth Baker, was eventually able to accept the recommendations of the Science Working Party, the Prime Minister, Margaret Thatcher, expressed her dismay at the length and prescriptive nature of the National Curriculum documentation. Thomson succeeded in convincing Baker that science should be allowed 20% of curriculum time, rather than the 10% favoured by the Minister. In the wider educational context, this proved controversial as did the formulation of the Attainment Targets in terms that carefully avoided the words chemistry, physics and biology in an attempt to promote a broad and balanced science throughout compulsory schooling. It is unlikely that science teachers failed to recognise that the content of the National Curriculum was structured around areas all too readily associated with one or other of the three basic sciences. At the ASE Annual Meeting in 1986, Paul Black sought to recommend a 'middle way' between the positions adopted by those who sought to integrate the individual sciences and others who saw them as different in quite fundamental ways, e.g., by co-ordinating the teaching of a topic such as energy. It is an issue that continues to divide science teachers to this day.

The SSCR was not the only way in which members of ASE influenced the inclusion in the National Curriculum of elements of the social, historical and technological aspects of science. In the early years of the decade, ASE had published two post-16 courses: *Science in Society* (Lewis, 1981) and *SISCON in Schools* (Solomon, 1983). Partly in an attempt to broaden the school science curriculum in order to meet the needs of the wide range of pupil ability found in comprehensive schools, the Association set up a Science and Technology in Society (SATIS) project, under the direction of John Holman and supported by the Gatsby Charitable Foundation and industrial sponsors (see Chapter 8, Case Study 2). Many ASE members were involved in writing the published units, working in collaboration with experts in a variety of scientific fields. The writing of the 14–16 materials began in 1984 and continued until 1991. The initiative was followed by another similar project for older (16–19) year-old pupils (directed by Andrew Hunt). The SATIS units helped to disseminate and legitimise a much wider range of classroom activities than was commonly found in school science at that time. This exploration of, and developing interest in, the teaching of some of the social, historical and technological aspects of science was reflected in the National Curriculum, particularly in the troubled formulation of AT17. It also raised complex questions about the interrelationships of science and technology, questions that became particularly important as design and technology emerged as a distinct component of

Figure 3.6: Kenneth Baker (right), Secretary of State for Education and Science, 1986-89, with ASE members at the Annual Meeting 1988.

the National Curriculum. That component owed much to the work of Paul Black and Geoffrey Harrison in a project supported by the Nuffield–Chelsea Curriculum Trust, which led to the publication of a policy statement entitled *In Place of Confusion*. In due course, the Nuffield Foundation funded a Design and Technology project, led by David Barlex.

The renewed emphasis on the technological aspects of education during the 1980s reflected a number of factors, most notably the shortage of practical skills among a large and growing pool of unemployed young people. Its most striking manifestations were the creation of City Technology Colleges (CTCs) and the Technical and Vocational Education Initiative (TVEI), the latter launched amid some controversy by the Department of Employment at the beginning of the decade. The Initiative provided over £900m to support work with 14–18 year-olds during the 1980s and led to a number of innovative approaches both to the upper secondary curriculum and its assessment. As far as ASE was concerned, it had already begun in the previous decade to develop closer links with industry, not least by inviting prominent industrialists, rather than distinguished academics, to assume the role of President. While this undoubtedly brought benefits, including financial benefits, to the Association, the relationship between ASE and school technology was never an easy one, partly because the Association was an organisation of science, rather than technology teachers, many of whom had initially trained as teachers of handicraft, art or domestic science. In addition, it was difficult for the Association to adopt a clear policy in relation to school technology when influential bodies such as The Engineering

Figure 3.6: The SATIS project. Resources from various phases of SATIS, ASE's family of influential curriculum development projects.

Council and The Royal Society expressed diverse opinions about the nature and place of technology in the school curriculum.

An examination for all: the GCSE

The introduction of the National Curriculum was not the only major challenge facing ASE and its members towards the end of the 1980s. After almost two decades of attempting to relate GCE and CSE examinations and a number of trials and pilots, a new examination, the General Certificate of Secondary Education (GCSE) was finally introduced in 1988. The development of this examination presented several challenges, not least the need to cater for almost the complete range of pupil ability. This led to differentiated content and examination papers, a practice known as 'tiering'. Whereas the CSE had made substantial use of coursework in both practical and written tests, the Ordinary level of the GCE had relied almost exclusively on terminal examinations. The use of teacher assessment in GCSE examinations reinforced questions about the reliability and methods of moderation of teachers' judgements that had long dogged the CSE. A further challenge stemmed from the increased attention given in the new examination to scientific processes and skills compared with the more traditional and familiar emphasis on scientific knowledge and understanding.

Those responsible for developing the GCSE were able to call upon a range of approaches to assessment that had been developed in the previous decade or so. APU had developed materials as a result of trials in the schools during the 1980s. In practical science, for example, two types of 'process-based tasks' had been identified and constructed. *Practical Tasks* involved activities such as measuring, observing and describing relationships between variables. *Written Tasks* involved handling data, graphing and planning investigations. A Graded Assessment in Science Project (GASP) developed the work of APU in order to establish criteria to measure progression in pupils' competence and, as noted above, the Technical and Vocational Education Initiative had supported a wide range of assessment strategies, including portfolio assessment of work done. This latter was widely used in the more vocationally-oriented General National Vocational Qualification (GNVQ), first piloted in 1992.

Although ASE had no formal role in these developments, the involvement of individual members, regional groups and committees was essential to their successful implementation. Unfortunately, much of the experience that ASE members had gained in constructing syllabuses and examinations was lost when the CSE examination boards were abolished, although two schemes (NEAB Modular and Suffolk Science), which had been developed by SSCR working groups, survived the changes to become GCSE 'subjects'.

GCE Advanced-level examinations were not immune to the pressure for reform in the light of the changes that had already taken place in the science curriculum of primary schools and that for 11–16 year-olds. Although yet another attempt at a major reform to the widely assumed 'gold standard' A-level examination, led by Professor Higginson, came to nothing, ASE members were able to take advantage of the lack of statutory specification beyond GCSE to develop innovative approaches to science education. In the mid- to late- 1980s, the University of York Science Education Group obtained the support of the Salters' Livery Company to develop chemistry and, later, science courses that introduced pupils to the applications and implications of science. These contexts were then used to define the content used to teach scientific concepts. These so-called Salters' courses, which survive to this day, incorporated a diverse range of teaching and learning activities, including practical work, data analysis, case studies and the use of ICT, then becoming much more widely available in schools. Another initiative, supported by Bath University and the publisher Macmillan Education, provided a range of textbooks to support the teaching of A-level science, which helped to promote a 'core-plus-options' approach to the curriculum. As an example, a module based on Medical Physics could be used to extend or enrich the physics curriculum.

1990–2000: Constant change and varied responses

Attempting to resolve problems of the National Curriculum

The speed with which the science National Curriculum and its associated assessment were introduced, allied with unresolved issues about AT1 and AT17, meant that trouble was soon forthcoming as teachers tried to come to terms with what was required of them. The seventeen Attainment Targets of the first version of the National Curriculum were almost immediately reduced to five in a document issued for consultation. This consultation led to a further important change. The number of Attainment Targets was reduced further to four and the first AT renamed 'Scientific Investigation'. This was soon commonly referred to as 'Sc1'. The remaining three ATs were thinly veiled versions of chemistry, physics and biology. Despite this 1991 revision and the guidance offered by the National Curriculum Council (NCC), problems soon emerged with Sc1 with its emphasis on scientific investigations conducted by pupils. Some influential members of ASE were forthright in their support of Sc1. Paul Black, for example, regarded Sc1 as a *'noble attempt to break away from the kind of experience that so many adults recall of their school science – practicals of little challenge following quite easy instructions and few demands to think'*. It is not too much to say that the Association supported Sc1, although often tacitly rather than explicitly, despite the many concerns expressed by members at meetings and in the Association's journals.

The concerns were reflected in the response of the membership to a report entitled *The Place of Investigations in Science Education,* prepared by a Task Group of ASE led by the Association's then Chair, Maggie Hannon. While the response predictably supported the centrality of practical investigations in school science education, many members felt that the report failed to show how such investigations could be accommodated within Sc1. ASE and King's College London later undertook research (AKSIS) and published examples of what might be done. Some of the outcomes of the AKSIS Project influenced the nature of Sc1 as formulated in the subsequent National Curriculum (2000) and were incorporated in the National Science Strategy Materials.

Despite the support and encouragement of Sc1 by the Association, the difficulties of implementing this element of the National Curriculum, and especially of accessing the higher levels of performance, precipitated a minor crisis during 1993, which required an almost unprecedented intervention by the Schools Examinations and Assessment Council (SEAC) at a time when GCSE examinations were only a matter of months away. The crisis was first overshadowed, then resolved, fortuitously, by the larger crisis in the entire National Curriculum and its assessment in which teachers of English played a key role. Further changes were thus introduced in 1995, following a major review by Sir Ron Dearing, and teachers were promised by the government that there would be no further changes for another five years.

In preparing his report, Dearing wisely chose to consult widely and ASE Regions and constituent Sections were asked by the Association to help frame its response to the Dearing proposals. In his capacity as Association Chair in 1994, Phil Ramsden played a key role in ensuring that the views of the membership were represented to Dearing's committee, circulating copies of an ASE questionnaire to establish the views of members in the Regions and Sections. In the following year, he presented in *Education in Science*, on behalf of the Association's Curriculum Issues Division, a five-year plan for science education for the year 2000 and beyond (Ramsden, 1995: 22). This outlined a five-stage programme comprising members' briefing, wide consultation across Regions, developing broad policies, agreeing specific proposals, and dissemination. Discussion in *EiS* for example, Goldsworthy (1997: 8) and Finegold and Wymer (1997:10), culminated in an introduction to the report that was sent to the Qualifications and Curriculum Authority (QCA) by the then Chair of the Association, Roger McCune (McCune, 1998: 17).

QCA provided support for the planning and teaching of the National Curriculum with Schemes of Work for Key Stages 1, 2 and 3 (ages 5–7; 7–11 and 11–14) (QCA, 2000). These were written by leading practitioners in the field, many of whom were recruited through ASE networks. Although intended to be guides to 'delivering' the National Curriculum, the contemporary demand for accountability, allied with worries over Ofsted inspections and reports, meant that schools often felt that they had to adopt the Schemes in their entirety. The outcome was that the Schemes acquired a reputation for stifling initiative and creativity.

Scottish developments

In Scotland, events during this decade followed a different path. ASE's policy statement on balanced science (ASE, 1990) did not sit well with the views of Scottish members, who strongly wished to maintain the teaching of discrete separate sciences post-14 and to work within the curriculum structures following the Munn Report (1977). After considerable lobbying by the likes of Gerry McKenna, Jim Auld, David Standley and Duncan Alexander, the Scottish Region of ASE was allowed to produce an alternative policy statement, *The Place of Science in a Balanced Curriculum* (ASE, 1991). Seeking the views of ASE members in Scotland was facilitated by an extensive database maintained by the Scottish Region, which enabled members' views to be canvassed and collected for the purpose of consultation. This database was known as ASETTS, an acronym rather quaintly derived from ASE Think Tank Scotland. For much of the decade, Elizabeth Sinclair maintained the database which, long before email and online surveys, was an effective means of gathering the views of members at a time when consultation deadlines allowed for the construction of questionnaires, posting to and from members and the collation of a representative ASE response. Keith Black was able to co-ordinate a consultation based on returns from over 70 members to the Scottish Examination Board Revised Higher Physics Arrangements, which followed on after Standard Grade replaced Ordinary Grade. The corresponding consultations for biology and chemistry generated almost as many responses from members.

Standard Grade Science was introduced as an alternative to the separate sciences and was initially designed to meet the needs of pupils of lower ability. Andrew Allardyce co-ordinated a group of ASE members to write support materials and ASE's SATIS materials were mapped on to the new courses.

The same decade saw the introduction of the 5–14 curriculum guidelines, where science was subsumed along with the social subjects and technology in Environmental Studies (SOED, 1993).

Changes in post-16 education in Scotland had been implemented following the publication of *16–18s in Scotland: An Action Plan* (SOED, 1983). Post-16 vocational and further education courses were modularised and the Scottish Vocational Education Council (SCOTVEC) was set up as an awarding body. As soon as this occurred, SCOTVEC modules started to be used in secondary schools. Duncan Alexander, one of the first members of ASE's Post-16 Committee, ensured that the Association was kept abreast of these developments as well as those of TVEI, which applied to Scotland as in the rest of the UK. In the following decade, the obvious duplication of SCOTVEC and SEB courses, along with concerns about the 'two term dash to Higher' and the parity in esteem of vocational and academic courses, led to the Higher Still Programme. SCOTVEC and the SEB were amalgamated to form the Scottish Qualifications Authority (SQA). Many ASE members were involved in these developments with Stuart Farmer being a member of the Higher Still Physics Groups and Chair of the SEB Physics Subject Panel for seven years, during which it morphed into the SQA Physics Assessment Panel. Ian Rowley remained a significant figure throughout this time, having become the HMI with national responsibility for physics.

An increasingly competitive environment

The GCSE examinations introduced in 1988 in England, Wales and Northern Ireland inevitably took time to be implemented satisfactorily. Concerns over coursework/teacher assessment survived the introduction of the new examination, along with a debate about the relative merits of terminal and modular approaches to teaching and examination. The expectation of government was that most pupils would take two science GCSEs in order to provide a broad and balanced science education. The evidence is that entries for the individual sciences at GCSE level fell throughout the decade, by the end of which around 80% of the age cohort followed the route leading to double certification.

In addition to the GCSE, a new system of vocational qualifications was introduced in 1993 and made available to schools. Unlike most vocational qualifications, such as BTEC, which had been restricted to colleges, General National Vocational Qualifications (GNVQs) were intended for post-16 students, although some schools chose to make them available at Key Stage 4 (age 14–16). The GNVQ appealed to the many teachers who saw it as a means of stimulating and engaging the interest and enthusiasm of those pupils disillusioned with what schools had hitherto been able to offer. However, the assessments required of those preparing pupils for a GNVQ qualification were burdensome compared with those of the GCSE and the comparability of standards became increasingly contentious. After repeated revisions to both content and assessment, the GNVQ qualification was phased out from the year 2000. The agencies responsible for conducting public examinations also changed. Universities lost their long-standing control of school examinations and new, commercially oriented organisations were established. It was not long before these organisations began to offer courses for teachers and to permit textbooks written by examiners associated with them to carry the label 'official'.

The changes to the National Curriculum, the problems associated with Sc1, and the development of GNVQ all took place while the governance and management of schools were also changing. The links between schools and their Local Education Authorities (LEAs) were weakened and schools were given more responsibility for the management of their own affairs. Senior management teams became larger and subject departments lost some of their financial autonomy. ASE sought to support its members by publishing *Getting to Grips with LMS* (Local Management of Schools). The loss of financial control by LEAs and a decline in the number of Science Advisers (in most cases active members of ASE) meant that the needs of science departments, for example, resourcing the teaching of practical science, were accorded a lower priority. The school system itself became even more diverse during the 1990s with schools offered financial inducements to become Specialist Schools, emphasising, for example, science, the arts or sport, while still being required to teach the National Curriculum. The election of a Labour government in 1997, after 18 years of Conservative administration, presaged further changes with Prime Minister Tony Blair highlighting the importance of *'education, education, education'*.

The introduction of a statutory National Curriculum, changes in the governance, management and financing of schools, the reform of public examinations and the increased emphasis on accountability transformed the political and economic contexts within which ASE was required to operate. The need to provide professional support and development for science teachers, including those working in primary schools, became more pressing. The programme of successive Annual Meetings/Conferences and the events organised by ASE Branches and Sections reveal a major commitment to informing teachers of changes, keeping them abreast of major developments within science itself and providing opportunities for debate, criticism and the exchange of professional views (see Chapter 5). The importance of this commitment, much of it reliant on the goodwill of speakers and ASE members, cannot be over-estimated.

It was a commitment that had to be discharged in an increasingly commercial and competitive environment. Once arguably the major provider of ongoing professional development for science teachers, the Association increasingly found itself during the decade having to position itself among a number of other providers, including examination boards, publishers, private companies and educational consultants. Schools, in turn, had to choose how to allocate the funds available to them to support the professional development of their staff, of which science teachers were but a part. Given the demands on teachers' time and the range of providers of professional development for science teachers, it is not surprising that membership of ASE showed a substantial decline during the decade. The Association was also obliged to adopt a much more commercial approach to some of its activities.

In addition to the programme of national and regional meetings, ASE continued to support the work of teachers by providing innovative and practical resources. SATIS developed new extension projects, notably for younger (under-8) pupils. A new series of internationally focused units became, firstly, *Science Across Europe* and, later, *Science Across the World.* Sponsored initially by BP and later by GlaxoSmithKline, the units stimulated exciting exchanges of schoolwork between pupils in many countries (see Chapters 2 and 8). Funding was also obtained for a range of publications linking science, technology and history (Solomon, 1996), and poetry and science, composed by the future children's laureate, Michael Rosen (ASE, 2000). A number of other publications depended solely on the work of authors and editors with the support of the ASE Publications Committee, e.g., *Creative Trespass*, another poetry for science anthology (Watts, 2000). Contemporary concerns about the under-achievement of some ethnic groups of pupils led ASE to set up a Multicultural Education Working Party. Building on work that had begun in the former Inner London Education Authority, the Group produced two handbooks of advice, guidance and practical activities for science teachers.

Some educationists (ASE members but not in an ASE capacity) were looking beyond the immediate problems of school science education to the review of the National Curriculum, due in 2000 at the expiry of the five-year moratorium on change following publication of the Dearing Report. Rosalind Driver and Jonathan Osborne of King's College London secured funding from the Nuffield Foundation for a series of seminars with a wide, but selective, membership to take a strategic look at the school science curriculum (Millar and Osborne, 1998). The Report, entitled *Beyond 2000* acknowledged that school science had two principal purposes:

○ to develop the scientific literacy of all students, to enable them to engage with an increasingly scientific and technological society; and

○ to provide the basic understanding of science needed by those students who would proceed to a scientific, or science-related, career.

The second of these objectives, the pre-professional function of school science, had long been recognised as a curriculum goal. Although the notion of scientific literacy is at least half a century old, its importance had been highlighted by a report from the Royal Society in 1983, which addressed the case for an increased public understanding of science. Since that date, several national and international measures of scientific literacy had served to confirm that much needed to be done to raise the general level of such literacy among the general public.

Beyond 2000 argued that the Double Award GCSE courses available to schools failed to meet either of these objectives well and were, at best, an unsatisfactory compromise. It recommended that the curriculum at Key Stage 4 should be much more flexible and that the aim of compulsory school science education should be to develop scientific literacy. The recommendation was supported by a number of short-, medium- and long-term proposals and advice that, to be effective, widespread innovation needed to be piloted. ASE members were well represented among the contributors to the seminars, which also involved participants from academia and the professional scientific institutions. There can be little doubt that *Beyond 2000* influenced not only the version of the National Curriculum introduced in 2000 but also a number of other later initiatives. Development of that curriculum was the responsibility of the science team at QCA, who have recalled the importance given to the views expressed at regular meetings with ASE.

After 2000: Adapting to the new millennium

The new millennium brought little respite from the pace of change within the system of public schooling that had characterised the closing decade of the twentieth century. That system became even more diverse, with a growth in the number of Specialist Schools and Colleges and the establishment of Academies, free from the control of LEAs and exempt from the obligation to teach the National Curriculum. Diversification is continuing in 2012 with, for example, the establishment of Technical Academies, University Technical Colleges, Studio Schools and Free Schools. The varying extent to which these institutions have to conform to the National Curriculum and government control, and their relationships with work placement learning, will have an impact on methods of science teaching.

From 2005 to 2010, there was significant investment in school building, much of it under the so-called Private Finance Initiative (PFI)

Building Schools for the Future. Many school science laboratories were modernised under this scheme.

Publicly-funded schooling also became more diverse as the education systems of the four countries within the UK continued to diverge. There was considerable innovation in the science curriculum in Scotland where the education system is different from the rest of the UK and there has never been a statutory National Curriculum of the kind that now characterises England. Prior to devolution in 1999, education in Scotland was the responsibility of the Secretary of State for Scotland and the Scottish Office at Westminster, rather than the Secretary of State for Education. With the formation of the Scottish Parliament, education became one of the key policy areas for the devolved administration: it is now the responsibility of the Cabinet Secretary for Education based at Holyrood. With such a distinctive education system, much of ASE's engagement with other Scottish educational organisations has been conducted by the Scottish Region of ASE, rather than by ASE staff and committees at UK level. Following moves towards devolution in the 1990s, the Region rebranded itself as ASE Scotland. Nevertheless, as in the rest of the UK, many of those active in Scottish science curriculum developments, particularly in physics, were also prominent ASE members, some serving as Chairs of ASE in Scotland and holding other significant Scottish and UK roles within the Association.

Following devolution, the Scottish Government instigated a National Education Debate and the Scottish Government launched Curriculum for Excellence (CfE). ASE members warmly welcomed the aim to produce *'a single, coherent, Scottish curriculum 3–18'* (Scottish Executive, 2004) rather than the rather piecemeal approach to different age ranges used previously. Rhona Goss, seconded to Learning and Teaching Scotland, was instrumental in developing the Science Experiences and Outcomes 3–15, as well as being a member of the Qualification Design Team writing the Revised Higher and Advanced Higher Physics Arrangements.

School science education was reformed in Northern Ireland, where secondary education retained its selective character much longer than elsewhere in the UK. The systems for monitoring pupils' progress also differed among the school systems in the UK. In addition, the results of international tests of pupil achievement such as TIMSS (Trends in International Mathematics and Science Study) and PISA (Program for International Student Assessment) have revealed significant differences in performance among the four 'home' countries. PISA also highlighted the fact that differences between the performance of schools within an education system, such as that of England, were often much greater than the differences between the education systems of different countries.

The recommendations in the *Beyond 2000* report led QCA to embark on a period of research and development. Groups were commissioned to refine the notion of scientific literacy and to explore how it might be promoted and assessed. QCA eventually set up a pilot of a new model for GCSE Science, which was run by the Awarding Body, OCR, with the development work being carried out as the *Twenty-First Century Science* project. This was a collaborative project involving the Science Education Group at the University of York and the Nuffield Foundation. In the light of this work, a revised version of the National Curriculum for Key Stage 4 science was produced for 2006. Much less prescriptive of scientific content than previous versions, this was presented as a single page entitled 'Breadth of Study', while 'How Science Works', a combination of intellectual skills, was presented as the essential component of compulsory science. In 2008, the Key Stage 3 science curriculum was revised in response to the changes introduced at Key Stage 4. The contents of *Education in Science* reveal that teaching 'How Science Works' was a major issue for science teachers. (Bell, 'Editorial', 2006: 3; Kibble, 2006: 13; Roberts, 2009: 30). A substantial review of the primary curriculum, which would have led to the combining of science and technology, and would have impacted on the secondary phase, was accepted by the Labour government but rejected by the incoming Coalition administration, before it could be implemented. New criteria for GCSE examinations led to a more flexible range of courses; the core GCSE Science, which covered the requirements of the National Curriculum, could now be combined with either GCSE Additional Science or GCSE Additional Applied Science. The expectation of government was that two GCSEs (20% of curriculum time at Key Stage 4) would be the norm. However, in 2008, the government required schools to provide pupils with an entitlement to study all three sciences as separate disciplines to GCSE level. Although regarded by some as regressive, this change proved popular with some schools, parents and pupils, and GCSE entries for these disciplines increased steadily at the expense of dual certification. The change was accompanied by a substantial support programme with ASE represented on the Steering Group. Mark Ellis, who directed the programme, considered that it was essential to recruit, through ASE, key people to promote the development.

The abiding concern for standards

The issue of standards was given ongoing prominence by the publication of unofficial 'league tables' and by concerns over the marks required to secure some grades in public examinations. After many years of unsuccessful attempts to change the A-level examination, reform in 2000 led to the separation of the traditional two-year A-level course into two one-year elements, known as AS and A2. Located within a National Framework of qualifications, the reform was intended to encourage a broadening of the post-16 education within both academic and vocationally-oriented courses. However, when the first A2 units were graded in 2002, some of the results were contested and the reliability of the system brought into question. Consequently, the assessment and grading procedures were revised[2]. The integration of vocational courses also did not follow as expected and the government responded by commissioning a further review under the direction of HMI Mike Tomlinson (a leading member of ASE who became its President in 2005). However, his committee's recommendation of an integrated academic and vocational system leading to a Diploma proved too radical for the government to accept. Vocational Diplomas were developed as alternatives to existing BTEC qualifications, but the development of three 'academic' Diplomas, including science, was abandoned by the Coalition government.

Concern over standards was not confined to A-level. The reliability of GCSE standards was also called into question, especially after the changes to the examination introduced in 2006. The wide range of assessment modes by the awarding bodies, particularly of 'How Science Works', led to criticism by the examinations regulator, Ofqual, and to the introduction of controlled assessment of practical work. During consultations about this change, ASE argued for more guidance to be provided *'on rigorous and different approaches by which practical work can be assessed, without reverting to the unimaginative and constraining Sc1 assessments of the past'*. To the relief of teachers, national curriculum tests in science (SATs) were abolished in 2008 (Bell, 2009: 3). QCA had already produced *Assessing Progress in Science* for optional use by teachers to complement the SATs and this was subsequently developed and published as *Assessing Pupils' Progress*. This offered fairly generic assessment guidelines to identify progression on the level scale in the context of particular curriculum elements, and a standards file provided examples of pupils' assessed work. The removal of the statutory tests had given teachers an opportunity to make greater use of assessment for learning, an approach that, by the end of the decade, was well-supported by a body of evidence derived from work at King's College London and the Assessment Reform Group (Harrison, 2011).

The abiding issue of standards was readily coupled with the concerns about the UK's future supply of qualified scientific personnel, concerns exacerbated by the decline that had taken place in the numbers of young people

---

[2]The public controversy surrounding the question of A-level grading and standards led the Secretary of State to sack the Chair of QCA. The Secretary of State's own resignation followed shortly afterwards.

choosing to study scientific subjects, the physical sciences in particular, beyond compulsory schooling. The concerns were the focus of numerous conferences and the Institute of Physics developed a radical new A-level, Advancing Physics, under the direction of Jon Ogborn, a long-standing and distinguished member of ASE. The concerns also found expression in a number of government and other reports, notably the 'State of the Nation' reports published by The Royal Society, a critical review of science education in Europe (Osborne and Dillon, 2008) and An Institute of Physics report *Shaping the Future* (Campbell, 2000). The 2002 report of a committee chaired by Sir Gareth Roberts, President of ASE in 2006, and entitled *SET for Success: The supply of people with science, technology, engineering and mathematical skills* (Roberts, 2002) was particularly influential, prompting action across several government departments. The Secondary National Strategy operated in science throughout the decade, ending in March 2011. In 2004, a Network of Regional Science Learning Centres was established, alongside a National Centre at York, with John Holman as Director. He subsequently became the first National STEM Director, and a National STEM Centre was opened at York in 2010.

ASE's ongoing influence

ASE and many of its members have been involved in a variety of ways with a range of developments and initiatives. Both Directors of the Secondary National Strategy for Science (SNSS), Des Dunne and, later, Pauline Hoyle, were active members of ASE and they made full use of the Association in developing and delivering the Strategy. The regional advisers worked closely with NAIGS (the National Advisers and Inspectors Group for Science), a special interest group within ASE, and with regional ASE groups. All the consultants engaged in developing the Strategy were expected to be members of the Association and the development of both the framework and the trialling and dissemination of resources involved ASE staff and members. There were close links, too, with the Science Learning Centre Network (NNSLC). In 2009, ASE, in partnership with the NNSLC and a number of other partners, began a major project, *Getting Practical – Improving Practical Work in Science*. The research and development was conducted mainly by ASE (see Chapter 8). The subsequent programme of professional development was designed and delivered by the NNSLC, with the participation of consultants from the SNSS. The wider ASE membership was kept abreast of the progress of the project through *Education in Science* (see, for example, Bell, 2008: 3; Westbrook, 2010: 36).

The year 2001–2, designated Science Year, involved a wide range of events, projects and resources, designed to stimulate interest in, and enthusiasm for, science and technology. It focused attention on young people between 10 and 19 years old and the adults around them, especially their teachers. Science Year was managed by the National Endowment for Science, Technology and the Arts (NESTA), with ASE as one of the partners (see Chapter 8). One interesting feature of the year was the organisation of a nationwide review of the curriculum involving over 350 students. The findings were discussed with the Schools Minister of the time. This exploration of student opinion was part of a wider study of the 'Student Voice' (see, for example, Osborne and Collins, 2000; Jenkins, 2006).

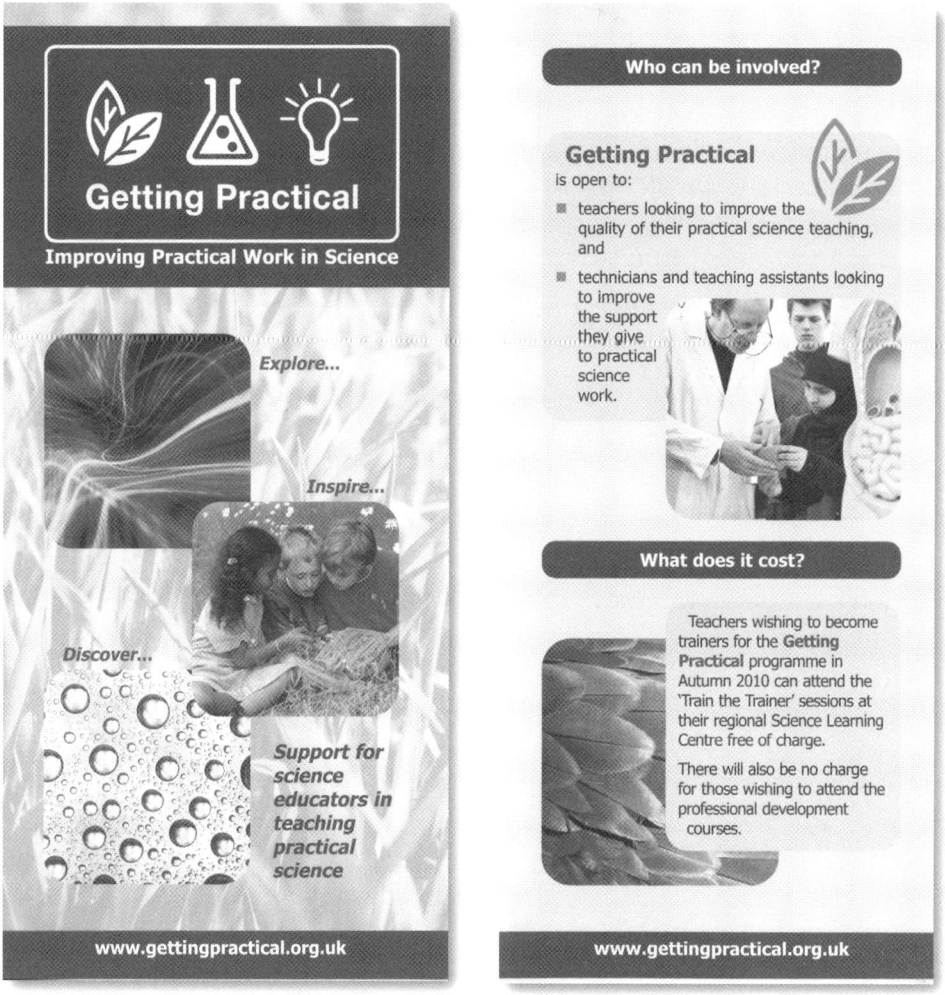

Figure 3.8: Getting Practical, the latest of ASE's collaborative curriculum development projects 2008 to 2010.

ASE was closely involved with the STEM programme and the Innovation Programme, both centrally and through regional groups (Holman, 2008), an involvement that John Holman believes was mutually beneficial. SETNET, later STEMNET, provided an infrastructure to allow pupils and their teachers to engage with a variety of science- and technology-related extra-curricular activities and produced directories of enrichment and enhancement activities in science, mathematics, technology and engineering, although, in some opinions, not without some risk of marginalising the role of the science teacher.

ASE itself has also responded to the rapid changes in information and communication technologies, notably the World Wide Web and the internet. The learning potential offered by these tools has already been explored by many science teachers, but it is clear that developments are at an early stage: science curricula, lesson outlines and plans, hints on teaching and a range of networking possibilities can readily be downloaded. Science teachers have at their disposal more resources than at any time in the past. School science is also becoming increasingly globalised and ASE's long-standing international connections are likely to grow in importance. Within the Association, electronic communication with ASE members and electronic publication, including the journal *Science Teacher Education*, the Regional newsletters and notices, are already commonplace. ASE's interactive website and other initiatives such as *upd8* and *Wikid* are rich resources for teachers. Members, officers and staff of the Association can now communicate rapidly with one another over any matter they wish. Virtual meetings, whether of committees or as #ASE chat, are recent substitutes for traditional meetings (see Chapter 5). The ASE of the future, therefore, will inevitably function in some different ways from the past.

One of the difficulties facing government seeking advice about the form, content and assessment of school science has long been the number and diversity of interested parties whose views did not always coincide. In an attempt to secure a coherent voice for school science, a consortium of those with a professional interest in this field was established in 2006 – the Science Community Representing Education (SCORE). ASE is a member of this organisation, which has a wide range of representation. In 2010, the Science Minister commissioned a series of reports on science education and policy in which ASE was involved and SCORE has itself undertaken important studies of several aspects of school science.

The reports of those studies and other documents will no doubt have some influence as governments continue to seek to improve school science education. In doing so, many of the issues that have marked the past 50 years will continue to demand attention: the relationships between the curriculum and assessment, the role of practical work, the need to provide a broad and balanced science education for all pupils and to raise their standards of achievement, the importance of securing an adequate supply of successful, well-qualified science teachers. However, in looking back over the period with which this chapter is concerned, policy makers would do well to note the comment of Derek Bell, formerly Chief Executive and one-time ASE Chair and subsequently Education Officer of the Wellcome Trust. Speaking at an event to mark the 21st anniversary of the introduction of the National Curriculum, he offered the following advice to the incoming Coalition government:

'...for teachers to use the curriculum as a launch pad, continuing professional development and support are essential. Throughout the National Curriculum's history, science teachers have perceived a shift towards prescribing how to teach rather than what to teach. This has caused a drop of teachers' professional confidence...professional support will allow teachers to implement the curriculum successfully, but, more importantly, it is also needed for them to engage in curriculum development, helping to ensure that an exciting science education is tailored to the interests and need of these students.' (Bell, 2010)

It is a succinct outline of the past, present and future role of the ASE.

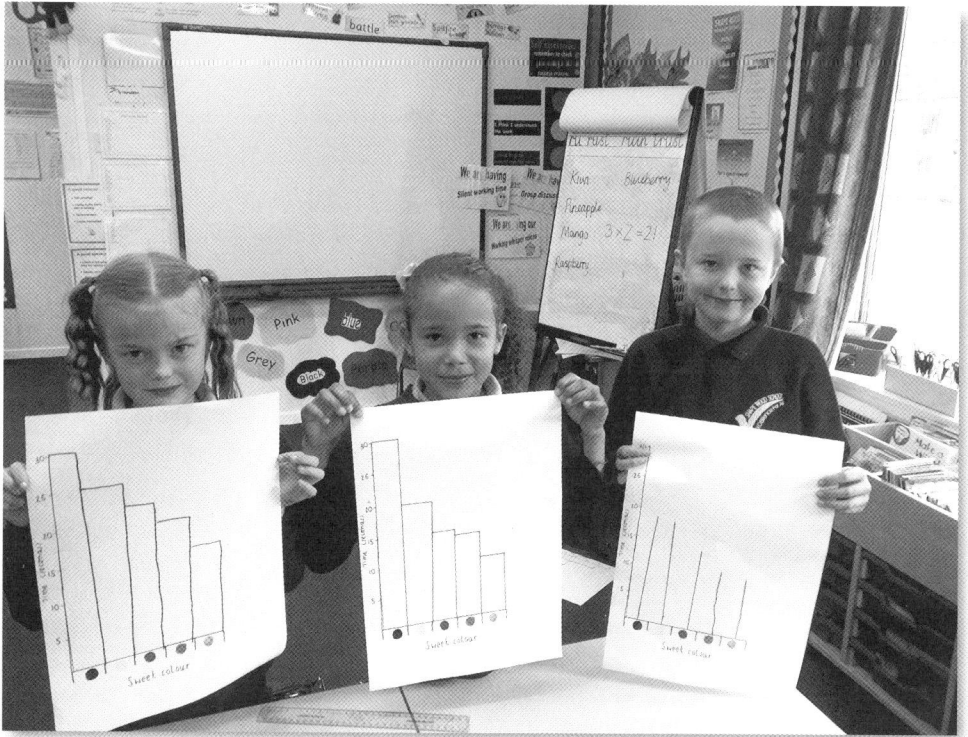

Figure 4.1: *Primary school pupils engaged in a science presentation to their classmates* (From Primary Science, *September/October 2011*).

4   The ASE and primary school science

Wynne Harlen

*'Science should be recognised – and taught – as a major human activity...
No system of education in the primary school can be considered
satisfactory that ignores this major human activity.'*

ASE 1963

The development of primary science during the past 50 years has been quite remarkable. In 1963 there were a few patches of exciting and innovative work in science in primary schools, but the large majority of children encountered little that would now be called learning in science. Fifty years later, science is accepted as a key part of primary education, no more to be neglected than basic numeracy and literacy. Perhaps only ICT, for reasons of rapid advances in computer technology, has seen similarly fundamental change.

Teachers and science education professionals, who have historically constituted ASE, have been instrumental in this transformation of practice. What they have done as an association could not have been accomplished by individuals acting alone or even in informal groups. Their work has affected the system and so has been of as much value to non-members as to members. Few primary teachers, being generalists, would describe themselves as 'science teachers'; probably none would have done so in 1963. Indeed, in the 21st century, only a small proportion of primary schools and teachers are members of ASE. However, its work has reached out beyond the membership; all can potentially benefit from the publications, policies and responses to government proposals created by members.

The roots of primary science

Of course primary science did not begin in 1963. The story of education in science for young children begins over a century before the establishment of ASE. For most of the 19th century, the 'object lesson' was the main vehicle for giving elementary school children some classroom experience of things in their environment. This was often a passive experience with little educational value, in which children were shown an object and asked routine questions about it, calling for memorisation rather than observation. Scientists in the British Association for the Advancement of Science (BA) began to express interest in elementary schoolchildren's education and advocated a wider range of methods. One attempt involved peripatetic demonstrators visiting schools with scientific apparatus to give experimental demonstrations, but only to boys. The teacher, present at the demonstration, was intended to consolidate what had been shown, but this was limited by time, equipment, and the teachers' own understanding.

However, it quickly became clear that peripatetic demonstrators were not the solution to the problem of providing children with the learning that was required. The BA and scientists such as T.H. Huxley and H.E. Armstrong considered that:

'The method of experimental inquiry is the only natural method of gaining a knowledge of scientific facts; but such a method is the very antithesis of the didactic method of instruction too generally in vogue...'

(From a report of the BA meeting published in *The School World*,
September 1908)

They recommended the appointment in each school of a teacher qualified in science to advise others and to teach science in some classes. As something that has not yet been fully achieved, this was clearly ahead of its time. Meanwhile, the 'object lesson' remained the dominant mode. However, its limitations became increasingly unacceptable and, by 1904, the Code of Regulations governing elementary schools made clear that science should comprise both observation and nature study.

The School Nature Study Union was established in 1903 to provide some support for teachers through its publications, including a journal entitled *School Nature Study,* and conferences encouraging nature walks and the greater use of school grounds. Learning out of doors was permitted by the Code of 1906. The adherence to the various revisions of the Code of Regulations is a reminder that the National Curriculum was not the first document to control what is to be taught in schools.

T.H. Huxley, H.E. Armstrong and the BA regarded an acquaintance with scientific method as more important than knowledge of scientific facts, since the *'scientific habit of mind'* would serve everyone in later life. However, as well as recognising the value of science for everyone, there was also concern for the education of future scientists. The issues of content versus process, and science for all and science for specialists, still debated today, are evident here. Early in the century for those children who attended elementary schools, this was their only formal education, many leaving at the age of 13. From 1907, however, the introduction of tests in the '3Rs' to select pupils from elementary schools for scholarships to transfer to secondary schools was accompanied by a relative neglect of other subjects. Thus the science education of all suffered for the sake of the few who would be selected to proceed to secondary school.

The Hadow Reports of 1926 and 1931 recommended a clean break at age 11, with all children proceeding from the newly-named primary school to secondary education, up to the leaving age of 14. The Reports advocated a child-centred approach, where the curriculum of the primary school would focus on *'activity and experience'*, rather than on *'knowledge to be acquired and facts to be stored'*. A direct challenge thus emerged for a recognisable, distinct and autonomous institution, with its own curriculum and pedagogy. The dire economic situation of the 1930s, followed by the Second World War, delayed the Hadow implementation. It was not until 1944 that the system of primary and free secondary education taking place in separate schools, the one leading directly to the other, became statutory as part of the 1944 Education Act.

In the 1950s, there were unprecedented changes and expansion in school science education as a whole. The demand for scientists and technologists in the post-war years brought about a need to sustain the flow of university science entrants. It was necessary to give attention to reform of science teaching in schools. The focus of attention for change in the state sector started at the top of secondary education and gradually worked its way downwards. When it reached the primary school, it became clear that the existing practices were highly unsatisfactory, both in helping children to begin to understand the scientific aspects of their world and as a preparation for secondary science.

In many primary schools, more informal methods were already taking hold. Infant schools were the earliest to make changes, adopting active methods that slowly spread to junior schools. Instead of giving facts, teachers were enabling pupils to learn from projects *'in which children take the initiative and acquire knowledge, not only from books, but also by exploring the school and its neighbourhood, and where facilities exist, by experimental work and observation in gardens and science rooms.'* These changes were encouraged by HMI, college lecturers and by publications from the Froebel Foundation, the BA and the Ministry of Education, all reflecting progressive ideas actively disseminated by pioneers such as Susan and Nathan Isaacs and Margaret Macmillan. Courses extending over several days were run by science HMI, including Len Ennever (who was later to direct the Science 5/13 Project), for invited participants from colleges and universities, inspectors and some key primary Headteachers. The purpose was to enthuse and inform those in positions to 'spread the word' about the importance of children's own practical investigations.

The interest of the professional associations

The voices of the Science Masters' Association (SMA) and the Association of Women Science Teachers (AWST) were rarely heard in matters of primary science education. As described in Chapter 1, the membership of these organisations was almost exclusively drawn from teachers in grammar schools and public schools with little contact with primary schools. Indeed, when the SMA and the AWST formed a joint committee with two other organisations (the London Association of Science Teachers and the Association of Teachers in Colleges and Departments of Education (ATCDE)) to give some guidance to *the many teachers who are endeavouring to widen the scope of Nature Study'*, it decided that *'before stepping into this field, the Committee... needed to strengthen itself by inviting a few people who are particularly concerned with the Junior School to join its ranks'*. The meetings of this Joint Committee resulted in the publication of a pamphlet, *Science in the Primary School* (AWST, 1959). The BA's continued interest in science education at this time took the form of a conference organised in 1961 in association with the ATCDE, with the proceedings of this conference published as *The Place of Science in Primary Education* (1962). The opening address was given by Nathan Isaacs and included the following words, which are worth contemplation given the 21st century emphasis on inquiry-based science education as if it were an innovation.

'The school...can provoke questions or expressly invite them; and it can use any that are suitable in order to launch groups of children on their own co-operative quests for the answers. They can be encouraged to consider and discuss, and to put out ideas or suggestions either by way of actual solutions or at least for next steps. They can be guided and steered, helped over difficulties, and offered hints in the right directions or suggestive leading questions. In all these ways each inquiry that has been set in motion can be carried forward,...and become an immensely educative experience for all the children who have shared in it. For not only have they thus built up by their own efforts some fresh scheme of connected knowledge and understanding, but they have also experienced for themselves some of the typical ways and methods by which such building up can be achieved.'

(BAAS, 1962:12)

ASE: establishing a policy for primary science

The lack of interest in primary practice on the part of the school science teaching associations came to a swift end once the SMA and the AWST amalgamated to form the Association for Science Education (ASE) in 1963. The gradual integration of primary science into all aspects of ASE's operation began with the setting up of a Primary Science Sub-committee of its Education Committee as one of the first actions taken by the new Association.

The first task of the Sub-committee was to produce a policy statement on primary science. As a result of the activities in the 1950s and early 1960s, there was a groundswell of support for active learning in the primary school and for the inclusion of science in the curriculum. The following extracts from the Policy Statement reflect the values that permeated development in primary science for the following two decades.

'Science should be recognised – and taught – as a major human activity... No system of education in the primary school can be considered satisfactory that ignores this major human activity.

'At this level we are concerned more with the developing of an enquiring attitude of mind than with the learning of facts...our aim should be to give significance to the facts which children will inevitably acquire; at no time is the imparting of factual knowledge to be regarded as an end in itself.

'Thus the teacher should not be restricted by a narrowly based syllabus, but must be free to follow whatever lines of inquiry seem to him to be promising in the teaching situation as it is at the time.

'In the interests of unity of learning and the integrated approach it is better that there should not be any special laboratory in the primary school. It is possible to do experimental work in the classroom.

'If there is insistence on "finding out by doing" during the initiation to science in the primary school ...we shall be training citizens who can appreciate the value of science and who are concerned about the possibilities of applying science to human problems.' (ASE, 1963)

The Statement also recognised that teachers would need help in many aspects, such as the selection of equipment and reference books, as well as in their scientific background and understanding of children's learning. As a *'step in the right direction that can be made immediately'* it was recommended that *'a basic Science is made compulsory for all students in Training Colleges'*.

Inevitably, some of these statements were interpreted as support for more extreme claims, such as that the content of children's science experience did not matter as long as the process followed certain lines. Also, the language of 'discovery' and 'finding out' implied an inductive view of science embodied in 'the scientific method'. The danger of misunderstanding was recognised in the influential report of the Central Advisory Council for Education (the Plowden Report) of 1967, which noted that *'For a brief time "activity" and child-centred education became dangerously fashionable and misunderstandings on the part of camp followers endangered the progress made by the pioneers'* (CACE, 1967: para. 513). In relation to science, extreme positions were taken about the emphasis on content or process and the notion of 'finding out' was embraced without attention to how learning was taking place. The distinction between the 'discovery' of ideas and the 'construction' of ideas was not made. It took several years of attempting to implement the advocated approaches for evidence to accumulate a more balanced view of the process of children's learning in science and how to help it. As time went on, there was a greater recognition of the importance of children beginning the progressive development of key ideas of science and that, therefore, content did matter.

The Sub-committee then set about providing the help that they acknowledged was needed, producing a series of five booklets under the general title *Science for Primary Schools,* published by John Murray for ASE between 1966 and 1970: *Children learning through science* (nine case studies of classes in action), *List of books, List of teaching aids, Materials and equipment* and *Using broadcasts.*

The lists were detailed and comprehensive, reflecting a considerable amount of work by the members of the Sub-committee. At the same time, members were contributing to ASE regional meetings and establishing the tradition of primary science exhibitions of work at the Annual Meetings. Other publications followed, first *Science for the Under-Thirteens* and then a series entitled *Science in Primary Education.* The first three of these were entitled: *The Present Situation* (1974); *The Role of the Headteacher* (1974); and *A Post of Responsibility* (1976). They proved very popular, as did a series of three booklets on teaching about energy: *Moving Things; Burning, Warmth and Sunlight;* and *Working with Electricity.*

Expansion and development in the 1960s and 1970s

At the time of the formation of ASE, there were signs of radical changes at national level, heralded by the first curriculum development projects in science on a national scale and by government action relating to the assessment of performance and the status of primary science. Although these initiatives did not involve ASE as an organisation, several were spearheaded by members of the Primary Sub-committee and other ASE members contributing as individuals.

The first two national projects in primary science were the Oxford Primary Science Research Project and the Nuffield Junior Science Project. Both emerged from a meeting in 1961 of a committee that included representatives of the inspectorate, LEAs, Institutes and Colleges of Education, schools, the Nuffield Foundation, the SMA and the AWST. The Oxford project, funded by the Department of Education and Science (DES), was a research and development project in primary science based at the Institute of Education of Oxford University. Its terms of reference indicated a focus on the learning of scientific concepts: *'An enquiry into the formation of scientific concepts in children under the age of thirteen; the development of teaching material for this age range; and the training of primary teachers in science'* (Boyers, 1967).

The Nuffield Junior Science Project was set up as part of the Nuffield Science Teaching Project (Collis, 2001). It began in January 1964 with aims that were clearly focused on developing children's process skills and understanding of science *'as a way of discovering which can be applied anywhere, at any time, with whatever material happens to be available.'* The aims of the Nuffield project were clearly different from those of the Oxford project. They were also distinct from those of the other initiative funded by the Nuffield Foundation at that time, the O-level projects in physics, chemistry and biology. Indeed, the leader of the Junior project, Ron Wastnedge, strenuously defended the informal methods being developed in primary schools and argued that these were more suitable in the early years of the secondary education than the formal methods and subject boundaries of the secondary school. The issue of transition from primary to secondary was thereby brought into focus, but even though the Junior Science project was intended to cover the 8 to 13 age range, in practice the project catered only for the junior range, ages 8 to 11 (Jenkins and Swinnerton, 1998).

The Nuffield Junior Science Project team of seconded teachers visited schools in order to identify aspects of good practice in teaching science that could be passed on to other teachers. Trials of materials for teachers began in 1965 in pilot schools. Local Authorities set up Teachers Centres and the newly established Schools Council for the Curriculum and Examinations ran introductory courses for teachers, area leaders and administrators. It was seen as vital that children should handle materials, and hear, smell and taste them where practicable. This first-hand experience was considered enough to be the basis for the formation of concepts. What students investigated was regarded as less important than how they investigated it. Thus the content encountered by students was spread widely and thinly.

The Nuffield Junior Science Project was far more influential than the Oxford project due to embracing the child-centred approach and the 'discovery learning' endorsed by the Plowden Report. This was despite the mixed findings from an evaluation commissioned by the Schools Council. The report (Crossland, 1967) found that teachers of junior classes were making progress in more active methods and were extending science beyond nature, but found nothing new in some classes, particularly in those infants' schools where progressive methods were already well established. The report found no evidence that the project had identified and communicated a progressive structure for students' learning in science. Of course, that was not intended but was a key point to be addressed by the project's successor.

The project that followed Nuffield Junior Science, in 1967, Science 5/13 soon formed its own ideas of how to develop science in the primary school (Harlen, 1975). Moreover, being a 'second generation' project, it had the advantage of being able to learn from the experience of other projects both in the UK and abroad. The director, Len Ennever, had been a key player in the promotion of primary science for over a decade. He also visited the projects for elementary school science that were by then active in the USA. These projects reflected the same content–process tension that was apparent in Britain. The experience of these projects helped to identify a need for a clear statement of what children should learn from their science work, and how this changed in the years from age 5–13. Thus the project identified objectives for children learning science, both in process skills and concepts, spelling this out at three stages of development, defined in terms of Piaget's description of cognitive development. Science 5/13 agreed with the Nuffield project in rejecting the ideas of producing kits and pupil materials. Its chosen way of helping teachers was to produce 'Units' relating to topics of interest to children and to provide background science for the teacher. The Units were described as illustrations of how teachers might help students achieve certain objectives, not presented as a course. To construct the Units, working groups of teachers were formed to discuss and try out initial ideas with their students. From the information gathered, draft Units were produced and trialled in pilot areas around England and Wales, with Scotland also as a trial area. A formative evaluation of these trials (Harlen, 1975) was aimed at revealing the extent to which the draft Units helped teachers to recognise and work towards learning objectives. The project was extended on several occasions, ending in 1975. The 26 Units published included 20 written by members of the team and 6 by Margaret Collis.

Meanwhile other projects were funded by the Nuffield Foundation, the Schools Council and LEAs, each extending the help given to teachers in various ways. For example, Learning Through Science produced workcards for pupils, Progress in Learning Science produced multimedia materials for in-service courses, the Teaching Primary Science project produced material for pre-service courses. Other projects and individual authors added to the materials and background information available to class teachers.

Assessment of achievement

The 1970s brought a new element into primary science education in the UK – the assessment of children's learning. In 1975, the Government-funded Assessment of Performance Unit (APU) was set up, and the science programme began in 1977 as a consortium of King's College London and Leeds University, under the direction of influential ASE members Paul Black and David Layton. From 1980 to 1984, the APU conducted annual surveys in science of national samples of pupils at ages 11, 13, and 15 in England, Wales and Northern Ireland. Surveys of a similar nature, initiated and funded by the Scottish Education Department, were started in Scotland in 1984. The APU was set up, among other purposes, to answer questions about what was happening to standards of education as a result of the rapid changes of the 1960s. In order to develop the assessment programme, it was necessary to decide what kinds of achievement should be assessed. The lack of consensus at the time about the aims of primary science and the absence of a common national curriculum made this difficult and there were objections that it was likely to impose uniformity on what was taught, rather than leaving this to schools to decide.

The APU assessment framework was a wide one, however, with an emphasis on processes and the inclusion of practical activities as well as written tests (Harlen, Palacio and Russell, 1984). The results were of considerable value beyond monitoring the performance of children. They provided evidence of the interdependence of process and the content used to assess it. So, for instance, in making observations, planning an investigation or interpreting results, the content on which these skills were used made a considerable difference to achievement. This was in direct conflict with the view that the subject matter was unimportant in the use and development of processes. Further, the findings provided evidence of children using non-scientific ideas in explaining scientific phenomena. At the secondary level, it was clear that these ideas were held despite science teaching and seemed to make more sense to the children than abstract scientific explanations. These findings, added to the research into children's own ideas both at primary and secondary levels, led to important conclusions about learning in science as the construction of ideas by learners rather than accepting ideas from teachers and others. In the late 1980s, the Science Processes and Concepts Exploration (SPACE) project, funded by the Nuffield Foundation, and based at Liverpool University and King's College London, studied children's ideas about a wide range of scientific phenomena. It created, with teachers, approaches to helping children towards more scientific ideas, starting from those that the children had worked out for themselves. The SPACE Project team, directed by Paul Black and Wynne Harlen, included active ASE members, notably a future Chair and later Chief Executive, Derek Bell.

Increasing activity and membership

For the first 16 years of ASE, primary science was making its mark through the activities of a Primary Sub-committee of the Education Committee. It was not until 1979 that primary science achieved full committee status with secretarial support and full records of meetings (Collis, 2001). The members of the Sub-committee comprised those most experienced and energetic in primary science at the time, including Ron Wastnedge, the co-ordinator of the Nuffield Junior

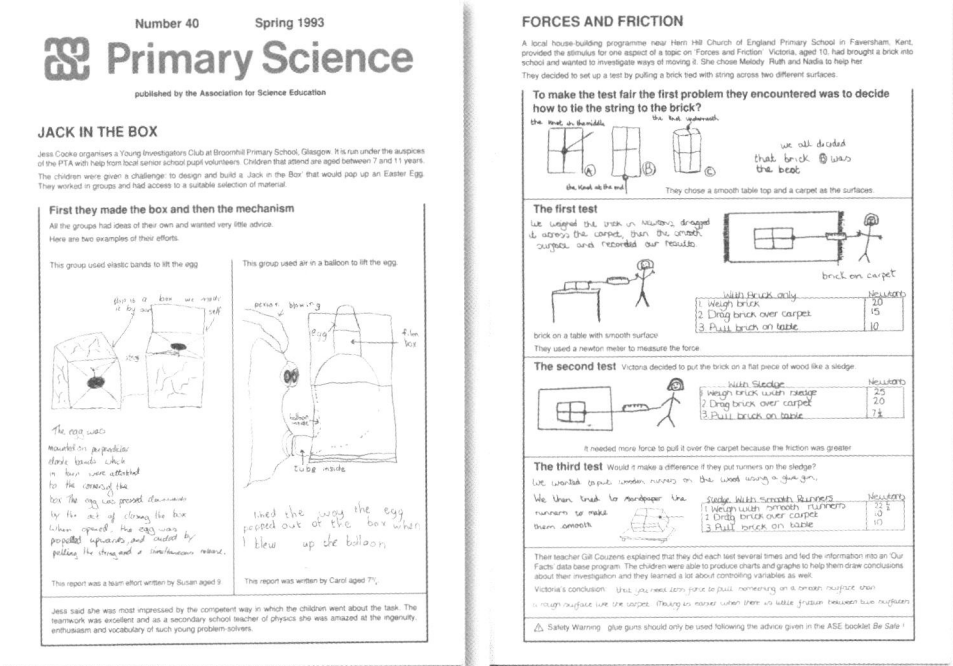

Figure 4.2: *Primary Science Broadsheet, Spring 1993. The first ASE periodical for primary science was introduced in 1980.*

Science project, and Margaret Collis, (see above and Chapter 2) who, after a few years, took over the Chair when the Sub-committee was reconstituted. Primary science gathered momentum in the 1980s from the continued development of classroom material and the publication by the DES of *Science Education in Schools,* underlining the importance of beginning science in the primary school (DES/WO, 1982), at the same time noting that '*Primary school pupils have still far to go in their awakening to science*' (para. 29). This document was somewhat dismissive of the work of the Nuffield Junior Science Project and Science 5/13, since these '*did not improve science teaching as much as was hoped*'. ASE's response to this was to suggest that this ignored the role of these projects in '*defining the directions in which further effort is required*'. Whether or not these and other comments were heeded will never be known, but the later *Science 5–16: A Statement of Policy*, drawing on the 1982 paper, expressed rather more wholehearted support for primary science. Its first paragraph proclaimed that '*All pupils should be properly introduced to science in the primary school, and all pupils should continue to study a broad science programme, well suited to their abilities and aptitudes, throughout the first five years of secondary education*' (DES/WO, 1985).

Despite the activities of the influential Primary Science Sub-committee, whose hard-working members laid some of the foundations for the role that ASE was to play in making science for children of all ages a reality, there were few primary teacher members of ASE for the first 20 years. Although the booklets they were producing proved very popular and the Sub-Committee members were energetic in promoting membership, the focus of the Association remained mainly on secondary science and it seemed to offer little to the primary teacher, who had to pay the same subscription as a secondary teacher. That was until 1983, when a range of actions was put in place to encourage primary teacher membership. ASE Council decided to institute '*a special Primary Teacher Subscription (in 1983–4 this was £5, compared with the ordinary member's subscription of £16), which provided a personal copy of* Education in Science *and the* ASE Primary Science' (Layton, 1984: 117).

A newly constituted Primary Science Committee (PSC) in March 1983 suggested that a collective primary membership was necessary as well as the individual membership and this was put in place in 1984. The Committee also wanted to strengthen primary science in the ASE Regions. Further, it asserted that '*If the ASE is to develop primary teacher membership then clearly it must provide a service which is both valued and of assistance to the class teachers on a regular basis*'. To provide this, a new journal was needed and a recommendation made to Publications Committee to this effect. Primary school members would then receive the new magazine and the broadsheet, *Primary Science,* (but not *Education in Science (EiS)* or *School Science Review*) in addition to other benefits of membership. The Chair of the Primary Committee (Colin Smith) was very clear that the new journal should reflect the difference between primary and secondary science and did not consider that *'attempts to encourage mutual understanding between primary and secondary sectors of science education should be aimed for'.*

In 1986, the General Secretary produced a paper proposing the election of honorary officers to ASE committees. These officers would be expected to act on behalf of ASE in their area of expertise as well as advising the committees and playing a full role, at a senior level, in ASE. The first primary science honorary secretary was Colin Smith, followed in 1989 by Hazel Ruddle.

Primary membership increased considerably in the late 1980s (800 subscribers in 1985, reaching a peak in 1988 when it constituted a quarter of the total membership), probably as a result of many factors in addition to the reduced subscription. From 1983, ASE published a series of short reports for teachers on the APU surveys, the first being *Science at Age 11* (Harlen, 1983), which increased awareness of primary science and of ASE. Then, from 1986 onwards, publication of the journal *Primary Science Review*, available only to members, promoted membership. In addition, the Education Support Grants to LEAs by the government (see Chapter 5 and Chapter 8, Case Study 3) meant that advisory teachers who were employed to develop science work in primary schools became members and encouraged others to join the Association. Many of the LEA Science Advisers, whose remit included primary science, and HE lecturers for initial teacher training in primary science, were originally secondary science specialists. They appreciated the support for their own professional development and the networking provided by ASE membership and they also promoted the Association to primary teachers. As primary membership increased, members whose professional background was in primary science increasingly became elected to regional committees and the various national committees, such as Publications, Safeguards, and Research. In 1999, a significant marker in establishing the primary presence in ASE was the appointment of Rosemary Feasey as Chair of the Association, the first person with a primary background to occupy that position.

Primary journals

The first regular publication for primary members was *Primary Science*, a four-page A4 publication produced three times a year. Publishing *'work done by practising primary teachers in ordinary classrooms'* (Rapson, 2001: 59), its purpose was to promote the child-centred philosophy of primary science and show how it was different from secondary science. The General Secretary, Brian Atwood, had initiated a meeting of a Working Group in 1979, in response to a request from Shirley Williams, Secretary of State for Education, for ASE to provide help for primary teachers. The Group devised *Primary Science* and became its Advisory Editorial Board. The first edition was published and circulated to primary schools in spring 1980. The Department of Industry provided some funds towards production and distribution costs and the BA provided access to work displayed in the primary school exhibits at its science fairs.

Despite bulk buying and distribution of *Primary Science* by LEAs to primary schools, many primary teachers remained unaware of its existence, as were most secondary teachers. Attempts at publicity through *EiS* and other journals were unsuccessful in increasing awareness. Although well-received by teachers, *Primary Science* attracted some adverse criticism at a Council meeting in 1982. To counter this criticism, it was suggested that the publication might be extended to include some items on curriculum issues. The Publications Committee declined to take up this suggestion.

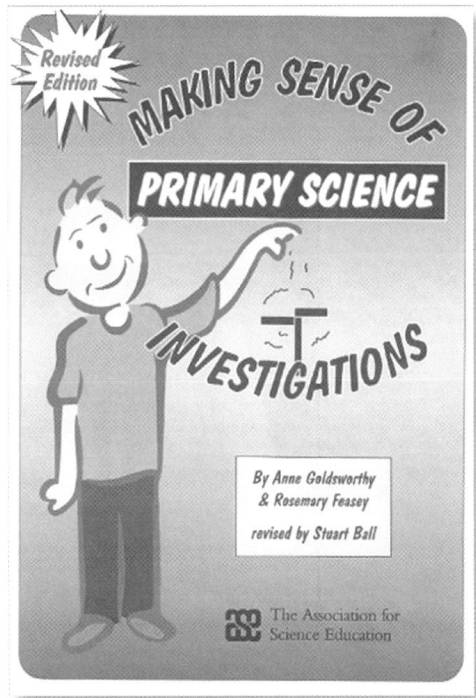

Figure 4.3: *Rosemary Feasey, Chair of the Association 1999 and the co-author of an enduring ASE publication,* Making Sense of Primary Science Investigations.

In 1983, the Editor of *Primary Science (PS)* became a member of Publications Committee and Helen Rapson, the founding Editor, attended the spring meeting that year. That meeting considered a paper from the Primary Science Committee, recommending the development of a new publication for primary subscribers as part of the membership package. This would be a 24-page A4 publication with news, articles, book reviews, and advertisements. It was the first step towards *Primary Science Review*. There was concern about the lack of material for *PS*, which problem only increased as time went on, in spite of the valiant efforts by Helen Rapson and later Audrey Randall. This did not diminish the value of the material that was published in *PS*, as the rising print runs (30,000 in 1985) and rapid sales of the bound collected edition of issues 1–9 showed. *Primary Science* continued until the end of 2001. In the final issue (number 66), its final editor, John Stringer, noted the constant difficulty in terms of securing sufficient material of the required quality to inspire fresh approaches to familiar topics.

When Council approved, in 1984, a primary membership, this initiated discussion about what publications could be offered to primary teachers as an incentive to join the Association. One suggestion was a collection of relevant articles from *SSR*, perhaps with some original material, as an annual publication. Another was a double-sided A4 newsletter. It was the latter proposal that was taken up and the first number was issued in June 1984. It contained articles about the APU surveys and about science projects and schemes. The *Primary Science Newsletter* was sent to members for a couple of years, but ended when its role was taken over by *Primary Science Review*.

Figure 4.4: Primary Science Review *covers from Autumn 1986, January 1997 and November/December 2005.*

After much discussion in various groups, in 1985, ASE Council supported the proposal for a new journal. An Editorial Board was appointed with Peter Ovens as Chair and, although he was *de facto* Editor, it was only in issue 13, Summer 1990, that he was formally described as such. A draft of the first issue of *Primary Science Review (PSR)* was circulated at a meeting of the Publications Committee just before the launch in June 1986 and Peter Ovens, who was made a member of the Committee, was congratulated on the outcome. The first issue was sent free to all primary schools, thanks to external funding, but contained a warning that individuals or schools would need to join the Association to obtain future copies. In addition to *PSR*, members received *EiS* and *Primary Science*.

Primary Science Review was published three times a year, then five times a year from 1991, with regular sections including a 'Viewpoint', Research Round-up, Notice Board, Postbag and Reviews. This gradually gave way to a less predictable layout, but the Reviews section always remained a key feature. The idea of a curriculum focus or theme for some but not all articles in each issue was introduced in 2000. Themes for each issue have always been decided well in advance, attracting new authors, and some commissioned articles have added to the value of the discussion of the theme. To celebrate 20 years of publication, in 2006 *PSR* blossomed into full colour from its early format of black and white with colour only on the cover. Then, after 100 issues, the journal's name was changed to *Primary Science* in 2008, that title having become vacant since the demise of the four-page *PS* in 2001.

In response to the growing interest in the learning of young children, a new journal, to be published in electronic form only, was proposed to ASE in 2010 by the Emergent Science Network. This organisation would produce the *Journal of Emergent Science (JES)*, which would have a target audience of early years professionals working with children up to 8 years of age as well as academics and further and higher education tutors. Its focus on research and its implications for practice made it distinct from, and complementary to, *Primary Science*. Council agreed to the publication being hosted on the ASE website, but without the status of a journal published and funded by ASE itself. The first and second issues were published online in 2011, free to all, but non-members had to subscribe from 2012.

Primary projects

IPSE

Apart from the production of journals and other publications, ASE has occasionally undertaken evaluation and development projects in primary science. The first of any size was what became known as the IPSE project, an acronym for both 'Initiatives in Primary Science: an Evaluation' and 'Implementing Primary Science Education'. The award of the contract to ASE by the DES was recognition of ASE's role in supporting primary science. The eventual outcome was far more than an evaluation; it made a major contribution to increasing the quality as well as the quantity of primary science education.

The IPSE project arose when, in 1985, as part of the Educational Support Grants scheme, the government invited LEAs to submit programmes of action relating to the teaching of science as part of the primary curriculum. In particular, proposals were invited for the appointment of advisory teachers, drawing on the successful work that had already been carried out in a number of different parts of the country. Local evaluation was to be included but, at the same time, the government set up a national evaluation, which was undertaken by ASE. The outcome was the publication by the Association of three books in 1988: the IPSE *Report*, *The School in Focus*, and *Building Bridges,* and a file of separate papers called *Snapshots*. Quite early in the project, the IPSE team developed a list of features of 'good primary practice' and published this in *Primary Science*

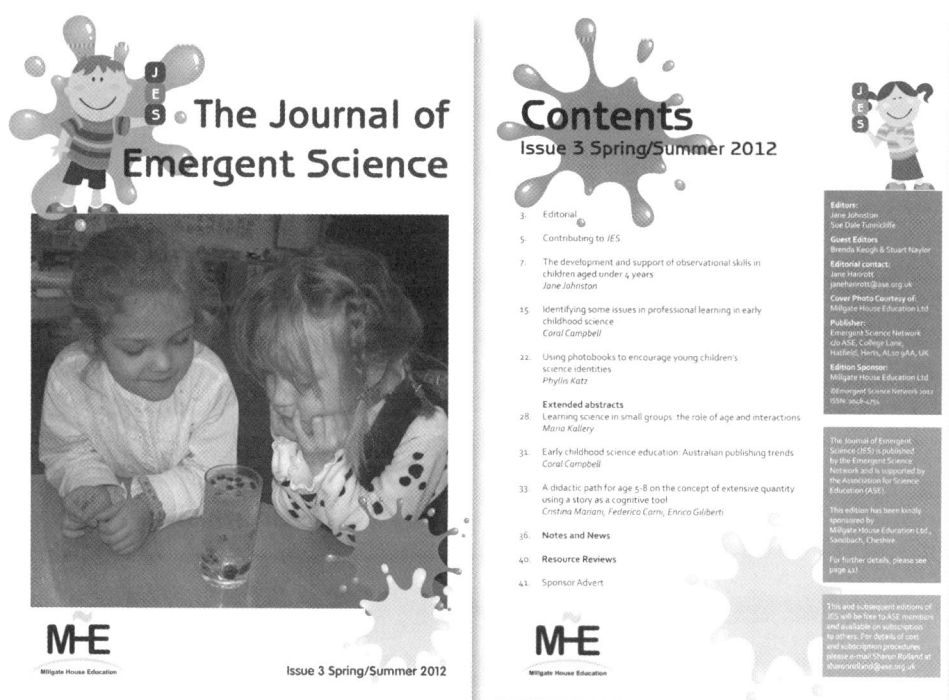

Figure 4.5: First published in 2010, the online Journal of Emergent Science (JES) *hosted on ASE's website, has a target audience of early years professionals.*

Review (Slade *et al.*, 1987). It consisted of a set of statements that could be used to indicate progression in changes in teachers and pupils as science was introduced. The *PSR* article in which this list was included was published as an appendix in the *Report*. The *Report* also included 34 recommendations, which contained valuable advice that retains its relevance to this day. Further details of IPSE are presented as Case Study 3 in Chapter 8 of this volume.

The impact of this project might have been greater had the *Report*, in 1988, not coincided with the publication of the Education Reform Act (ERA), the first draft of the National Curriculum and, at the end of the year, the publication of the report of the Task Group on Assessment and Testing (TGAT). It was 'all change' and heralded a move away from local decisions about priorities and solutions to local problems and towards meeting specified national requirements.

The Five Year Study

The Five Year Study, begun in 1996, was an initiative of the Primary Science Committee. The idea was to use adults, mostly teachers, to interview individual children about their experience of science, their view of scientists and their understanding of some key scientific ideas, and to do this annually for five years to see how their ideas changed and how their interest in science developed. It was not intended as formal research, but as *'an informal descriptive study'* (Wright *et al.*, 2001: 26). An article by members of the Primary Science Committee in *PSR*, to mark the end of the project, highlighted the difficulties of some primary schools in catering for children who were able in science. A summary of the project was produced in 2002.

SATIS 8–14

SATIS 8–14 (Science and Technology in Schools 8–14) was a project of ASE that followed the secondary school SATIS project (see Chapter 3). Published in 1996, for Key Stages 2 and 3 (age 7–11 and 11–14), SATIS 8–14 materials were intended to enrich work in the (English) National Curriculum for both science and technology, putting these subjects into social, industrial, agricultural, and health and safety contexts. However, since Key Stage 2 teachers were not required by the National Curriculum to teach about the implications of scientific and technological developments, the uptake by primary teachers, beyond the enthusiasts, was disappointing (see details in Case Study 2 in Chapter 8).

AKSIS

As the National Curriculum was put in place, there were several changes both in the structure of, and in the balance between, the processes of investigation and the knowledge and understanding of science concepts. The attention given to developing teachers' own understanding of scientific ideas in the specification for government funding of 20-day courses tended to increase the separation between process and knowledge of science. The belief that the two should work together to develop pupils' understanding was the basis for a collaboration between ASE and King's College London, known as the AKSIS project. The project sought to ensure that:

'scientific enquiry should be at the core of school science; that it should develop pupils' understanding of the nature of scientific activity and the relation between data and scientific theories'

(Goldsworthy, Watson and Wood-Robinson, 2000: Introduction)

AKSIS was a three-year research project (January 1997 to December 1999), funded by the Wellcome Trust. The aim was to identify aspects of investigations where pupils were having difficulties and to produce publications that would give practical suggestions, trialled in schools, for teachers of Key Stages 2 and 3 to use. The topics of the publications are indicated by their titles: *Getting to Grips with Graphs*; *Developing Understanding*; and *Targeted Learning*. The project was followed by the AKSIS INSET Project, 2000–2002, which helped primary schools to use the AKSIS materials in creating school-based professional development. This extension work was developed by Anne Goldsworthy, the primary practitioner on the AKSIS team and a former Chair of the Primary Science Committee.

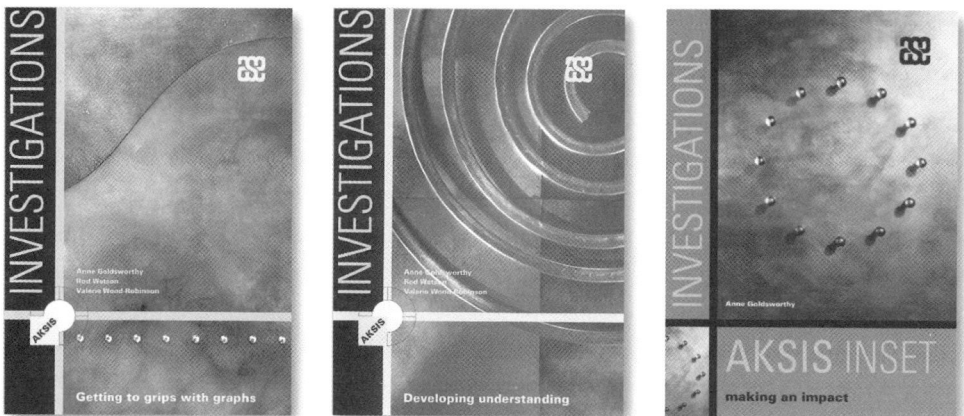

Figure 4.6: *The publications of the AKSIS project proved popular with teachers and were influential in taking forward scientific enquiry in the primary classroom.*

Inspiring and responding to curriculum change

ASE has always been active in responding to invitations to give evidence to government inquiries and to proposals for change in the curriculum. An early example is the submission to the House of Commons Education, Science and Arts Select Committee enquiry into Achievement in Primary Schools in 1984. This submission described the role of ASE, staking out its claim to be an important voice in matters relating to primary school science. It pointed out the Association's participation in maintaining quality in in-service courses for primary teachers, through its validation of certificates and diplomas: the ASE Certificate being for teachers with no background in science and the ASE Diploma for those aspiring to curriculum leadership or management within their school. The written submission emphasised that the greatest need was for training and adequate resources. Members of the Primary Science Committee also appeared before the Select Committee to give evidence following the written submission. One of the questions raised concerned the possibility of specialist science teaching in primary schools. In response, Edwyn James, one of the ASE group, proposed that it might be possible for one teacher to teach the science in another's class or that there might be peripatetic advisers visiting schools – foreshadowing the introduction by several LEAs of science advisory teachers made possible by the Educational Support Grants.

Activity in relation to national policy proposals stepped up a gear in response to the national assessment and curriculum developments. In early 1987, the Primary Science Committee was preparing a contribution to the debate about ASE's policy, and members were assigned to produce written contributions on various topics. However, the shadow of the National Curriculum was cast over this activity and the idea of a paper was not pursued. Instead, the Committee considered, jointly with primary technology colleagues, collaboration on the primary contribution to ASE's submission to the National Curriculum Science Working Group (SWG). In early 1988, the Primary Science Committee received a report on the presentation to the SWG. The presentation covered both primary and secondary science education, including the proportion of curriculum time to be spent on science and the relationship between science and technology at the primary level, progression, attainment and assessment, as well as the matter of balanced science and single and double awards at secondary level. In addition, a working group of the Primary Science Committee, the Examinations Committee and the Executive Committee drew up an ASE response to the Task Group on Assessment and Testing (TGAT) report.

In August 1988, the Secretaries of State for Education and Science and for Wales published the SWG proposals for the National Curriculum together with their comments and invited views on both to be sent to the National Curriculum Council (NCC). The publication brought relief to some teachers and consternation to others; relief that the report did not specify activities or how science should be organised within the school or classroom and consternation about the amount to be covered. Raising science to the status of a 'core' subject meant an increase in the amount of time spent on it for many teachers. The report recommended that one-eighth of curriculum time should be spent on science and technology, averaged over the primary years. The comments of the Secretaries of State requested a 're-examination' of matters relating to the number of profile components and insisted on the use of the 10-level scale proposed by TGAT for all attainment targets.

As the response to the proposals from the Centre for Research in Primary Science at Liverpool University pointed out that:

'The truly radical nature of the proposals for the implementation of science at the primary phase cannot be over-emphasised. Even in those primary schools in which good practice can be recognised, that expertise is almost invariably limited to less than the whole school staff. Science in primary schools lags well behind the kind of confidence and expertise which has accumulated and permeated the profession in, say, language and mathematics.'

The response went on to argue for sustained, classroom-based INSET geared to existing practice.

By the spring of 1989, teachers had their copies of the National Curriculum document. The pages of *Primary Science Review* began to reflect efforts to come to terms with it. For instance, one science co-ordinator at a first school described the challenge of implementation in a school without an existing science scheme. She wrote *'I began by reading the original document several times until the terms became familiar'* (Peck, 1989). These were terms such as 'Programmes of Study', 'Profile Components' and 'Attainment Targets'. Teachers of 7–11 year-olds had longer to become used to the new regime than teachers of 5–7 year-olds, who were expected to implement the new curriculum in the autumn of 1989.

ASE responded to this momentous change for primary science by producing a free *PSR* supplement on the National Curriculum. Several of the articles discussed assessment, an area of particular concern to primary teachers, since prior to the National Curriculum, there was very little assessment of science, formal or informal, at the primary level. The section on assessment included an article about the development by one of the consortia commissioned by SEAC to research, develop and trial Standards Assessment Tasks (SATs) at Key Stage 1 (age 5–7). The work by this and two other groups working independently began before the final versions of the National Curriculum had been distributed. The work of two of these groups was terminated prematurely and the Key Stage 1 SATs were developed as a combination of practical activities and written tasks, reduced further to written tasks only in 1992 and by subsequent legislation until they were removed entirely and replaced by teachers' assessment for all subjects in 2004.

The TGAT report intended that teachers' assessment should have a key role in the national assessment, using data collected by teachers as part of teaching. Since primary teachers would have to carry out this assessment in all three core subjects, it made sense for there to be some common approach. Producing this was one of the tasks taken up by the Core Subjects Development Group, made up of representatives of ASE, the Association of Teachers of Mathematics, the Mathematical Association and the National Association for the Teaching of English. The Group began working in preparation for the National Curriculum and produced *Making it Work for the Primary School*, a successful publication that sold almost 30,000 copies. After the second publication in the series, *Teacher Assessment: Making it Work for the Primary School,* was produced, the Group proposed to produce a new journal, entitled *Primary Associations*. A first edition was produced in May 1991, but very few subscriptions were received, the second edition was delayed and the journal folded at the end of that year. The Primary Science Committee in 1993 recorded concern that the joint Associations group was becoming *'too political'* and, consequently, ASE decided to distance itself from it.

Meanwhile the National Curriculum was undergoing a series of changes; first, in 1991, when the original 17 Attainment Targets (only 14 applying at the primary level) were reduced to four, one called 'scientific investigation' and the others concerning life, materials and physical properties. This changed the structure and there was growing discontent as teachers tried to reconcile the new demands with their existing practices. ASE set up a Primary Curriculum Task Group to find out how teachers were coping and what help they needed. The results were published in *The Whole Curriculum in Primary Schools: Maintaining quality in the teaching of primary science* (1993). This report addressed some of the issues concerning topic work, which had been severely criticised in an NCC report:

'*Some schools have simply overlaid the requirements of the National Curriculum onto systems of curriculum organisation based largely on topic work. There is often a reluctance in such schools to dispense with the familiar topics and themes which lie outside the National Curriculum.*'

(NCC, 1993: para. 4.12)

123

Jenny Begg, the Chair of the ASE Task Group, insisted that the issue was not a matter of topic work versus subject teaching, but was *about the best way to teach children through relevant contexts using a balance of approaches at different times* (Begg, 1993: 5). In response to continued concerns about overload, Sir Ron Dearing was asked to review the situation. His interim report was carefully studied by ASE and by the professional associations of the other core subjects. Some concerns were expressed, particularly about the proposal to focus on 'basic skills' (not including science) at Key Stage 1. The final report at the end of 1993 recommended a radical revision of the National Curriculum, aimed at reducing the content. This was welcomed by ASE, as was the proposal that teachers and Headteachers should be included in the advisory groups undertaking the revision. Draft proposals for consultation produced in May 1994 included somewhat less curriculum content, and the reduction of the 10-level scale of Attainment Targets to 8-level descriptions for each subject. Whilst being broadly welcomed, there was some concern about the top-down presentation. As pointed out by Roy Richards in a *PSR* editorial: *'page after page of the new proposals head off with "Pupils should be taught..."'* This 'lead in' terminology persisted despite comments right through the Dearing Review drafts and into the aborted proposals of the Rose Review in 2010 (see below). But the most welcome outcome of the Dearing Review was the promise of a moratorium on changes to the National Curriculum for five years from 1995. Despite this, the content was further reduced in revisions carried out in 1999, mainly to accommodate an increased focus on numeracy and literacy and, in 2002, the National Curriculum was extended to include the foundation stage.

National testing and assessment

In 1995, ASE sought the views of its primary members on the first Key Stage 2 SATs, which coincided with the implementation of the 1995 curriculum. As the tests in 1996 were the first to be based on the 1995 curriculum, the survey was repeated to explore any perceived changes. Teachers' perceptions of the tests were on the whole surprisingly favourable, with little difference between the years. Comments indicated that they felt that the tests were fair. One wonders, then, why, ten years later, the tests were perceived as not giving a true reflection of children's achievement in science and as having a detrimental impact on the curriculum content and pedagogy. A hint can be found in the survey results, which showed an increase in just one year in the number of schools spending time on revision and 'mock' tests. The use of test results not only to monitor national levels of achievement but as a surrogate for a measure of teaching quality meant that testing acquired an increasing stranglehold on teaching in the year of the tests, and often in the previous year also. The pages of *PSR* reflected the growing practice of abandoning all new science early in the final primary year to practise on past SAT papers (for instance, Harrison, 2001). The effect of coaching was noted by markers (Coleman, 2001). Research began to be published showing that what this did was to distort the results, as children learned to pass tests rather than develop the skills and understanding that the tests were intended to assess (ARG, 2002).

Whilst reflecting the criticism of the high stakes use of test results, ASE put its weight behind the use of formative assessment. Sessions at Annual Meetings, regional conferences, pages of *PSR* and other publications were used to share ideas about how to gather and use evidence about children's learning, how to give feedback to help learning, involve children in understanding the goals of their work and begin to take part in self- and peer-assessment.

The impact of the literacy and numeracy strategies

The national tests results for science rose sharply and reached the target level by 1999, but results for English language and mathematics failed to do so. Government concern about basic numeracy and literacy levels gave rise to more direct guidance in teaching, in the form of the National Literacy and Numeracy Strategies. Although not statutory, schools were strongly advised to follow the frameworks and to show that they were giving priority to government targets in numeracy and literacy. The effect was not only to elevate the status of these subjects and to separate them from other subjects, but also to downgrade others, including science. An ASE survey (ASE, 1999) confirmed that the time for science had declined from 1997 to 1998, that it had been put 'on the back burner' at Key Stage 1 (Murphy, 1999). In 1998, the QCA produced *A Scheme of Work for Key Stages 1 and 2* in order to save schools time in planning, with a second version in 2000. It was advisory only and ASE urged its members not to give up an existing scheme, reminding schools that the National Curriculum was a minimum entitlement and that it was appropriate to extend children's experiences beyond it.

Throughout the first few years of the 21st century, there was rising discontent with the effect of the various pressures on primary science. As time for science teaching was squeezed by attention to the literacy and numeracy frameworks, teachers found even greater difficulty with the curriculum, which they increasingly saw as overloaded and over-prescribed. This led to greater use of transmission than inquiry-based teaching, a situation exacerbated by the impact of testing. Relevance of science to children's everyday experience and environment was sacrificed and, not surprisingly, there were reports of pupils' interest in science and confidence in their ability to learn science being lowered (TIMSS study of 2007, see Sturman *et al.*, 2008 and Royal Society, 2010).

Science was not the only subject causing dissatisfaction. English had been reduced to reading and writing; mathematics to arithmetic; and all the other subjects, including science, were squeezed into little more than half of school time. This situation gave rise to two reviews of the primary curriculum. The *Cambridge Primary Review*, funded independently by a charitable foundation and covering all areas of the curriculum, assessment and provision for primary education, began in 2006 and published its final report in 2010 (Alexander, 2010). The government's review, confined to the curriculum, began work in January 2008, under the leadership of Sir Jim Rose, and published proposals for a new primary curriculum in 2009. ASE made written submissions to both reviews and took part in the national soundings of the Cambridge Review. However, since the Rose Review made definite proposals for a completely new curriculum, the first since 1989, particular attention was given to ensuring that ASE's views were brought together and effectively presented. The process involved senior members of ASE staff, the manager of SCORE (see Chapter 3), a representative of NAIGS (the National Advisers and Inspectors Group for Science) and ASE members with expertise in primary science. A summary of the response was published in *Primary Science* (ASE, 2009) and the full response made available to members on the ASE website.

In the event, the new Coalition government, formed after the general election of 2010, refused to proceed with the Rose Review proposals. Instead, in 2010, it set up an expert panel, supported by the Department for Education, to provide detailed advice on the construction and content of the new National Curriculum for 5-16 year-olds. In particular, advice was sought about whether subjects other than English, mathematics, science and physical education should be part of the National Curriculum or should have non-statutory programmes of study. It was clear, however, that science would be part of the statutory curriculum and ASE made a detailed submission, including a clear statement that a curriculum should set out learning and not teaching. It also provided a detailed example of how learning at the end of Key Stages 1 and 2 should be part of a progress towards the development by pupils of an understanding of key ideas in science.

Sustained pressure from ASE, from SCORE and groups concerned with assessment no doubt had some part in bringing about the decision to abandon national tests for Key Stage 2 in science in 2010 and to replace them by sample testing, which involved only a small number of schools. This sample would enable national achievement to be monitored year by year. The position in relation to the testing of mathematics and language was not changed, but many of the arguments that applied to science were equally valid for these subjects and there was clearly a need to rethink the purposes and procedures of testing at the primary level. So, in 2010, the government set up a panel, chaired by Lord Bew, to consider the testing and accountability system for primary schools. The recommendations in the final report included the continuation of sample testing in science, although recognising that it was relatively new and its *'effectiveness is not wholly clear'* (DfE, 2011). The position would also need to be reconsidered in the light of the National Curriculum Review.

Primary science and technology

Since the early days of stepping beyond nature study, the activities called 'science' have also included much that could equally be called 'technology', although sometimes '…and technology' has been added to 'science' without a great deal of justification. Many of the activities suggested in schemes such as *Science 5/13*, *Learning Through Science* or *Science Horizons* could be described as technology. In topic-based work, it was generally thought not necessary to make a distinction between science and technology. The 1963 ASE policy statement on primary science made no mention of technology neither did government documents on science education in the 1970s and 1980s. Interest was at the secondary level in recognition of the need to produce more and better-prepared technologists. The APU, for instance, produced a framework for assessment of design and technology and commissioned a survey of the performance of 15 year-olds in this area.

A publication in 1977 from the National Centre for School Technology (Evans, 1977) attempted to define technology in terms that could be applied at the primary level, as designing and making something to solve problems. However, this was challenged as being too narrow, and notably by making no reference to problem creation (Harlen, 1986). ASE's policy statement on technology (1989) emphasised the importance of technology education for all pupils throughout their compulsory schooling. It stated that this technological education should consist of acquiring technological literacy and technological awareness and the development of technological capacity through involvement with extended interdisciplinary technological tasks. The later 1991 policy statement indicated that, whilst science and technology were *'inextricably interwoven'* in practice, it was important *'not to deny the distinctive features or the separate identify of either'* (ASE, 1991).

When the National Curriculum was being created in 1988, the matter of whether science and technology at the primary level would be treated as a single element or separate subjects came to a head. At first, the intention was to consider both together at the primary level only and the Working Group on Science was extended by four members concerned specifically with primary technology. At the secondary level, a separate Design and Technology Working Group was set up a few months after the Science Group had begun working and had produced its interim report. The Science Group did not find a way to produce a combined curriculum and so its final report contained a separate section on technology at the primary level, comprising four attainment targets and programmes of study. However, in his letter to the Secretaries of State accompanying the final report, the Chair of the SWG, Jeff Thompson, recommended that the technology proposals be considered by the Design and Technology Working Group. The National Curriculum for science was subsequently published without any section on technology and the two remained separate in the later revisions. The four attainment targets for technology were present in the original Order for Design and Technology, but were reduced to two in a new proposal in 1995 and eventually to one in the 1999 curriculum. This gradual reduction was regretted by Roy Richards in an article in *PSR* as indicating a loss of creativity and originality and a risk of being too prescriptive. ASE has continued to support primary teachers in their design and technology teaching, with frequent articles in *PSR/PS* recognising the particular goals of this work within activities that also aim to develop scientific capabilities and understanding.

The separation of technology from science in the National Curriculum for England and Wales is in contrast to the Scottish 5–14 curriculum guidelines, introduced in the early 1990s, where science was subsumed along with the social subjects and technology in Environmental Studies. The 2004 Curriculum for Excellence (CfE), however, identifies 'Sciences' and 'Technologies' as two of the eight distinct Curriculum Areas within *'a single, coherent, Scottish curriculum 3–18'*.

Encouraging and celebrating best practice

Regional meetings and particularly the national Annual Meeting, now Conference, of ASE have been a key source of professional development for primary teachers. The informal exchange of practice through exhibitions of children's work, as well as the formal sessions and workshops, have spread new pedagogical and content ideas. The Annual Conference has also been the opportunity for celebrating excellence through hosting the presentation of the primary science teaching Awards, first supported in 1993 by the *Times Educational Supplement* and Pfizer. Later, following the establishment of the

AstraZeneca Science Teaching Trust in 1997, the Award became part of the Trust's actions to improve the education and training of primary science teachers.

ASE also recognises expertise in science teaching through the award of CSciTeach (see Chapters 2, 5 and 8). The first awards were made in 2006 and, since then, many members involved in primary teaching and in the support of primary teachers have gained the award. The ability to reward teachers in this way is not only a recognition of past achievement, but also creates networks of mutual support among recipients and encourages them to mentor other potential applicants.

As well as rewarding individual expertise, ASE recognises the importance of creating good practice throughout the primary school and has been instrumental in establishing, in partnership with Barnet Local Authority and the National Network of Science Learning Centres, the Primary Science Quality Mark (PSQM). The Wellcome Trust funded a two-year pilot trial in a few local authorities in 2008/9 and the highly positive results of an external evaluation of the trials supported a rollout across the UK, which began in 2010 with further funding from the Wellcome Trust (see Chapter 8 for details of PSQM). Whilst schools are pleased to display their awards, it is the process of developing confidence and knowledge in managing science across the schools that is most valued. Award-holding schools are required to belong to ASE, which has resulted in an increase in school membership, and raised awareness, of the Association.

In conclusion

There are many aspects of the work of ASE that influence, or have been influenced by, developments in primary science education. Several publications should be mentioned, perhaps particularly the best-sellers: the successive editions of *Be Safe!*, advising on health and safety in primary science and technology, and the various editions of the *ASE Guide to Primary Science Education,* which have been valued particularly by student and newly qualified teachers. There are also multiple channels for professional development, considered in Chapter 5, and enriching activities through links with countries outside UK. The over-arching theme across all areas of ASE activity, however, is of caring and sharing to extend opportunities for young children to enjoy science and for their teachers to provide the best conditions for children to develop their understanding of science and scientific activity.

Figure 5.1: ASE provides professional development for all members: technicians and teachers at the National Technicians' Conference, 2012 (from Education in Science, *September 2012).*

5 The professional development of science teachers: the role of ASE

Phil Ramsden

'A good teacher will be forever bringing his skills and knowledge up to date.'

HMI Report, 1985

Although terms such as continuous professional development (CPD) and in-service education (INSET) were largely unknown in 1963, developing the professional expertise of their members had long been a central concern of the Science Masters' Association (SMA) and the Association of Women Science Teachers (AWST). Such concern was to continue to frame the work of the Association for Science Education (ASE).

Teachers helping teachers

Much of what is now described as CPD went on informally, with individual teachers sharing ideas and expertise within one school. Beyond this, ASE members in 1963, most then working in independent and grammar schools, had long relied on provision by the Association. This included articles in *School Science Review*, the regular programmes of activities provided by the Branches, and the Annual Meeting, with its important Members', Manufacturers' and Publishers' Exhibitions. Most of the articles in *SSR* sought to update members' scientific knowledge, although contributions about the teaching of new or familiar topics were also long-standing features of the journal. As an example, the March 1967 issue of *SSR* consisted of 14 articles, with titles such as 'Chlorine' and 'Some Aspects of the Ecology of the Shropshire Meres', along with a review of 'American School Chemistry' and an exploration of 'Science Teaching and Social Change'. In its early days, the *ASE Bulletin*, later *Education in Science* (*EiS*), also played a part in updating teachers' scientific knowledge. A section of *SSR* formally entitled 'curriculum development' was introduced in the 1960s.

Of course, ASE was not alone in seeking to promote school science education by supporting the work of science teachers. A variety of organisations and institutions offered 'refresher' courses where, as the name implies, science teachers were given an opportunity to familiarise themselves with recent developments in science. The courses varied in length. Some were as short as half a day or one evening, others lasted a week in the school holidays or were provided over a series of Saturday mornings. The courses were organised by the universities and colleges, the professional scientific societies, Local Education Authorities (LEAs), the then Ministry of Education and charitable organisations such as the Salters' Company.

At first, the Branch and other activities of the fledgling ASE followed the pattern established by its predecessor organisations. The sessions advertised in the Branch, later Regional and Section, programmes show that change came slowly and that ASE Regions continued to provide the type of meetings that had been successful in past years. This was only to be expected, because the membership of Branch committees changed slowly in response to the changes taking place in the membership as whole.

Although the broad pattern of meetings arranged by the Branches remained largely unchanged, the programmes were very diverse, with visits continuing to prove very popular with members. In the first year of ASE's existence, Branch visits included the BBC Engineering Department in Birmingham, the Inde-Coope Brewery in Essex, Oxford Technical College, the Hilger and Watts Instruments factory, Atlantic College in Wales, Cheltenham Ladies' College, The Wildfowl Trust, Hinckley Point Nuclear Power Station in Somerset, and the British Jute Trade Research Association in Dundee (the latter being part of an extensive programme of visits during the Annual Conference of the Scottish Branch). Another popular element of a Branch programme consisted of a lecture on a scientific topic of current interest. In 1963–4, Branch meetings accommodated several of the significant recent scientific developments with meetings bearing titles such as 'New horizons in organic chemistry', 'Modern Physics', 'Photoreceptors', and 'The behaviour of plastic materials'.

The impact of external reforms

The 1960s were a period of major change for school science teachers as the global movement to reform school science education gained momentum (see Chapters 3 and 4). This drew attention to the need both to modernise the content of school science syllabuses and to develop new approaches to science teaching. The decade also saw the introduction of a radically different new examination, the Certificate of Secondary Education (CSE) and the requirement of LEAs to develop schemes for the introduction of comprehensive secondary schooling. Inevitably, ASE sought to help its members familiarise themselves with these and other developments. The South West Branch held a very successful meeting in 1964 on the forthcoming Certificate of Secondary Education, which was attended by over 100 teachers. Similar meetings were organised by other Branches across the country. Members of the Northern Ireland Branch heard about programmed learning on a visit to Stranmillis College in 1965 and, in the same year, the North East Branch visited Kenton Secondary School for a talk on comprehensive education by its Headteacher.

The development and publication of the Nuffield Science Sample Schemes in O-level biology, chemistry and physics constituted an obvious need for a large number of meetings and courses to which the Association and its Branches promptly responded. Almost every Branch held at least one and often several meetings about what quickly came to be referred to as Nuffield courses. These meetings were often addressed by teachers, almost all of them ASE members, who were involved in the development or/and the trialling of the Project materials. The Yorkshire Branch held an over-subscribed 'Working Day' on 'Teaching Modern Physics' at Huddersfield New College in March 1964, which covered both Nuffield O-level and the new Advanced level syllabuses. As well as issues of pedagogy, the Nuffield courses, especially those in physics, also introduced many new experiments, such as those involving radioactivity, for which new apparatus had been specially developed. As had been the case with the SMA, Branch meetings of ASE all over the country became occupied with trying out and testing new items of science teaching equipment. Many of these meetings were run in conjunction with the manufacturers, who would not only make the apparatus available but also provide some welcome refreshments!

In Scotland, major changes were introduced by the Scottish Education Department in the form of Alternative physics and Alternative chemistry syllabuses at O- and H-Grades. The 1962 Annual Conference of the Scottish Branch of the SMA was, in effect, the launchpad for these new syllabuses. The Conference was addressed by two physics teachers from Scottish schools, both of whom, according to a subsequent report in SSR in 1962, 'succeeded in conveying to those present – and it seemed to be a record crowd – something of their own buoyant enthusiasm for physics as an adventure and a challenge'. One of these, Jim Jardine, who had also contributed to the Nuffield developments, entitled his demonstration 'Physics is Fun', a title he went on to use for his well-known textbook. Scottish science teachers inevitably needed to familiarise themselves with the new syllabuses in physics and chemistry, and the necessary programme of professional development was mainly the responsibility of the Colleges of Education. Nonetheless, ASE members were fully involved in contributing both to the weekend and week-long summer courses organised by the Colleges and the various meetings organised by the Association itself in Scotland.

Following the election of a Labour government at Westminster in 1964 and Prime Minister Harold Wilson's reference to economic growth in the context of the *'white heat of technological revolution'*, the relationships between school science and technology received considerable attention. As far as ASE was concerned, science teachers had a particular responsibility to promote technology, not least in response to claims, notably from some university engineering departments, that science teachers promoted only 'pure' science courses amongst their brighter students. The challenge to the Association had been laid down by HRH The Duke of Edinburgh, the Patron of ASE, in his speech to the first ASE Science and Education Conference in April 1963. The Duke championed the engineer as *'the means by which we are all able to enjoy the fruits of science'* and, to drive home the message, his full speech was circulated to members as a loose insert in the *ASE Bulletin* of April 1963. However, as McCulloch *et al.* (1985) have shown, the attempts of ASE to be involved in the development and accommodation of technology as a component of the school curriculum were fraught with difficulty, not least because of tension and conflict between competing interests. Articles and letters in the Association's journals reflected an ongoing and lively debate, while several Regions organised meetings concerned with 'Applied Science' and a curriculum initiative known as 'Project Technology'.

Ongoing concerns

It should not be assumed that the need to address a wide range of curriculum and pedagogic initiatives during the 1960s prevented ASE from giving attention to a number of other concerns. Topics such as examination 'post-mortems', microscope maintenance and laboratory safety had long been staple items of Branch meetings. To these were now added electronics, chromatography and SI units, along with the familiar annual features of Branch summer programmes that took the form of an outing to a nature reserve, animal sanctuary or similar venue, which served an important social as well as educational function. Lecture demonstrations also continued to enjoy great popularity with members. Given by one of a small band of gifted individuals from within or outside ASE, many of these occasions were a masterly combination of instruction and entertainment. The ears of the audiences at several Branch meetings were left ringing as Dr Shaw from Nottingham University took his eagerly-awaited demonstration lecture on 'Explosives' around the country. Physics teacher and long-standing ASE member Colin Siddons of Bradford was invited to visit many Regions with his various demonstration lectures. Unlike those who attended Dr Shaw's lectures, teachers were able to take from Colin's plenty of ideas for demonstrations that they could legitimately take back to school!

A number of points are worth emphasising in connection with meetings of this kind. Attendance was not restricted to ASE members and the meetings commonly took place in teachers' own time, in the evenings or on Saturday mornings. Attendance was entirely voluntary and did not require permission or funding from the school where a teacher worked. Not surprisingly, those who chose to attend the meetings valued them in terms of their professional development. The meetings also served to consolidate teachers' sense of ownership of, and responsibility for, school science education. During the 1960s, that sense was strengthened by the role that science teachers, many of them prominent ASE members, were playing in reforming school science curricula and examinations. It was further reinforced by the role that teachers came to play in the development and operation of the CSE examination and by the publication by the professional scientific institutions of new journals devoted to science education. *Education in Chemistry* first appeared in 1964 and was soon followed by *Physics Education* and, later, by *The Journal of Biological Education*. All three seemed to offer something of a threat to the dominance of *The School Science Review,* although, for a variety of reasons, this soon proved not to be the case.

By the late 1960s and early 1970s, the expectation was growing amongst teachers that being out of school to consult with other teachers and to attend courses was an integral part of the job. While associations such as ASE can take some credit for this change in perspective, increasing LEA involvement in curriculum development was also a factor. Many LEAs appointed science advisers and set up Teachers Centres, over 300 of which were opened in the 1960s with more following in the 1970s. As well as offering a venue for courses and meetings, the Centres also held resource collections and encouraged teachers to form interest groups, e.g. a chemistry teachers' group or an environmental science group. However, not all LEA Centres had facilities for doing practical science and relatively few were concerned exclusively with science education. This was not the case with the large number of specifically-designated Science Centres that were set up by, and within, universities and colleges. Many of those involved in the various Centres were also members of a local Branch of ASE, which continued to offer its own programmes. Such was the proliferation of courses and meetings available to science teachers that some duplication and clashing of dates was inevitable. In some parts of the country, attempts were made to minimise these problems by producing and circulating to schools a termly information sheet, listing all the courses and meetings on offer in a geographical area. Success, however, was limited by the willingness, or efficiency, with which an organiser of meetings and courses provided information, and by an inevitable degree of competition among institutions and departments seeking to promote contact with local science teachers.

In the decade or so after 1963, the Annual Meeting of ASE reflected changes already evident in the programmes organised by the various Branches and Sections. While the total number of talks and lectures increased only slightly between 1965 and 1971, from 29 to 34, the nature of the talks and lectures changed considerably. At the 1965 Annual Meeting held in Imperial College, London, most of the sessions were lectures on science, with only two or three giving attention to wider educational issues. By the time of the 1971 Annual Meeting at the University of Sussex, science and science education commanded an equal share of the overall programme. A parallel shift in focus is evident in the main articles of SSR and in the growth of the sections devoted to curriculum development, 'Science Notes' and the reporting of the Members' Exhibition at the most recent Annual Meeting.

Building upon foundations

When ASE was formed in 1963, it had fewer than 10,000 members. By 1980, membership had increased to almost 16,000. This increase in membership was accompanied by a corresponding increase in all aspects of ASE activity, including the size of its journals, and the numbers of meetings, conferences and other forms of professional support for science teachers. The June 1968 issue of SSR consisted of no fewer than 441 pages, of which 134 were devoted to advertisements by publishers and apparatus manufacturers. In the 1970s, the courses and meetings organised by ASE and its Branches faced growing competition from many other providers, including the Science Centres and Teachers Centres, the professional scientific institutions and the universities. The staff in university departments of education put on many short courses for serving teachers, often in conjunction with the university science departments, local industry or examination boards. As an example, the University of Leeds Department of Education offered 59 courses during 1977, which attracted a total of 3487 science teachers. Initiatives of this kind were common in most part of the country. The proliferation of courses reflected not only the growth in the number of providers but also the wide range of issues that needed to be addressed.

The September 1971 issue of *EiS* advertised meetings concerned with 'Assessment in the sixth form', 'Non-exam. science courses' , 'Nuffield courses', 'Physiology', 'Vocational science' and 'The use of lasers', alongside the enduring topics of 'Safety in science laboratories', 'Experiments old and new' and 'Microscope maintenance'. Unsurprisingly, given the teaching experience of most ASE members, two of the major concerns during the 1970s were the growth of mixed ability/non-streamed teaching associated with the development of comprehensive secondary schooling, and the raising of the school leaving age to 16 in 1973. Any local meeting to discuss issues relating to the teaching of science to pupils of widely different ability always attracted a full house.

The Association responded by setting up a Working Group to collate information and advice from members about 'mixed ability teaching' and this resulted, in 1975, in an ASE publication, *Non-Streamed Science: A Teachers Guide*. Some of the summer courses offered in 1974 by the Department of Education and Science, the successor to the Ministry of Education, also addressed this issue, ASE members being informed of the course via *EiS*. In March 1976, the topic was the focus of a special ASE-sponsored three-day invitation conference in Nottingham of science advisers and tutors in colleges and departments of education.

The role of science in secondary education has been a source of recurrent debate since science was first schooled in the mid-nineteenth century. The advent of comprehensive secondary schooling and the raising of the school leaving age (RoSLA) reinvigorated that debate throughout the 1970s and beyond. In its submission to a House of Commons Select Committee enquiring into 'Attainment and the School Leaver', ASE instanced the case of a survey involving over 500 fourth year pupils (age 14–15) in 25 schools in England in which 59% of these pupils studied only one science subject and 14% studied none, leaving only 20% studying two sciences and 6% studying three. The Association went on to assert that *'there was reason to believe that figures now being collected for the whole country will show a similar pattern'*.

This clearly unsatisfactory state of affairs prompted a number of responses. Some schools used the flexibility of Mode 3 CSE examinations to develop broad courses in science for those pupils judged unlikely to succeed at the more demanding O-level examinations. Not surprisingly, the more effective of these courses featured regularly in the meetings organised by ASE Regions and Sections. A very different curriculum initiative, The Schools Council Integrated Science Project, funded by the Schools Council and referred to as SCISP, offered a broad, balanced and innovative course in science leading to a double qualification at O-level. As early as 1971, the Southern Counties Region of the

ASE organised a meeting to inform members about SCISP and similar meetings were subsequently held elsewhere. Such meetings were often led by teachers with experience of teaching this integrated, pattern-based curriculum. Although the initiative found favour with a significant number of schools, the take-up of the Project materials was relatively modest. SCISP, however, had at least two important consequences. It encouraged the notion of breadth in compulsory school science education and established that it was possible to design and implement a broad and balanced science course that led to double certification.

The effects of LEA developments

The raising of the school leaving age stimulated a great deal of development work to devise curricula and teaching approaches for pupils who would otherwise have left school at the end of their fourth year (now Year 10 in England) of secondary education. The new courses often involved practical subjects, which were sometimes taught in new purpose-built facilities, the so-called 'RoSLA blocks', some of which remain in use. Much of this development work was done by LEAs, with working groups of teachers meeting in the newly opened Teachers Centres under the leadership of the LEA Science Advisers. The numbers of such Advisers had increased substantially in the later 1960s and, in the early 1970s, they formed a Special Interest Group (SIG) within ASE known as the Science Advisers Group (SAG). This Group held meetings throughout the year and, after 1967, met regularly at the ASE Annual Meeting. By 1971–2, membership of the Group had reached 80 and during that year the members met to discuss teacher training, visited newly-built and refurbished laboratories in schools in Yorkshire, and held a weekend summer conference which included an exchange of ideas with the Schools Department of the BBC.

In the coming decades, as Advisory Teachers were appointed and some Advisers became involved in Ofsted inspections, SAG expanded to become, first, NSAIG (the National Science Advisers and Inspectors Group), and then NAIGS (the National Advisers and Inspectors Group for Science). Those involved in NAIGS are ASE members and they have played an important role, not only in meeting the needs of the group to which they belong, but also in contributing to the wider programme of INSET activities provided by ASE. NAIGS members meet regularly, including at the ASE Annual Conference, and are still a SIG within the Association. In 2004, ASE members in university and college teacher training departments followed the example of the Science Advisers and Inspectors and set up their own SIG, the Association of Tutors in Science Education (ATSE) and, like NAIGS, the tutors hold their own Annual Conference.

The rapid growth of LEA involvement in science curriculum development and professional development presented ASE with something of a dilemma. The North and East Midlands Region of the Association recognised this in its Annual Report of 1971–2, commenting that *'many past ASE responsibilities have now effectively and rightly passed to organisations such as LEA teacher centres and subject centres based at universities'*. Noting that *'as the ASE is the only national body concerned with the whole spectrum of science teaching'* it had a *'vital role to play'*, the same Report went on to express the view that the role of ASE in providing INSET was *'diminishing'*. In practice, the fact that the Science Advisers were active members of ASE and closely involved in its national and regional activities meant that the Association retained a degree of involvement with the curriculum developments taking place in various parts of the country under the aegis of the LEAs. In addition, the Association was itself directly involved in producing resources designed for use with those pupils who came to be referred to as 'the least academically motivated'. Aware that individual teachers and small groups around the country were trying to overcome the lack of published resources suitable for use with these pupils, the Education (Research) Committee of the Association established a project in 1974 to help remedy this deficiency. *'The Contribution of Science to the Curriculum of the Least Academically Motivated Pupils in the Secondary School'* almost immediately became known as LAMP (see Chapter 3). Science teachers working in groups all over the UK became involved and materials were shared and evaluated. Progress reports regularly appeared in *EiS* and speakers talking about LAMP materials and approaches featured in many Section and Region meetings. In 1977, the first of a series of ASE LAMP publications was launched, making the materials and ideas available to all.

New examinations and legislation

The introduction of the CSE examination in 1965 presented many schools with a variety of problems. Decisions had to be taken about whether to enter pupils for this examination or the Ordinary level of the GCE and whether to do so for all or for selected subjects. School timetables and staffing then had to be arranged to accommodate the decisions that had been made. This dual system of CSE and GCE examinations was clearly unsatisfactory and, in 1970, the Schools Council decided that there should be a common system of examining at 16+. From that date onwards, reports of progress towards creating a common system of examining at 16+ featured prominently among ASE activities at both local and national level. An article in *EiS* in 1974 reported good progress by the working parties in science subjects established to undertake the necessary developmental work. Many of those serving on the working parties were ASE members and they helped the GCE and CSE examination boards to develop joint schemes. Although these schemes became popular, it was still necessary to award successful candidates either a GCE or a CSE certificate on completion of their studies. From the perspective of the 21st century, it is difficult to imagine a system of public examinations involving eight GCE boards and fourteen regional CSE boards accompanied by an ongoing debate about the relationship between the two types of qualifications. The weaknesses inherent in that system were not to be overcome until the introduction of the GCSE examination in 1988. Nonetheless, much of the developmental work that had been done within the framework of a common system of examination was put to good use in schools and it formed the basis of many regional meetings of the Association.

Any developments in public examinations at 16+ inevitably had implications for A-level GCE examinations taken two years later. Although attempts at reform of the latter during the 1970s came to nothing, the ongoing debate was a common feature of Branch meetings across the country. So, too, were other developments that affected the work of school science teachers. These included the *Health and Safety at Work etc. Act 1974*, legislation that outlawed curriculum differentiation on the basis of gender, and developments in vocational education, notably the Certificate of Pre-Vocational Education. Fundamental issues about the inter-relationships of school science and technology remained unresolved and were to continue to cause difficulty in the following decade in the construction of a National Curriculum for England and Wales. The notion of 'broad and balanced science' also began to receive increased attention, although without any clear agreement about the interpretation to be given to either adjective.

ASE conferences and Annual Meetings

Some of the issues discussed in the ASE Regions derived from, or were submitted for consideration at, the Annual Education Conference of the Association. This was a delegate conference, as distinct from the Annual Meeting which anyone could attend, and was held in the spring. The first such Conference, in 1963, was a relatively brief affair and involved little in the way of discussion. By the 1970s, however, the Conference had come to be based at the University of Nottingham, where regional delegates met for a weekend to discuss major issues relating to school science education. The deliberations of the Conference often informed ASE policy-making, and full reports of the meeting were published in SSR and EiS. Each Conference had a theme addressed by a keynote speaker. Regions were made aware of the theme in the autumn preceding the Easter vacation in which the Conference took place and invited to express their opinions about the issues to be discussed. Themes included Science in the Middle Years (1971), Towards a Scientific Culture (1974) and Science Education 16–19 (1978). When appropriate, Regions could submit papers summarising the discussions that had taken place in Regional meetings. These papers were then laid on a table in the library of St. Catherine's Hall at the University, where they could be consulted by delegates attending the Conference. The Annual Education Conference quickly became a means for the Association to disseminate to the Regions, via their delegates, news of developments and initiatives at the national level. This information could then be passed on to ordinary members of the Association via regional newsletters or bulletins. The interchange did not always work smoothly, partly because the diversity and number of inputs from the Regions played havoc with the Conference timetable. The 1972 Conference, for example, sought to consider the elements of a new ASE policy statement that reflected the ongoing changes in the structure of secondary schooling and the form and content of school science education. In the event, Conference delegates spent much time discussing topics such as the work of the Open University, Common Examinations at 16+, environmental education, science in general studies and science resources.

The 1977 Conference was addressed by Norman Booth HMI, a Staff Inspector and a senior member of the Inspectorate. Aware of the significance of Prime Minister James Callaghan's speech at Ruskin College the previous year, he urged the Association to play a major and proactive role in developing

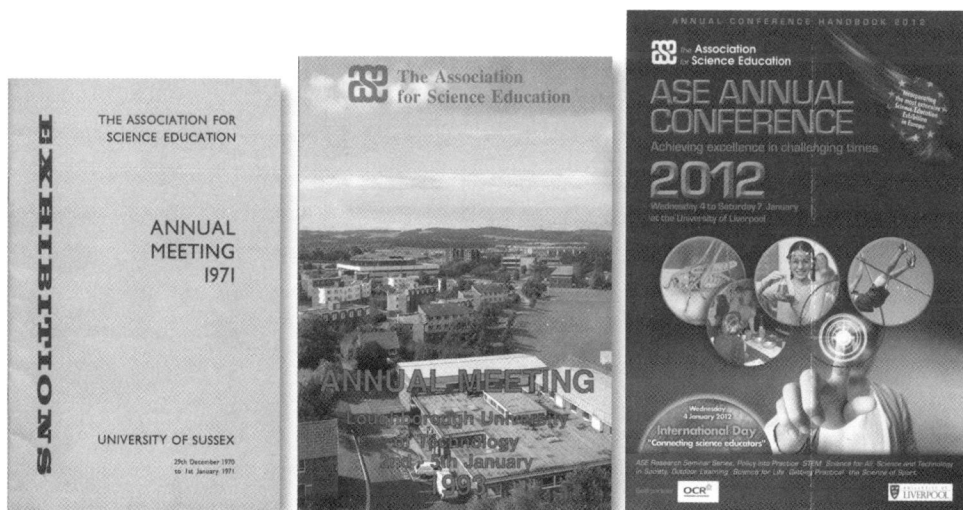

Figure 5.2: The Annual Meeting has become the Annual Conference with an increasingly diverse programme.

school science education in the coming years. The history of the Association's activity in response is further detailed in Chapter 3. In outline, when ASE was invited to submit its views on school science education to a House of Commons Committee in 1977, it became obvious that its previous 1971 policy statement was seriously out of date. Although a short term response was quickly formulated, a much more substantial and considered policy document was needed. That document was eventually produced only after dissent and conflicts of personality had almost threatened to sunder the Association (Jenkins, 1998). In the event, this was avoided, but the process of formulating the policy document occupied not only regional meetings but also prompted correspondence and comment on a hitherto unparalleled scale, although the number of ASE members at some meetings was often a small proportion of the regional membership. Continued

Figure 5.3: Colin Siddons (left, see page 135) demonstrating to Shirley Williams, Secretary of State for Education and Science, at the Annual Meeting at Liverpool 1978.

professional development was now involving science teachers in a hotly contested debate about what they were seeking to achieve in the context of school science education for all pupils. An Association policy statement, *Education through Science,* was finally published in May 1981, although it is better described as a 'framework for policy decisions' than as an overt agreed policy.

Unlike the Education Conference, which was by invitation to ASE officers, regional delegates and official guests, the ASE Annual Meeting was open to all members of the Association as well as to guests. By the 1970s, it had already begun to move away from the pattern long established by the SMA, although a number of key features remained, including holding the Meeting early in the New Year. In 1963, the newly-formed ASE had 9183 members in various categories, of whom 8238 were ordinary members based in the UK. By 1982, the corresponding figures were 16,159 and 14,090. In the intervening years, school science education had undergone major changes and science teachers had faced many new challenges. The growth in membership and these changes and challenges were reflected in the size and programme of successive Annual Meetings. In addition to the usual exhibitions and visits, the 1971 Annual Meeting, at the University of Sussex in Brighton, offered members 15 scientific lectures and 19 talks about various aspects of science education. By 1980, when the Annual Meeting was in Hull, the programme included 15 substantial symposia covering topics such as 'Falling rolls and the science curriculum', 'Science 9–13: what should Middle Schools do?' and 'The Use of computers in Science Teaching'. These were sessions of several hours' length, which featured a number of speakers, each addressing an aspect of the topic, with opportunities for discussion and group work. Scientific lectures (24) still featured prominently on the programme, along with 16 talks relating to science education, but the form (and eventually the title), of the Annual Meeting was to continue to evolve in response to what were identified as members' needs.

Towards an entitlement to CPD

In his speech at the Annual Meeting in Hull in January 1980, Sir James Hamilton, the Permanent Secretary at the Department of Education and Science, set out the challenges facing education in the coming decade and attempted to indicate the new Conservative government's likely approaches to issues such as examinations at 16+, science and technology and teacher supply. He ended by calling upon the Association to *'continue to demonstrate the reasoned and analytical approach to education, which you have demonstrated in the past'*.

It is not too fanciful, in retrospect, to see this as something of a green light to ASE to become much more fully involved at a national level in the many developments in science education that Hamilton made clear the government expected to see. By May of the following year, the uncertainty and difficulty surrounding the Association's policy for school science had been resolved. *Alternatives for Science Education*, published in full in the September 1981 issue of *SSR* (pages 5–52), and as a separate pamphlet, highlighted the need for the '*development of a more effective programme for in-service training and support for teachers of science*'. The importance of such training and support was underlined in a report (*Science Education 11–18 in England and Wales*) published by The Royal Society in 1982 and officially endorsed three years later when the government issued its long-awaited policy statement for school science, *Science 5–16,* (DES/WO, 1985).

Arguably, the need among school science teachers for continued professional development had never been greater and the Association was not slow to respond. The national science-monitoring programme was generating important insights into pupils' scientific thinking and understanding of scientific processes and the resulting publications of the Assessment of Performance Unit (APU) formed the basis of many local and regional ASE meetings, as well as featuring in the programme of several Annual Meetings. The close involvement of ASE in the Secondary Science Curriculum Review (SSCR), directed by Dick West, led to the establishment of many local groups that produced a wide variety of curriculum materials, and the work of these groups soon featured in local and regional meetings. A Children's Learning in Science Project (CLISP), directed by Rosalind Driver (also an ASE member) was likewise generating results, which not only revealed the ideas about the natural world that children brought to their science lessons, but also exposed how resistant such ideas were to change. The consequent pedagogical challenges were clear and of importance and interest to science teachers, and many Branch meetings were devoted to exploring how best such challenges could be met.

In the wider context, work was well under way for the introduction of the GCSE examination to replace the existing wasteful arrangements at 16+ and on the development of a Certificate in Pre-Vocational Education (CPVE). Although the recommendations in a report of a committee chaired by Professor Gordon Higginson about the future shape of A-levels were eventually rejected by government, change eventually came with the introduction of Advanced Supplementary (AS) examinations. A Technical and Vocational Initiative (TVEI) launched by the Department of Trade and Industry in 1981 was funded on a large scale and seemed to have significant implications for school science teaching. Issues associated with the Initiative dominated the Annual Meeting in Cardiff in 1987, despite the fact that fewer than one in ten LEA science advisers had any direct influence over the way TVEI programmes developed at the local level. As far as ASE was concerned, one unanticipated benefit of TVEI money or, more particularly, the funds associated with a TVEI extension programme, was a substantial increase in the number of teachers who received financial support to attend Annual Meetings of the Association. The Nottingham (1988) and Birmingham (1989) Meetings each attracted over 5000 attendees, making them the largest ever held. One LEA adviser alone brought over 600 science teachers to Nottingham.

The programmes of Branch meetings of the Association reveal an almost bewildering array of topics of concern to members. In addition to learning and engaging in discussions about some of the government and other initiatives referred to above, meetings were held with titles such as 'Software Evaluation', 'Multicultural Science', 'The Role of Farms and Farm Units in Environmental Education', 'The Management of School Science Departments', 'Balanced Science', 'Science for All' and 'Biotechnology in Schools'.

Science in primary schools was also clearly rising on the political agenda (see Chapter 4). An HMI survey in 1980 had concluded that *'Few primary schools visited in the course of the survey had effective programmes for the teaching of science'*. However, despite much encouragement by HMI and efforts by ASE at local and national meetings, there was no major improvement throughout the early 1980s. In 1985, the government provided funding through an Education Support Grant (ESG) for LEAs to appoint advisory teachers to support science teaching in primary schools over the next two years. Over 200 such ESG advisory teachers were appointed and primary school science began to gain some momentum. (See Chapter 8, Case Study 3.) Only a tiny proportion of primary school teachers had a significant qualification in science, especially physical science, and few had experience of teaching it. The need for professional development was urgent and ASE was an obvious source of help. Already ASE provided validation of some CPD by primary teachers, through its validation board, which had been established in 1981 to approve course proposals and scrutinise examiners reports for the awards of the ASE Certificate and ASE Diploma (see Chapter 4). Within the next two years, the Association gained 4500 primary members and local committees arranged meetings devoted to aspects of primary science. A journal, *Primary Science Review,* was launched in 1986 (see Chapter 4) and this quickly became a valuable source of information and ideas for primary school teachers. Almost inevitably, several newly appointed advisory teachers were already ASE members and many more joined the Association after taking up their appointments.

The advent of the National Curriculum

Despite the myriad of initiatives with which science teachers were coping, few, if any had any inkling of the major change that was to come next. This was an initiative that dwarfed in scale everything that had gone before it and which would influence science education to the present time: the introduction of a National Curriculum in England and Wales.

In July 1987, the newly-elected Conservative government issued a Consultation Document, colloquially referred to as the 'Red Book'. The outcome of the consultation was the publication of a detailed and prescriptive National Curriculum, accompanied by an initially unworkable strategy for reporting pupils' levels of attainment (see Chapters 3 and 4). For the rest of the decade and well beyond, issues surrounding the implementation of the National Curriculum dominated much local and national ASE business outside Scotland.[1] The late 1980s also saw the introduction of a new curriculum in Northern Ireland; the first time, in the Province, that the science curriculum for 4–16 year-olds was set out in legislation. ASE members served on the Working Group set up by the then Minister of Education (Dr Brian Mawhinney), which published its proposals in 1989. After a period of consultation, the new curriculum was introduced for implementation from 1992 onwards.

In the 1989/90 school year, 50% of the meetings of the Yorkshire Region were devoted to aspects of the National Curriculum, a proportion mirrored in other parts of the country. The period witnessed some of the most well-attended Region and Section meetings ever held, with teachers sometimes queuing for admission, and organising committees having to get larger rooms at short notice to accommodate them. Such a surge in interest in ASE meetings would have been all the more welcome had it not been driven by anxiety and uncertainty on the part of teachers about what they seemed to be asked to do. Despite this emphasis on the National Curriculum, ASE Regions and Sections still offered meetings on the issues of enduring concern to science teachers, as well as visits to universities, colleges, agricultural institutions, the manufacturing industry and the ever-popular breweries and distilleries.

Many ASE regions had organised one-day conferences often with several speakers and a choice of workshops; they were sometimes called the region conference and were a major undertaking for volunteers with no paid help. When ESG funding was extended to support the appointment of secondary science advisory teachers, in 1987/8 they co-operated with the SSCR to establish Area Science Conferences. Held annually, in the summer months, these Conferences

[1]For details of developments in Scotland, see Chapter 3, page 89

often encompassed two or more ASE Regions. These used the expertise of the advisory teachers and their connections with speakers of national standing to put on a host of very successful CPD sessions during a one- or two-day event. One of the earliest of such Conferences was arranged in 1989 by a group of advisory teachers from the North West and Yorkshire Regions of the ASE who met, over a period of about six months, with the SSCR regional officer in Manchester to plan an event. The outcome was a two-day conference, with keynote inputs from the professional officers of the National Curriculum Council and the Schools Examinations and Assessment Council, followed by 28 optional workshop sessions. The Conference took place at Salford University on Friday 23rd and Saturday 24th June and was then repeated on the following Friday and Saturday at Sheffield University. Each attracted over 200 delegates. In Autumn 1989, ASE appointed its first Field Officers and one of their tasks was to co-ordinate the Area Conference in their regions. This enabled them to fill the administrative/ organisational gap left when the SSCR ended and the regional officers moved on (two became Field Officers). Any surplus made on the Area meeting could then be used to offset part of their salaries. In November 1990, ASE Council formally approved Area Meetings as *a new type of meeting to be known as Area Meetings serving a cluster of regions'*. The title was later changed to 'Area Conference', since it was considered that this could help teachers to argue for

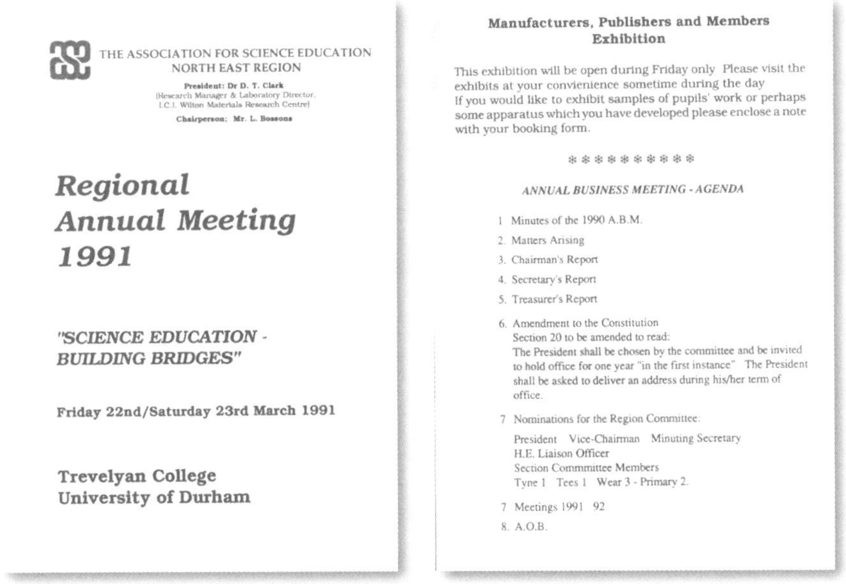

THE ASSOCIATION FOR SCIENCE EDUCATION
NORTH EAST REGION

President: Dr D. T. Clark
(Research Manager & Laboratory Director,
I.C.I. Wilton Materials Research Centre)

Chairperson: Mr. L. Bossons

Regional Annual Meeting 1991

"SCIENCE EDUCATION - BUILDING BRIDGES"

Friday 22nd/Saturday 23rd March 1991

Trevelyan College University of Durham

Manufacturers, Publishers and Members Exhibition

This exhibition will be open during Friday only. Please visit the exhibits at your convenience sometime during the day. If you would like to exhibit samples of pupils' work or perhaps some apparatus which you have developed please enclose a note with your booking form.

✱ ✱ ✱ ✱ ✱ ✱ ✱ ✱ ✱ ✱

ANNUAL BUSINESS MEETING - AGENDA

1. Minutes of the 1990 A.B.M.
2. Matters Arising
3. Chairman's Report
4. Secretary's Report
5. Treasurer's Report
6. Amendment to the Constitution
   Section 20 to be amended to read:
   The President shall be chosen by the committee and be invited to hold office for one year "in the first instance". The President shall be asked to deliver an address during his/her term of office.
7. Nominations for the Region Committee:
   President Vice-Chairman Minuting Secretary
   H.E. Liaison Officer
   Section Commmittee Members
   Tyne 1 Tees 1 Wear 3 - Primary 2.
7. Meetings 1991 92
8. A.O.B.

Figure 5.4: Part of the programme of a Regional Annual Meeting, 1991.

release from their schools. The same reasoning led the ASE Scotland Annual Meeting to become the ASE Scotland Annual Conference in 1999, and the ASE Annual Meeting to become the Annual Conference in 2005.

It is clear that the 1980s were a period of unprecedented demand for support from science teachers and that ASE responded to the challenges facing a membership that increased to a record 25,000 by the end of the decade. As noted above, attendance at Annual Meetings increased and, in 1989, the Annual Meeting was spread for the first time over four, rather than three, days in order to accommodate all the sessions in the programme, the growth in primary membership to around 6000 being a key factor. The numbers of lectures and symposia had doubled since the Hull Annual Meeting in 1980 and the special lecture category included the 'National Science Teachers Association (NSTA) Exchange Lecture' and the 'Secondary Science Curriculum Review Lecture', alongside the Presidential Address. However, the greatest growth in the programme was in talks and discussions, which had increased from 16 in 1980 to 105 in 1989, a reflection of the enormous changes and challenges facing school science education. The 1980s also saw the emergence of a new form of session, the booked course. These were typically half-day sessions for which delegates paid extra, in return for which they came away with either printed resources or artefacts made during the course, e.g., electronic devices, which they could use in their schools. As might be expected, such courses were focused on specific areas of science and were run by experts in those areas. Despite their extra cost, the booked courses proved popular and, by 1990, the Annual Meeting programme included 48 of them. The number of exhibitors at Annual Meetings also more than doubled, much of the growth stemming from so-called 'Special exhibitions' mounted by multinational corporations and non-commercial bodies such as charities and learned societies. These exhibitions were often sources of free teaching resources, such as posters and worksheets, many of which served to load down the carrier bags readily provided for delegates.

In 1985, an HMI report, *Education Observed (3): Good Teachers,* had emphasised that '*A good teacher will be forever bringing his skills and knowledge up to date. This need not be confined to local authority in-service training, but membership of professional associations, visits to other schools as well as school-based activities can all contribute*'. For school science teachers at least, it must have seemed that, by the end of the 1980s, the importance of CPD had largely been accepted. If so, it was due in no small measure to the work of ASE.

The ongoing challenges of the National Curriculum

The introduction of a statutory subject-based National Curriculum presented ASE with several challenges. Some were fundamental; how should the Association respond to what some of its members saw as an attack on their professional independence and judgement? Many teachers reacted adversely to the detailed prescription in the Statutory Order for Science and there were letters in *EiS* implicitly or explicitly urging the Association to have nothing to do with the government's initiative. ASE should *'make clear, particularly through its relationships with the government's curriculum and examination bodies its continued adherence to the principles of liberal education and professional independence'*. It was a course that the Association wisely chose not to follow, although it missed no opportunity to highlight weaknesses in the National Curriculum and to represent the views and concerns of members, as they sought to implement a statutory requirement that was often under review even as they did so. It is worth remembering that, by the early 1990s, ASE membership was at a peak of well over 20,000 members, of whom 6000 worked in primary schools. It was the latter who relied very heavily on ASE for support in discharging their statutory obligations, the more so as ESG support for primary advisory teachers was scaled down.

A more particular and severe challenge came from the difficulties that secondary school teachers experienced as they attempted to teach and assess pupils' competence at conducting scientific investigations, a requirement of the 1991 version of the National Curriculum, then based upon four Attainment Targets (ATs) rather than the initial seventeen. It was the first of these ATs, commonly referred to as Sc1, which caused particular difficulty for science teachers. Sc1 placed an emphasis on individual pupil investigations and, although teachers' reactions to it were complex (Donnelly *et al.*, 1996), criticisms of Sc1 were often seen as undermining the role of practical work in school science. This led the General Secretary of the Association to write a 'steady the ship' editorial in the April 1993 issue of *EiS,* in which he observed that *'the legal requirement to teach the national curriculum can only extend to that which is humanly possible'*. Not surprisingly, 'teaching and assessing Sc1' figured prominently in local and regional meetings. Members' individual opinions were also surveyed and these helped to frame the Association's input to the debate that led to another revised National Curriculum in 1995.

'Scientific Investigations' constituted the focus of a number of other initiatives involving ASE. Following its long tradition of publishing books and pamphlets of use to science teachers, the Association published *Making Sense of Primary Science Investigations*, written by two of its members, Anne

Goldsworthy and Rosemary Feasey. This was a highly successful venture that was used in a large number of INSET meetings. This success encouraged ASE to bid to the Wellcome Trust for funds to support a project designed to help teachers teach the skills of scientific investigations in their schools at Key Stage 2 (primary) and Key Stage 3 (secondary). The successful bid led to the so-called AKSIS project (ASE King's Science Investigation in Schools), managed jointly by the Association and King's College London (see Chapter 4). The project materials were well-used in local ASE meetings and in many day-long courses; they were later re-worked to facilitate school-based INSET and their use in this way continues to the present day.

Unlike England, Scotland has no national curriculum so that many of the issues facing science teachers there were different. ASE played a key role in helping teachers to implement curriculum changes in the late 1970s and, in the 1990s, members responded to consultations on a draft 5–14 Environmental Studies programme and on reform of the curriculum of the upper secondary school. These responses were co-ordinated by the Committee of the ASE Scottish Region which, like its counterparts elsewhere in the UK, found itself with a greatly increased workload (see Chapter 3). The Region Committee in Northern Ireland found itself equally busy, supporting curriculum reforms through its bi-annual regional meeting and through its links with the science advisers of the Education and Library Boards, most of whom were themselves ASE members. In 1985, ASE co-operated with the Northern Ireland Science and Technology Regional Organisation (SATRO) to establish the Northern Ireland Science Education Forum (NISEF). This brought together and supported key stakeholders in science education in Northern Ireland and provided a valuable means of exchanging information and ideas for both individuals and organisations.

Towards the new millennium

As a new millennium approached, ASE began to look towards the form and content of school science education after 2000 and this was the theme of the 1992 Education Conference. The Conference Chair and Chair of the ASE Education (Research) Committee at the time, John Avison, subsequently wrote in *EiS* of the enthusiasm and enjoyment at the Conference as delegates discussed subjects such as life-long learning, scientific literacy, the entitlement of learners, ethics and science, as well as the central issue of the science curriculum itself. However, maintaining this wider perspective in the face of the immediate pressures of 'delivering' a National Curriculum proved difficult and it was not helped by the decision in 1993 that the Education Conference would cease to be an annual event. Instead, bids could be put forward and the Conference would take place only if a bid presented a sufficiently strong case. In 1994, the ASE Primary Committee made a successful bid, but no bids were made in the following year. Subsequent conferences were no longer confined to Nottingham and, to all intents and purposes, the Education Conference has ceased to be a regular source of CPD for active ASE members and a source of ideas for regional meetings.

The issues raised at the 1992 Education Conference were revisited in 1995 when ASE established a Curriculum 2000+ Task Group to make proposals about school science education in the new millennium. ASE in Scotland had also been considering the future and its views were represented on the Group. In its consultation phase (phase 2), Regions and Sections were asked to hold meetings on this matter using a series of workshop materials developed in the first phase, in order to structure discussion and collect ideas. Many such meetings were held during 1996 and the ideas generated were accommodated in a report published in *EiS* in February 1998. The report represented ASE's first contribution to the next review of the National Curriculum to be completed by the year 2000. The next step involved developing the details of any new science curriculum but, in September 1999, ASE Council disbanded the Task Group *'due to overlap with other issues'*. The disbandment of the Group may also have owed something to the growing pressure on ASE's resources at a time when another group, funded by the Nuffield Foundation,

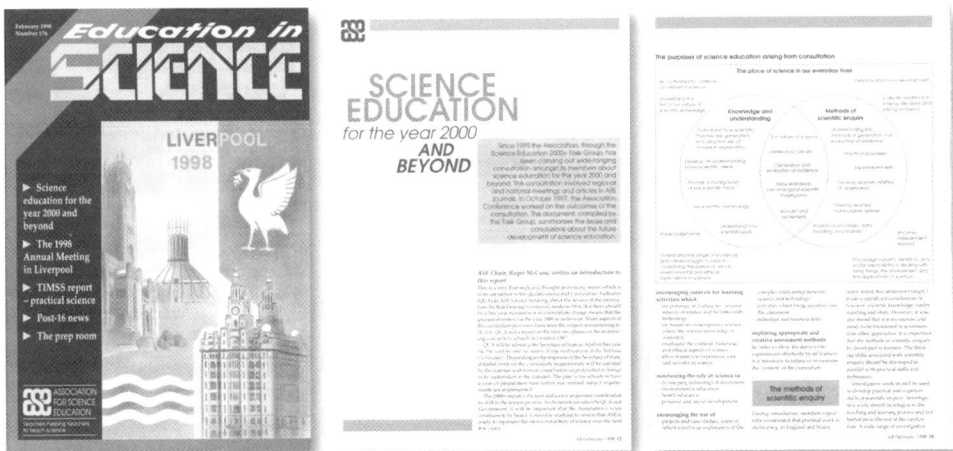

Figure 5.5: ASE was active in the discussion about the future of science education in the new millennium.

had produced a report entitled *Beyond 2000* that, in due course, was to prove highly influential. Although ASE Council held in 2001 a special session called 'Science 2020', no task group was established or reconvened.

Consideration of what the future might hold for the school science curriculum did nothing to weaken the commitment of the Association to advancing school science teachers' expertise. This remained central to its work. It acquired an added importance as the support for professional development by LEAs gradually reduced when the funding for teacher support was transferred to schools. In April 1992, an article in *EiS* announced the setting up of ASE INSET Services under the directorship of Malcolm Oakes. Chapter 8, Case Study 6 offers an account of the range of work of this highly successful initiative. Although the emphasis was on secondary school science, many primary support programmes were also run, despite the difficulty of securing primary school teachers' release from classrooms and the relatively small amount of money available specifically for the science component of the primary curriculum. ASE INSET Services also initiated a programme of workshops for technicians that covered the skills needed in each of the science areas and in the management of technician teams. ASE INSET Services initiated the Certificate of Continuing

Figure 5.6: A group of technicians, including a member from The Netherlands, engaging in CPD at the National Technicians' Conference, 2012 (from Education in Science, September 2012).

Professional Development. Independent evaluations of the activities of ASE INSET Services were unreservedly positive and the scale of its activities in promoting the professional development for science teachers and technical staff can speak for itself. The achievements were unquestionably significant, even if the detailed consequences of those achievements at school level inevitably remain elusive.

As Peter Borrows has shown elsewhere in this volume (see Chapter 6), the final two decades of the 20th century also saw ASE increasingly turning its attention to supporting the work of laboratory technicians. When Area Meetings were introduced, they began to offer courses for technicians. Following a particularly successful initiative by the Midlands Area Conference in 1996, it was decided to have an Annual ASE National Technicians Conference. In the following year, this ran alongside the Midlands Area Meeting at Solihull College. The Conference remains a major component of ASE's work. Further initiatives for the provision of CPD for technicians are detailed in Chapter 6, including technician events at Annual Meetings/Conferences.

As for the science teachers themselves, it was clear what they wanted from the INSET courses provided for them, irrespective of the provider. A survey of 130 teachers conducted at the Sheffield Annual Meeting in January 1992 suggested that they wanted to be more in control of their INSET, so that it was tailored to their needs. While they *saw it as vital to their professional careers'*, they cautioned that *'as soon as INSET moves away from immediate classroom practice and science curriculum implementation, the majority see it as irrelevant, theoretical and idealistic'*. In Scotland at this time, teachers did get greater control of their own CPD when the Education Authorities devolved their INSET budgets to individual schools, with some of it being made available to fund teachers' attendance at meetings and courses of their own choice. This resulted in a surge in attendance at meetings organised by local Sections of ASE, where the emphasis very often was on immediate classroom practice. Everywhere, health and safety was seen as an area of immediate concern, and ASE published several packs of training materials, targeted at different audiences, for CPD at courses, meetings and in-house (see Chapter 7).

'Immediate classroom practice and science curriculum implementation' have arguably constituted the routine business of ASE and its predecessor organisations. Thus, throughout the 1990s, meetings were held to discuss teaching science to pupils with special educational needs, assessment for learning, environmental education and earth or space science, as well as to provide teachers with an opportunity to learn about new technologies such as the concept keyboard. As the decade progressed, fewer meetings focused directly

153

on National Curriculum issues, although meetings such as 'Using green plants in primary schools' could clearly be linked to it. Earth science and astronomy topics proved especially popular. The firmly established industrial and nature reserve visits continued, often being extended to members' families, and providing pleasant outings in the summer months (in contrast to so many ASE meetings in poor winter weather referred to in this book!). Safety in school science teaching also remained a perennial concern and the decade saw attention being given to issues surrounding inspection by Ofsted. By the end of the 1990s, the use of the internet in science teaching had come to feature prominently in meetings.

As far as the ASE Annual Meeting was concerned, the 1990s saw a fall in the number of delegates from the record attendances at the end of the 1980s. Even so, a figure of 4000+ was reached on several occasions. In contrast, the number of sessions continued to increase, the Millennium Annual Meeting in Leeds hosting a record 530 events over five days, two days of which were devoted to international topics. Although there had long been sessions devoted to international aspects of science education throughout the Annual Meeting programme, the practice of having an International Day had started in 1998 at Liverpool, where several simultaneous international conferences, some lasting several days, preceded the Annual Meeting. From then on, there was always an International Day, but international travel arrangements at the millennium dictated that overseas delegates needed to stay for close to a week in order to minimise travel costs. As a result, a more substantial dedicated programme was devised and it is a tribute both to the overseas visitors and to the standing of ASE that so many delegates were willing to leave their home countries to attend at a time of global celebration of the new Millennium. In the second half of the 1990s, the Annual Meeting featured an increasing number of events for technicians and Friday came to be considered as the main Technicians' Day. A specific day also came to be identified as the main primary focus day.

By the end of the final decade of the 20th century, it had been decided to discontinue symposia, principally because many attendees had become increasingly reluctant to commit a whole morning or afternoon to a single topic, the more so if they were only day visitors. Talks and discussions, however, had continued their rapid growth throughout the decade. By the time of the Millennium Meeting in 2000, there were 291, including 32 on the International Days. A new category of session had also appeared in the 1990s, the workshop. The workshop differed from talks and discussions in offering some form of hands-on activity, making models, doing experiments or reviewing or producing resources; the 2000 Meeting accommodated no fewer than 120 workshops.

CPD in the new millennium

Following the General Election of 1997, the Labour Prime Minister, Tony Blair, identified *'education, education, education'* as a priority for his administration. It was not long before the consequences of this policy became clear, when funds were made available to rebuild schools and to refurbish and modernise school science laboratories. With the aim of raising standards, a 'Key Stage 3 Strategy' was introduced in January 2001 and subsequently extended to secondary schooling as a whole. Structured around five themes, of which science education was one, the Strategy made money available to LEAs to support the appointment of science consultants to deliver INSET programmes designed to facilitate the implementation of the government's policy. These programmes were substantial, involving several days per year for teachers from every secondary school and the production of a wide range of high-quality supporting materials. Once again, ASE found itself facing the possibility that the Association's own work in the area of science teachers' continued professional development, especially at the local and regional level, might be jeopardised, this time by the government's initiative.

Figure 5.7: The Science Learning Centres provide an opportunity for co-operation.

In the first year of operation of the Strategy, attendance at many Region and Section meetings of ASE inevitably declined as the pressure on teachers' time increased. However, as on many occasions in the past, the Association quickly found itself involved with an initiative the origins of which lay elsewhere. Close links were established with the management of the National Strategy, and the Association became involved in the training of the consultants, many of whom were already active ASE members, via its network of Field Officers. Close links were thus developed between these Consultants and the local ASE committees and these links enabled the local committees to plan programmes that complemented, rather than competed with, those provided as part of the National Strategy. ASE had also been successful in bidding for funds to develop some of the training materials used in the National Strategy, which thereby served to raise the profile of the Association among science teachers in general. When ASE launched *upd8,* its new 'download and go' resource linking science in the news to classroom activities, this was hailed in the June 2003 *EiS* as a *'runaway success'*. In its first term of operation, the site attracted 1300 subscribers and it is likely that the active recommendations of Key Stage 3 consultants played a significant part in bringing this about. Consultants were also generous in giving their time and expertise to speak at ASE meetings on topics related to the Strategy; their inputs were particularly valuable during the pilot phase of the Key Stage 3 Strategy when involvement was limited to 17 LEAs.

A further challenge to the role of ASE in science teachers' professional development came after the Labour government, re-elected in 2001, began the process that was to lead to the setting up of Regional Science Learning Centres and a National Science Learning Centre. The Association and ASE INSET Services took an active interest in the consultation that led to the establishment of the Centres and were involved in bidding for some of the contracts for the Regional Science Learning Centres, eventually becoming a partner in one of them. Field Officers were encouraged to link the Centres to their Regions and many were given a working base in them. The Association also became closely involved in the development and management of the National Science Learning Centre. As with earlier initiatives, the science educators successful in being appointed to posts within the Centres were, in most cases, already active members of ASE and well-known to other members.

The CPD provided by the Regional Centres was largely on a day basis. This had the effect of minimising competition with the programmes of ASE Regions and Sections, because these normally took place in the evenings or Saturday mornings. Good links with the Centres also meant that their facilities were often used for ASE meetings. In addition to allowing access to excellent facilities, these links served both to publicise the new Centres amongst teachers and to emphasise their close links with ASE. From time to time, the Centres and ASE Regions have run joint meetings. Both the Regional Centres and the National Centre promoted ASE membership as a good way for science teachers to keep abreast of new developments in science teaching, and this included displaying ASE publicity on their premises and also inviting ASE Field Officers to bring materials and displays to Centre courses. The net effect of all this activity and co-operation was that ASE-led CPD activity came to be seen by teachers as linked closely with the Science Learning Centres and in no way as competing with them. As happened with the National Strategy, staff from the Centres were willing to contribute to both area and local ASE meetings.

With September 2001 to August 2002 officially designated 'Science Year', the National Endowment for Science, Technology and the Arts (NESTA) sought to increase the engagement of 10–19 year-olds with science. In addition to the many national and local activities, ASE obtained funds to set up a team to produce imaginative teaching resources. The role of ASE in Science Year is detailed in Case Study 5 in Chapter 8. The CDRoms and 'KitPot' produced by ASE for Science Year provided the Association with a splendid opportunity to organise local meetings, introducing the CDRoms as they became available and suggesting innovative ways in which the new items of equipment could be used in schools. Meetings such as 'Getting the most out of the ASE CDRoms' were common. One of the pieces of equipment given to primary schools was a small digital microscope with software to link it to a computer and several secondary schools used this as a basis for transition projects; the use of this microscope often featured in local ASE meetings.

When the Science Year ended, the various initiatives it had prompted were carried forward under the name of Planet Science. Funding from this source and from the Royal Society provided finance for an ASE project entitled Laboratory Design for Teaching and Learning. The outcome was a CD that allowed teachers to design their science laboratories on a computer screen, move virtual furniture around and add equally unreal pupils and then view the results in 3D (see Chapters 7 and 8). Although the CD stands alone, it was widely used in Region and Section meetings and Area Conferences.

The Laboratory Design for Teaching and Learning Project is an illustration of ASE identifying a specific need on the part of its members and responding appropriately. Such was also the case with a *Getting Practical* project that began in 2009. The project was prompted by widespread anxiety, not simply among ASE members, that the pressures of assessment, concerns about health and safety issues and inadequate technical support were jeopardising the position of practical work in school science teaching. As the result of an inquiry by SCORE (Science Community Representing Education), upon which ASE is represented, the government funded a project, Improving Practical Work in Science, to be managed by the Association. The project led to a training-the-trainer programme (Getting Practical), in which science teachers from England and Northern Ireland helped colleagues to clarify the purposes of practical work and enhance its effectiveness. When the project ended, the training was incorporated into the work of the Science Learning Centres and of CLEAPSS, each of which had been involved in the original developmental work.

The responsiveness of the Association to members' needs is equally clear in the format of its Annual Meeting. Following the Millennium event, the 2001 meeting was designated the Centenary Annual Meeting to celebrate a hundred years since the inauguration of the APSSM (see Chapter 1) and it featured the Science Teacher Festival exhibition, curated by Mick Nott. Since 1999, the detailed programme for the Meeting had been entitled *Conference Handbook*, but the strapline on the Centenary Conference Handbook read '*Training Conference for all Science Educators*'. This presaged the change of name, in 2005, to Annual Conference, in order to facilitate members' attendance, to which reference has already been made. When visits associated with the Conference became less popular, they were dropped from the programme. In 2008, the notion of an 'Open Conference' appeared for the first time on the programme. Offered as a kind of 'Speakers' Corner', this allowed delegates to drop in and out of twenty-minute presentations in a corner of the Exhibition Pavilion. It also allowed them to hear something about a topic to which they had neither wish nor time to devote an hour in an already busy schedule.

When the government asked the Qualifications and Curriculum Authority to set up a working group to consider the revision of GCSE courses in science, ASE was invited to become a member. The group commissioned a number of studies and working papers and its work eventually led to the specification of a Double Award GCSE course, which was piloted in 80 schools between September 2004 and July 2006. Science teachers inevitably wished to learn of the development of the pilot course that came to be called *21st Century Science*. This pilot had a seminal influence on all the new GCSE courses developed for teaching in 2006. Throughout 2005 and 2006, ASE Regions and Sections put on many meetings to allow teachers to find out more about the radical changes planned for science to 16+. Contentious changes in the methods of coursework assessment and an increased emphasis on science in the context of use led to some lively meetings.

Following the publication of its *Science and Innovation Investment Framework*, the government sought to achieve '*a step change in the quality of science teachers and lecturers in every school, college and university*'. From 2008 onwards, all pupils who had scored a minimum of level 6 in the Key Stage 3 SATs became entitled to follow GCSE courses in the three sciences of physics, chemistry and biology. It thus became important to '*give teachers without a subject specialism in physics or chemistry the deep subject knowledge and pedagogy to teach these subjects effectively*'. The necessary training, free to teachers and schools and lasting for up to 40 days, was managed by the Training and Development Agency for Schools (TDA) and developed in conjunction with the Science Learning Centres, though many of the trainers were ASE members working as independent consultants. More narrowly focused courses were also offered by the professional scientific societies, e.g., the 'Chemistry for non-specialists' run by the Royal Society of Chemistry.

It is clear, therefore, that the first decade of the new millennium was characterised by a large number of government initiatives directed towards enhancing science teachers' knowledge and expertise with the ultimate twin goal of raising standards and encouraging more pupils to opt to study science, especially physical science, beyond compulsory schooling. Perhaps somewhat unexpectedly, the overall pattern of, and attendance at, ASE meetings seems to have been much as before, although with considerable regional variation. One consequence of the emphasis on improving secondary school science was a relative neglect of science education in primary schools in which the focus of government concern and attention was literacy and numeracy. The Primary Science Committee of ASE was sensitive to this shift of emphasis and responded by fostering links with the National Science Learning Centre that led to a joint National Primary Science Conference. This ran very successfully for the first time in 2010 and then again in 2011 and 2012. Another initiative, involving ASE and the Science Learning Centres, to promote the professional development of primary teachers is the Primary Science Quality Mark (PSQM), detailed in Chapters 3 and 8.

Following the grant of its Royal Charter in 2005, the links established by ASE with the Regional and National Science Learning Centres have led to perhaps one of the more striking features of CPD in the first decade of the new millennium, the introduction in 2008 of a programme to develop a framework for accrediting science teachers' professional development. Local and regional ASE meetings are able to contribute to such a programme, which is designed to lead to the award of Chartered Science Teacher (CSciTeach) (see Chapter 8). That award is a just recognition of the dedication of the many science teachers who have turned out, often on dark and cold winter evenings, or sacrificed time that could have been spent with their families, in order to further their knowledge and skill in the laboratory and classroom. It is a development that no one could have imagined when ASE was founded in 1963.

As the millennium enters its second decade, ASE Regions and Sections are networking through new kinds of less formal CPD meetings. Emulating the *Café Scientifique* model, Café ASE invites an 'expert' to introduce a topic, perhaps controversially, which the audience of teachers, academics, parents and journalists then discuss, with the opportunity to feed opinions back to ASE. Meetings advertised as TeachMeets provide opportunities for science teachers to meet face-to-face and exchange teaching ideas and tips through short inputs of only a few minutes, using a variety of presentation formats. Networking using the ASE website forums and social media sites enables informal CPD opportunities to be shared, not only throughout the UK membership, but also with the whole world of science education. Virtual online meetings are conducted weekly through #asechat, a discussion group conducted via Twitter and designed to complement, but not compete with, current discussion groups such as #ukedchat, #mathchat and #scichat.

No doubt innovative ASE members will continue to find new ways to satisfy the ASE's former slogan, used as a strapline on *EiS* through the 1990s and into this century, of *'Teachers (and technicians) helping teachers to teach science.'*

Figure 5.8: *NAIGS Annual Conference at Newcastle, County Down, Northern Ireland (see page 138). Peter Borrows (seated front), Phil Ramsden (standing) and colleague advisers enjoying field work on Slieve Donard.*

Figure 6.1: *One of the first school technicians to be awarded Registered Science Technician status, Selina Coleman, with Vince Cable (right), the Secretary of State for Business, Innovation and Skills and Lord Sainsbury (left). Selina was presented with her RSciTech certificate at the Strengthening our Technician Workforce Conference organised by Lord Sainsbury and the Gatsby Foundation in May 2012.*

6   The ASE and laboratory technicians

Peter Borrows

'Technicians should be considered full and valued members
of a science department and take part in all departmental
activities including relevant meetings.'

ASE, 1998

As early as the 19th century, a few schools employed laboratory assistants or stewards but, from the 1950s, they became known as technicians, in line with a Ministry of Education definition:

> *'Technician: these would have undergone specialist training,*
> *combined with practical work, and would need a good knowledge*
> *of basic mathematics and science.'*

The idea was that several technicians might support one science teacher, just as an industrial scientist was supported by several technicians (MoE, 1956; Pearson, 1999).

The key to understanding the relationship between technicians and ASE is to realise that, although the Association has had a 'technician committee' ever since its formation, the role of that committee has changed over time. The original concern was with the number (and qualifications) of technicians that a science department needed in order to support the curriculum satisfactorily and this long pre-dates the formation of ASE. As time went by, however, the committee became more concerned with supporting the growing number of technician members of the Association. This chapter follows these two strands but develops them further into the increasing and valuable contributions made by technicians to the work of ASE.

ASE's views on technical support

Irrespective of the role played by technicians within the Association, ASE and its predecessors have long had a clear view of the necessity of a sufficient quantity and quality of technical support if science is to be taught effectively. In 1938, the General Committee of the SMA adopted a report on laboratory assistants. Just before ASE's formation, the SMA, AWST, NUT and Joint Four Secondary Associations published a joint pamphlet, which concluded that only 8% of Local Education Authority (LEA) schools had a satisfactory level of provision.

In the first year of ASE, the Reading Branch, reporting to the whole Association, began an enquiry into the training and employment of technicians. It reported the results of a questionnaire sent to all LEAs, representing 3599 schools, with 9286 teachers working in 8330 laboratories supported by 1688 full-time technicians and 437 part-timers. The report proposed four levels of technician: Junior, Qualified, Senior and Chief. One LEA relied exclusively on paid help by pupils, so some things have improved in the past 50 years!

In 1963, Council of the new Association agreed to the continuation of all existing sub-committees, with the existing membership. However, the Laboratory Technicians Sub-committee was reported as 'non-active' in 1964, having a convener only. It took some time to reconvene the Sub-committee. In 1966, a request for information, especially about the position in girls' schools, apparently produced little response. A year later there was a major information-gathering exercise for use by the Dainton Committee (see Chapter 3), which included questions on technicians. Based on 875 responses, ASE published, in EiS, *The Supply of Laboratory Technicians*. This discussed working conditions, training and qualifications. It made recommendations to LEAs, ASE itself and the Department for Education and Science (DES). It suggested a points-based system for calculating the number of technicians needed, with points allocated according to the size of the school and extra points for laboratories in separate buildings, large classes, teachers who were not scientists, etc. It also suggested an adaptation of the Science Laboratory Technicians' Certificate, which was administered by the Institute of Science Technology (IST) in conjunction with the City and Guilds of London Institute.

In 1971, a 're-constituted Sub-committee on Laboratory Technical Assistance' was set up, with an ambitious brief. A questionnaire in EiS elicited a poor response and the report was inconclusive. A fresh Sub-committee followed in 1975, which produced an interim report discussing the categories of technician and the tasks each should carry out. Of the six committee members, two were technicians and one was a technician-trainer. A further contribution appeared in EiS a few months later in 1976, including the parody *The Secret*

Life of Anne Sillary. It published a formula for the number of technicians, based on the number of pupils of various ages, which resulted in several supportive letters in the next few issues of *EiS*. The 1981 ASE policy statement, *Education through Science,* stressed the need for appropriate levels of qualified technician support. It condemned the use of unpaid child labour, but accepted that paid, but unqualified, staff might have a role alongside qualified technicians. In 1980, the Laboratory Technicians Sub-committee published a rather impassioned plea for teamwork in science departments and for technicians to be given a role in curriculum development. The committee then stood down. Four years later, ASE adopted *'four areas of priority for 1984/5'* of which one was *'the promotion of resources of trained manpower and ancillary assistance for science teachers'.*

In 1985, a technician suggested the formation of a joint ASE/IST committee. Doubts were expressed by the Education (Co-ordinating) Committee, because some employment issues were felt to be outside the remit of ASE. However, members were asked if the previous Sub-committee should be re-established and what its role might be. It was re-established in 1987 with Mick Revell as Chair. Members included some technicians, as well as practising teachers, science advisers and HMI. *Technical Support for School Science* was published in 1990. This discussed historic resourcing levels and devised a new formula based on the number of science teaching periods. Job descriptions for various grades of technician were suggested, and the report included a lengthy list of contacts for technician networks. It also introduced the concept of the 'service factor'. As this dropped from the recommended level of 0.85 down to 0.45, fewer and fewer of the identified functions could be delivered. This ground-breaking idea was adopted, with refinements, in later publications of both ASE and CLEAPSS (see Chapter 8).

The Association subsequently adopted a suite of policy statements, including *The School Science Technician Service* (ASE, 1992). Largely based on the 1990 report, this said that appropriate technical support should be provided for all schools, including:

○ a sufficient number of trained and qualified technicians

○ specialist technical support for primary teachers

○ an entitlement to initial training and induction

○ adequate in-service training

○ a career structure that recognised and rewarded training, experience and management skills

165

○ a properly validated training programme

○ clearly defined job specifications.

It also recommended, for secondary schools, the following formula:

> Minimum number of technician hours/week
> = total number of science teaching hours/week x 0.85

Following the 1990 report, the Committee was re-constituted, variously calling itself the (Second) Laboratory Technicians Task Group or the Laboratory Technicians Sub-committee. Of six members, one was a technician and one a technician-trainer. The Group's survey of technician provision in a 5% sample of schools identified the value of having an ASE membership category for technicians, with a clearly-defined range of services. The resulting report, *School Technicians: an Invaluable Asset* (ASE, 1994), included statistics about the profile of the technician workforce. It noted that:

○ the tasks carried out by technicians varied in the degree of competence and skill required; as a result, the use of some skilled technicians was not cost-effective

○ there was a lack of national guidelines on conditions of service, which might provide protection from exploitation

○ most employers failed to meet the basic legal requirements on health and safety training, both induction and ongoing

○ some technicians lacked support and advice (e.g. because of ignorance about ASE, CLEAPSS, and SSERC, and a lack of local support).

In 1994, the Science Advisers' Group published the results of a survey across nine LEAs, which confirmed the under-provision of technician support.

By 1995, the Third Laboratory Technicians Task Group had been set up to:

○ work closely with…others to promote technician training

○ consider the need for, and if necessary produce, a series of module descriptors for a suite of modular skills-based training materials for technicians…modelled on NVQ and aim(ing) to parallel at least levels 1 and 2

○ co-ordinate technician training at the ASE Annual Meetings of 1996, 1997 and 1998 o identify key elements in the service which ASE could provide for its technician members

o promote the needs of the technician members with Region and Section Committees

o ensure a steady supply of articles in *EiS* of interest to technicians.

The Task Group was to have a 3-year life and comprised five members, of whom two were technicians. It was very successful in meeting its terms of reference, although some of the objectives took many years to reach fruition. One of the main outcomes was that, in 1998, a fully-fledged Technicians Committee (an ASE 'service group', like the Safeguards Committee) was set up, with six technicians and two non-technicians on it, the latter intended to achieve some continuity.

When ASE revised its policies (ASE, 1998), the section on technicians repeated most of the demands of the 1992 policy but, significantly, added that *'Technicians should be considered full and valued members of a science department and take part in all departmental activities including relevant meetings'*.

Training for technicians' careers

Most of the reports on the need for technicians in schools also commented on the training or qualifications required. Indeed, the original SMA report suggested a syllabus. Some LEAs had their own training schemes or organised training at local colleges. ASE was represented on the Advisory Committee for the Science Laboratory Technician's Certificate of the City and Guilds of London Institute. Later, there were BTEC courses but, by the early 2000s, Further Education-based training became increasingly uneconomic. From the mid-1980s, CLEAPSS had been running one-day courses for technicians on particular topics. The ASE publication of *School Technicians: an Invaluable Asset* resulted in a number of developments over the next few years, for example, the introduction of the ASE Health & Safety for Technicians course (see Chapter 7).

In 1995, the Association was contracted by the Department for Education and Employment (DfEE) to develop occupational standards for laboratory technicians. Ken Gadd chaired the Steering Group. The Laboratory Technicians Working in Education NVQ was to have three levels, Level 1 being the same as an NVQ for a laboratory technician in any environment. Levels 2 and 3 each had mandatory units and a choice of optional units. It was later extended to Level 4. The team of 30 who defined the new NVQ included 25 technicians.

In 2000, a further survey was carried out, jointly with the Royal Society. The report (Royal Society/ASE, 2001) commented on the number of technicians, their working environment, job descriptions, career progression and training. A joint working group was established, chaired by Sir John Horlock, and this published what amounted to a manifesto, *Supporting Success* (Royal Society/ASE, 2002). A group of technicians gave evidence to the House of Commons Select Committee on Science and Technology. This was followed by a report, *Supporting Success: Developing a Career Structure*, to the Department for Education and Skills (DfES) (Royal Society/ASE/CLEAPSS, 2003). Written by David Moore, then recently retired as the ASE Chief Executive, it drew heavily on CLEAPSS publications (CLEAPSS, 2002). It recommended:

○ a four-level career structure with core job descriptions, supported by NVQs

○ discussions with the National Joint Council, the Secondary Heads Association and other workforce unions

○ the development of specialist modules for science technicians (and teaching assistants working in science)

○ the National Network of Science Learning Centres to be encouraged to develop courses to support the career structure

○ funding to establish a technician assessment and support centre, offering NVQ accreditation.

A publicity leaflet (ASE/Royal Society/CLEAPSS, 2004) was launched at the National Technicians' Conference in July 2004 and circulated widely to Headteachers, LEAs and science departments. The leaflet was endorsed not only by ASE, the Royal Society and CLEAPSS, but also by the DfES, the Welsh Assembly Government, eight teacher, Headteacher and local government unions, learned societies, the sector skills council (SEMTA) and awarding bodies (Edexcel, VQSET). Despite such universal support, the long-term effects were, sadly, very limited, largely because implementing the proposals would have cost money and budgets had generally been delegated to schools.

In 2006, ASE submitted evidence to the House of Lords Select Committee on Science Teaching in Schools. The Committee noted: '*A motivated and well-trained supply of technicians is an essential component of effective science teaching. We therefore wholeheartedly endorse the ASE's proposed career structure for technicians, the new NVQ and the virtual assessment centre. We recommend these proposals to the Government, and in addition invite them to consider whether the career structure could be linked to advisory salary scales, in an attempt to increase the almost universally low level of pay for technicians.'*

As a follow-up to the report *Supporting Success,* ASE submitted a joint bid with the Design & Technology Association to the Gatsby Foundation for funding for what became known as the techcen project. This was *'a pilot to provide flexible training and assessment for science and design and technology technicians'* (SWDB, 2009). techcen set up a virtual national assessment centre and an e-portfolio for technicians (see details in Chapter 8). Although techcen was undoubtedly successful, and TDA funded it for a further year beyond the Gatsby grant, funding could not be obtained beyond the pilot phase and it finally closed in 2010.

In 2008, ASE responded to the Science Council as part of its submission to the House of Commons Innovation, Universities, Science and Skills Committee inquiry, *After Leitch: Implementing Skills and Training Policies.* The main thrust of the response was on the importance of access to funding for technician training. In 2010, the Association submitted a detailed response to a TDA consultation document on school support staff, and made a strong case for:

o the importance of skilled and experienced technicians (and TAs) working alongside teachers

o the explicit recognition of the role of science technicians in the structure of the workforce

o the need for funding for training.

The sad fact is that, despite the Ministry of Education's 1956 assertion that technicians are people who have specialist training, and all the investigations and representations and ASE's considerable efforts over 50 years, most schools still have inadequate support and there is still no career structure for technicians, nor any systematic training. Recent developments by ASE (for Science Council Registered Technicians) and CLEAPSS (for a suite of training courses) may begin to change that, but history suggests that it is unwise to be too optimistic.

Technicians as ASE members

The intention of the founders, in choosing the title 'The Association for Science Education', was for the Association to be more inclusive than its predecessors. Layton (1984) reports that a technician did attempt to join the SMA in the 1930s but his application was met by prevarication. However, in the 1970s, the General Secretary of ASE, Brian Atwood, made clear that technicians would be welcomed as members.

At that time, technicians joined as 'Ordinary Members', paying the full subscription (or occasionally having it paid by the school). Following the recommendations of the Task Group, it was agreed in 1994 that technicians be offered a special membership of the Association, at a reduced rate, initially as a pilot scheme. Technician members would receive *EiS* but not *SSR*, although they were given collections of relevant reprints. The strategy was very successful, with over 500 joining within the first few months and 1500 by 1997. The *Prep Room* page was started in *EiS*. With successive editors Bob Worley and Chris Peel (both from CLEAPSS), it became a regular feature, usually a double-page spread, discussing matters of particular interest to technicians.

Over the years, technician membership has grown and now accounts for about 11% of ASE membership. Technicians play a full part in the Association. Those making their mark as the first technician in various positions include Marie Lindars, serving on the Health and Safety at Work Sub-committee in the 1970s (see Chapter 7), Pauline Anderson, elected as Chair of an ASE Region (Scotland) and Ann Ratcliffe, co-opted onto Council. The first technicians to act as Chair and Secretary of the Technicians' Committee were Gill Halton and Wilson Agnew. Sue Sharpe was the first technician elected as a region representative on Council and the first to be elected an Honorary Member of the Association. One technician (Simon Quinnell) has been awarded CSciTeach. However, no technician, so far, has served as Chair of the Association.

Throughout its history, ASE has had a committee concerned with technicians but, for much of the time, it focused on schools' needs, rather than reflecting the needs of technician members. This did not change until 1998, giving rise to the view occasionally expressed by technicians that, until then, they had not been 'trusted' to run their own committee. However, technicians are now a well-established and respected part of ASE membership, playing a full part in the work of the Association on Council, in regions and on national committees, such as the Safeguards Committee.

Technicians' events and publications

As technician membership grew, there were efforts to increase what the Association offered them. The programme for the 1968 Annual Meeting carried a notice saying that the Institute of Science Technology would be displaying material covering their work, especially that of technicians in teaching establishments, with the following paragraph: '*The qualifications open to laboratory technicians provide a means whereby juniors can be given training and certification leading to rising scales of pay. Members should find this display useful in assisting their own laboratory staff to provide them with the ancillary help, which will enable their own teaching time to be that much more productive.*'

This ignored the possibility that technicians might be ASE members themselves and, sadly, many technicians have subsequently found that training and certification do not necessarily lead to rising scales of pay.

During the next 25 years, there were many events at the Annual Meeting on the theme of technicians. There was a discussion of the Interim Report at the 1974 meeting and one member contributed a paper to a symposium in 1975 on 'Pupil-power, administering a laboratory without a laboratory assistant'. At 'The Use and Abuse of the School Science Technician', in 1977, over half the audience of 53 were practising technicians. In 1978, there was a symposium *'mainly intended for technicians'* with a mixture of talks and hands-on activities, and this format was repeated in 1979 and 1980. Later events included 'Training School Laboratory Technicians – is your School Technician a Hazard?' (1982) and 'School Laboratory Technicians – Crisis or Crossroads?' (1989). There was a follow-up at the 1990 Meeting, with technicians encouraged to attend.

Figure 6.2: Technicians' Committee, past and pesent, congratulating Sue Sharpe at the ASE Annual Dinner 2008. Left to right: Wilson Agnew, Michelle McGaughey, Gill Halton, Sue Sharpe, Julia Bostock, Lynn Moon, Phil Muggins, Pauline Anderson.

Following change in the Association's rules to create a special technician category of membership, at the 1995 Meeting there were presentations of the work of the Task Group and INSET courses specifically aimed at technicians, on microscopes and computers. The work of the Task Group then ensured a full programme in subsequent years. The day-long ASE Health & Safety for Technicians course was delivered at the 1996 Meeting and there were workshops on data logging and a talk about NVQ developments. In 1997, there were symposia on the 'Technicians Task Group: Working for You', talks on 'Glass for Technicians', the Health & Safety course and other technician events. There was a similar pattern over the next few years. Gradually, Friday came to be identified as the main Technicians' Day, with a full programme, although there were events on other days too. From 2008 onwards, CLEAPSS started organising drop-in practical sessions, aimed at both technicians and teachers and repeated on two or three days.

In addition to the Annual Meeting, Area Conferences often included sessions for technicians and/or the Health & Safety for Technicians course. In

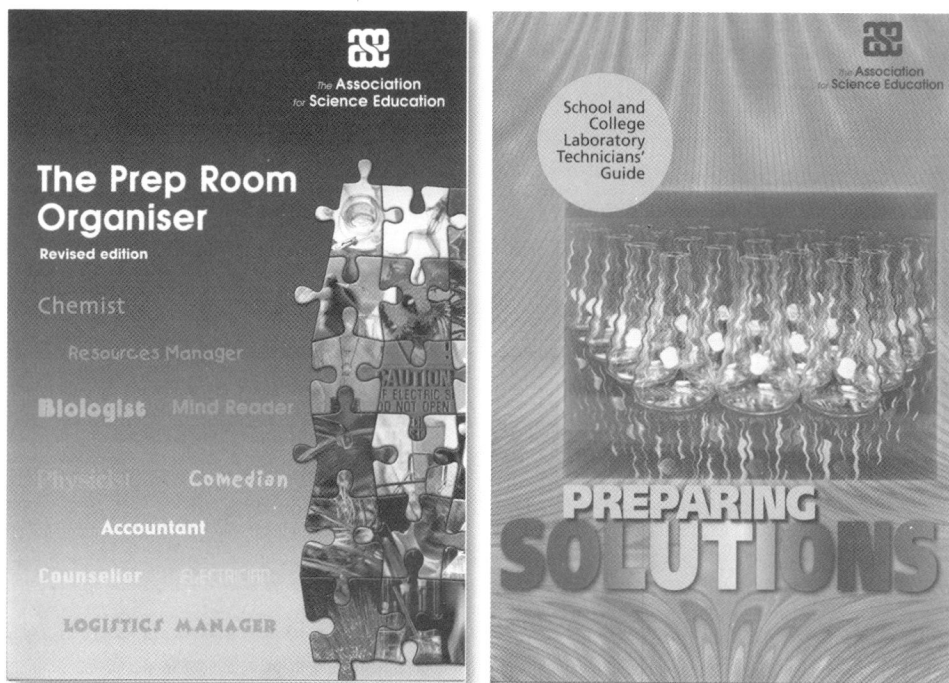

Figure 6.3: A selection of publications for technicians.

1997, a one-day Technicians' Conference was run in June at Solihull College. Attracting almost 400 visitors, it exceeded the safe capacity of the room booked and had to be moved to a marquee ('The Tent'). Because of windy weather, this was not entirely successful – or safe! The following year a two-day event was tried, but it then returned to a one-day meeting, moving around the country. In 2010, it became a joint, two-day conference with the National Science Learning Centre at York and it continues to recruit good numbers. Several regions started organising parallel conferences, although most did not continue for long. As a mark of the value of the Annual and Technician Conferences, it is worth reporting that at least two Dutch technicians have attended both for many years.

ASE Regions encouraged technicians to join their committees and started organising special events for them. Sometimes, this took the form of technicians meeting mid-afternoon in a local school to share ideas. Elsewhere, the committee invited a recognised trainer (e.g. CLEAPSS) to run a one-day course, with priority being given to local ASE members. In some regions, a Technicians' Section was set up, organising its own events but, like many other ASE sections, most had disappeared by 2011.

In the early 1980s, ASE published a series of *Technicians' Guides* (ASE, 1981–1983) under the general editorship of Eric Deeson. Typically with about 40 pages each, they sold for £1. The aim was to provide direct help *'for those technicians who had not had the opportunity to gain adequate training and experience'*. Some of the authors, but not all, were technicians. In 1997, the Laboratory Technicians' Task Group published *The Prep Room Organiser* (ASE, 1997). This included sheets prompting technicians to ask questions and write down information as they acquired it, in a systematic way. The loose-leaf format was intended to encourage users to add to, and adapt, the suggestions. It was based on work done by the Warwickshire Technicians Self-Help Group. A second edition appeared in 2003 (ASE, 2003). In an echo of the original series of *Technicians' Guides*, the Committee produced three practical manuals for technicians (ASE, 2005, 2008). However, it is surprising that there have not been more publications coming from the Committee in recent years, although perhaps it would have been difficult to compete with CLEAPSS.

Over the 50 years of ASE, technicians have progressed from being mere assistants to members, to the status of being influential members of the Association, in their own right.

Education
in Science
Number 246 ■ February 2012

The Association
for Science Education

The magazine of the Association for Science Education

Figure 7.1: Dr Hal Sosabowski at the 2012 Annual Conference in Liverpool. ASE has always promoted exciting science activities in the context of authoritative health and safety awareness and procedures.

7   Safety, laboratories, units and nomenclature: ASE's contribution

Peter Borrows

'That's banned, isn't it? It must be true – it was in the Sunday Times!'

Part 1 Health and safety support

After *The School Science Review*, the booklet *Safeguards in the (School) Laboratory* is probably the oldest surviving relic of the Association's inheritance. This flagship booklet had been started by the AWST in 1933 as *Safeguards in the Laboratory: '...to help inexperienced teachers to avoid some of the commoner laboratory mishaps and to guide non-scientific headmistresses in laboratory administration from the point of view of safety'.*

The 'first edition' compiled by the SMA and the AWST was published in 1947, with three further editions until the fifth – the first ASE edition – in 1965. The word 'school' was inserted into the title with the fourth edition. Further editions followed with the price rising from £0.15 in 1972 and £0.35 in 1976, to the most recent (11th edition, published in 2006), selling in 2011 at £12 for members, £18 for non-members (ASE, 1965, etc.). A Slovenian translation of the 10th edition, *Varno Delo V Šolskem Laboratoriju*, was published in 1999.

No copy of the 1947 edition has been located, but two things are striking about the others:

o how much thicker the booklet has become over the years

o how few people have been involved in producing all these editions.

The AWST booklet comprised three pages (of which two were about first aid) and the second edition of the joint booklet 6½ pages, with about 210 words per page. It and the next three editions were little more than a slight expansion of the AWST booklet. The 11th edition comprises 142 pages, with about 630 words per page. This 66-fold increase in wordage will no doubt confirm some readers' worst fears about health and safety being an invention of the 1990s, going mad and ruining good science teaching, but this is not really the whole story. In fact, health and safety was a matter of considerable debate in the early days of the Association. For example, following a letter in 1965 from the Explosives Branch of the Home Office about accidents involving chlorates outside school, there was extensive correspondence in the *ASE Bulletin* about their use within schools.

The Laboratory Safeguards Sub-Committee
This Sub-committee continued from the SMA days. For the first 20 years or so, its role was mainly to produce new editions of *Safeguards in the School Laboratory*. Other aspects of health and safety were dealt with by other committees. For example, in 1965, an accident involving Schultze's macerating fluid was discussed by the Science and Education Committee, which resolved to put an article in the *ASE Bulletin* and to write to the supplier. Gradually, however, the Sub-committee's role expanded and, at the time of writing, there is discussion about whether it should become a standing 'specialist group' type of committee. Minutes exist for 1973 and for 1977 onwards; all but 1973 are very detailed. In the 50 years of the Association's history, there have only been four Committee Chairs: George Andrew (pre-1961 to 1977), Peter Borrows (1977 to 1998), Phil Bunyan (1998 to 2005) and Ralph Whitcher (2005 to date).

The ASE's Science and Education Committee took the view that Sub-committees were convened for particular tasks. If one was 'active', the members held the appointment until the task was completed. After this, a Sub-committee would have a convenor only, ready and waiting should the need arise to reactivate it. The Safeguards Sub-committee was recorded as 'inactive' in 1966, but this does not accord with the experience of the present author from 1966 to the late 1970s, because the Sub-committee always held at least one meeting a year (more if a new edition of *Safeguards* were in preparation). ASE members often wrote to Headquarters to report accidents, and letters would appear in *EiS,* with comments from the Chair, who then reported these to the Sub-committee.

In 1970, the Education (Co-ordinating) Committee (Ed(C)) discussed a letter expressing concerns over safety in large classes, especially in 'difficult' schools. Concerns had also been raised by ASE Regions. It was agreed that the correspondence should be taken into account in producing a new edition of *Safeguards in the School Laboratory*. The Sub-committee was to be re-established and it was also asked to produce a booklet on common laboratory hazards, with cross-references to authoritative sources. It has to be said that there was much more extensive advice elsewhere than in the 1965 edition of *Safeguards*, e.g., in Sutcliffe (1950) and MoE (1960). In 1971, the ASE General Secretary was asked to arrange liaison between the Chair of the Sub-committee and Edgar Jenkins, who was producing a booklet on safety under the auspices of STEP, the Science Teacher Education Project. In the event, no liaison took place, there was no separate booklet on common hazards and class size was not mentioned in the 1972 edition, although it did have more than three times as much information about hazards than the 1965 edition. In 1972, the General Secretary arranged a meeting between the Chair and Secretary of the Sub-committee and the Chair of Ed(C) to discuss issues that were giving rise to some dissatisfaction. At the meeting it was agreed to widen the membership of the Sub-committee. The Chair would advise on individual problems and *'guide along an understudy'* (who turned out to be the present author). Matters came to a head with the implementation of the Health and Safety at Work, etc. Act 1974 (HSW Act) in 1975, when health and safety took an increasingly high profile. ASE Headquarters was receiving increasing numbers of queries from members about health and safety issues and it became clear there was a need for regular articles in the Association's journals. The Laboratory Safeguards Sub-committee was not to be given the role, however – a new committee was set up (see page 178).

As for advising on individual problems, each issue of *EiS* had responses from the Sub-committee about reports of accidents and incidents or comments on queries from members (see below). From 1979, the Sub-committee met at least twice per year, often termly, with additional meetings as required when preparing a new edition of *Safeguards* or other publications. Although most of the Association's sub-committees were appointed with a time-limited brief, Ed(C) acknowledged in its *Annual Report* in 1985 that, in effect, Safeguards had become a 'standing committee'.

With the re-organisation of the Association's structure from 1992, the Committee became a 'service group', reporting to the Guidance Division of Council. It was re-named the Safeguards in Science Committee, to reflect an increasing role in primary school science. In the remainder of this chapter, it is referred to as the Safeguards Committee.

On the 50th anniversary of the first edition of *Safeguards*, *EiS* (1997) carried an article discussing how the booklet had changed over the years. In all, only twenty-two people have written the seven editions about which we have information. The size of the Committee increased from four members in 1965, to five in 1976 and gradually to twelve by 2006. Long service and continuity is the hallmark of the Committee. The present author is still a member after 45 years, and other longstanding current members are Joe Jefferies and John Tranter, with over 20 years' service each. Other long serving members have been John Carleton (31 years), John Wray (18 years) and Dick Orton (15 years). However, with the later editions, a few members of the Committee were not involved in writing the booklet, which was delegated to a Task Group.

One concern expressed from time to time has been about the selection of Committee members. There is a need for a balance of subject expertise and an understanding of the legal issues and potential legal liability of the Association. Developing such understanding requires a long-term commitment, which does not sit comfortably with regular democratic committee elections. As an experiment, in 1986 the Committee held an open meeting as part of the Annual Meeting at which a number of interested people were invited to participate in the discussion. As a result, two attendees (Ray Vincent and Phil Bunyan) were invited to join the Committee (and 25 years later are still on it). The strategy has been repeated several times with similar success.

Members of the Committee have never been paid for their work on ASE safety publications. Involvement in the writing teams is seen as a professional

Figure 7.2: *The Safeguards in Science Committee, 2006.*
Left to right, back row: Ray Vincent, John Lawrence
Main row: Phil Stone, Phil Bunyan, Joe Jefferies, John Tranter, Ralph Whitcher. Colin DuQueno. Allen Cochrane
Front row: Esther Little, Peter Borrows

service, freely offered to the Association. Committee members have contributed extensively to the *ASE Secondary Handbook/Guide* (ASE, 1993, 1998, 2006, 2011) and other publications, and have served on the Editorial Board of *SSR* since 1993. In 1982, the Chair of the Committee, the current author, was awarded the first ASE/NSTA Exchange Lectureship and went to Chicago to deliver a lecture-demonstration, 'Minimising the Hazards'. Amongst other things, this included demonstrating the thermite reaction, making chlorine and exploding a can of glue on the 25th floor of the Hilton Hotel!

In 1972, a group of teachers from the Oxford and District section offered ASE a short leaflet intended to teach pupils about laboratory rules and the reasons for them, which was then published as *Safety in the Lab* (ASE, 1972). The Safeguards Committee made a number of changes to this for the second and third editions (ASE, 1982, 1990), but thereafter it was seen that too big a rewrite would be necessary and it was discontinued.

The Health and Safety at Work, etc. Act 1974 and its consequences

The HSW Act had a major impact on the Association's approach to health and safety. LEA safety officers were placing undue reliance on regulations aimed at the industrial situation and some LEAs were banning the use of particular chemicals on the basis of unsubstantiated rumours. Ed(C) was told that the DES was unlikely to produce any report on the implications of the HSW Act for several years. The Safeguards Committee was seen as not having the necessary expertise and perhaps not the right approach and there was no one body to which those involved could turn for reliable advice. In 1975, Ed(C) set up a Health & Safety Sub-committee chaired by Dr Peter Merriman (a former teacher, but then in the rapidly expanding Health and Safety Department of the Chemical Industries Association, CIA, and a co-opted member of Ed(C)). The Sub-committee eventually included an HMI, a representative of the Health and Safety Executive (HSE), four teachers, a local authority adviser and a technician, and it published a series of articles in *EiS*. Jointly with the British Committee on Chemical Education, it organised a symposium at the 1977 Annual Meeting. To avoid duplication, it was agreed that this (Merriman's) Sub-committee should be concerned with the implications of legislation and the Safeguards Committee with technical expertise. One person, the current author, was a member of both, soon becoming Chair of the Safeguards Committee.

In March 1978, ASE convened a conference with Norman Booth (former Staff Inspector for Science, and the then President of the Association) in the chair. Representatives of HSE, CLEAPSE, SSSERC (see Chapter 8), manufacturers, the Nuffield Foundation, examination boards, HMI and science advisers took part. A series of articles was written, mainly by conference participants, and refereed by Merriman's Sub-committee. These were published in *EiS* between 1979 and 1982 and later reprinted, with minor amendments, as *Topics in Safety* (ASE, 1982). After the publication of *Topics in Safety,* Merriman's Sub-committee continued in existence as the Safety in Science Group, but the composition changed, with two representatives from CLEAPSE, two from SSSERC, two equipment suppliers, a science adviser and observers from the HSE and HMI. The Safeguards Committee itself continued to deal with practical/ technical matters (e.g. how to avoid unexpected hydrogen explosions), but would regularly refer to Merriman's group matters of more quasi-legal concern, e.g. the necessity of laboratory coats for pupils, and qualifications (or lack of) of those teaching science.

In 1988, following pressure from CLEAPSS and SSSERC, a further conference agreed to produce a new edition of *Topics in Safety* (ASE, 1988). Writing was in the hands of an editorial committee, chaired by Neal Stears, from the Science Advisers' Group, and representatives of relevant bodies. Some chapters had minor changes, others were completely rewritten or dropped and there were new ones, some of which had first appeared in *EiS*. The editorial emphasised that the publication was not intended as a complete safety manual, but that it mainly focused on areas of contention.

A third edition of *Topics in Safety* was published in 2001 (ASE, 2001). Again, it was preceded by a conference of interested parties, which then appointed an Editorial Committee. For the first time, the DfEE, the Institute of Physics (IoP), the Royal Society of Chemistry (RSC), SAPS (Science and Plants for Schools) and the NCBE (National Centre for Biotechnology Education) were represented. However, HMI and HSE did not take part and members of the Safeguards Committee formed over half the Editorial Committee. There were several completely new chapters (e.g. on working with DNA, on the role of technicians and on manual handling) and others were totally rewritten. Publication was sponsored by the Esso company.

At the time of writing, work has started on a fourth edition of *Topics in Safety.* This will not be published on paper but, rather, will gradually appear as a collection of essays, updated as necessary, freely accessible to members on the ASE website. Now firmly under the wing of the Safeguards Committee, there will not be another national conference. ASE, with its partners CLEAPSS and SSERC, are clearly established as the authorities on health and safety in school science.

ASE's interest in health and safety cannot be discussed without reference to the role played by the organisations now known as CLEAPSS and SSERC. These had been set up in the early 1960s as a direct result of the concerns of a few members of the SMA, shortly before it became ASE, to find ways of improving the quality of equipment for teaching science. The Association's collaboration on health and safety with these two organisations is described in Chapter 8, Case Study 8, where details are given of the matters mentioned briefly in the paragraphs below.

ASE, CLEAPSE (later CLEAPSS) and SSSERC (later SSERC) were set up at the same time as the Nuffield science teaching projects (see Chapter 3) and they were part of the movement for curriculum reform. One of the particular concerns had been to improve the teaching of modern physics, including practical work involving the use of radioactive sources. In addition, the Nuffield science teaching projects specified the use of low-voltage power supplies. Both radioactivity and mains power at pupil workplaces were very contentious at national and/or local government level. The combined efforts of ASE and CLEAPSE, over many years, eventually resulted in a largely sensible conclusion for the benefit of science education. ASE and CLEAPSS have also provided mutual support on committees of the British Standards Institution, particularly with respect to fume cupboards, and have jointly liaised with textbook publishers on health and safety matters. Sometimes, however, the editors of ASE's own publications needed reminding of the existence of the published advice so, in 2010, an internal policy statement, *Health and Safety in the Association's Publications and Projects*, was placed on the members' part of the ASE website.

As well as working with employers' organisations, the Safeguards Committee has also worked with government education departments. In 1976, it played an important role in publicising the Administrative Memorandum AM7/76, *The use of asbestos,* despite having misgivings about whether there was any real risk from some of the asbestos products (e.g. asbestos-cement bench mats), which were to be phased out. Similar misgivings arose in 1987 when the government issued advice that neither blood sampling nor cheek-cell sampling should take place in schools. The Committee had a major success when ASE was asked to rewrite the 1978 DES booklet, *Safety in Science Laboratories,* and was able to change that advice (DfEE, 1996). In the 1990s, the Safeguards Committee began receiving complaints about how health and safety issues were handled in Ofsted inspections in England, with inspectors sometimes unduly criticising relatively trivial matters and sometimes simply being wrong. Accordingly, in collaboration with CLEAPSS and the Science Advisers' Group, two guides were produced for the use of Ofsted inspectors.

Safety in primary science

In 1981, the Safeguards Committee recognised the need for a safety publication for primary schools. Science advisers and the Primary Science Committee were consulted, but progress was slow. *Be Safe!* was finally published in 1988 (ASE, 1988). It owed its origin to an Inner London Education Authority (ILEA) document, which had served as a useful checklist. This was substantially re-drafted and widely circulated for consultation before appearing as the ASE booklet.

Soon after its publication, the government in England introduced a National Curriculum. A decision was made to produce a second edition of *Be Safe!,* closely aligned with the needs of the National Curriculum and including quotes from it. This was published in 1990. However, Scotland did not have a National Curriculum and did not use the key stage terminology, so there was a call for a separate Scottish edition. Including extracts from the *5–14 Guidelines for Environmental Studies* and with editorial support from SSERC, this was published in 1995.When the third edition of *Be Safe!* was published in 2001, with sponsorship from the oil company Esso, the lessons had been learned and a conscious effort was made to ensure that the new edition was acceptable across the UK. As a result, the book carried endorsements from the education departments in England, Northern Ireland, Scotland and Wales.

The fourth edition, published in 2011 (ASE, 2011), was endorsed by the Northern Ireland, Scotland and Wales education departments, but the newly-elected coalition government in England declined to do so, although Ofsted did. In Wales, endorsement was conditional on producing a Welsh-language version (in preparation at time of writing). The fourth edition was sponsored jointly by CLEAPSS and SSERC, who paid for a writing weekend near the start of the process. The fourth edition put rather more emphasis on using science and design and technology as vehicles for teaching health and safety, and tried to cover a wider age range and a broader range of topics.

Be Safe! has proved to be ASE's bestseller. Some 34,000 copies of the third edition were sold and there have been several imitators. In 1991, the National Association of Advisers and Inspectors in Design and Technology published *Make it Safe!* in an almost identical format. The Science Teachers' Association of Ontario obtained ASE permission to publish Canadian, Ontario, and French-language (*Soyez Prudents!*) editions. A similar co-operation with the Irish Science Teachers' Association led to an Irish edition, *Be Safe! Bí sábháilte!* These overseas editions took almost all the text and artwork from the ASE book but added extra material to suit local curricula. This collaboration must be one of the most successful achievements of the ASE's international role.

Advice for members

Association members have always written to the Safeguards Committee for information and advice about particular problems. Letters to the editors of the Association's journals usually attracted a comment from the Chair of the Committee, who then reported such correspondence at Committee meetings. There was only a handful of letters in the 1960s, but the implementation of the HSW Act in 1975 resulted in a flood of correspondence. By the late 1970s, most issues of *EiS* carried a page – sometimes more – of comments from the Committee. As the 1980s progressed, more and more letters came in, most requiring individual replies. Minutes of the Committee meetings record 15 queries in 1977 rising to 81 in 1989. Generally, the Chair was expected to respond, but the query might be passed to another Committee member with specialist expertise, or be dealt with by the relevant member of Headquarters staff. This correspondence placed an increasingly heavy burden on the Chair. However, in 1996, CLEAPSS publicised its *Helpline* (see Chapter 8, Case Study 8). The ability of ASE members to contact the Association's staff, officers and committees for advice is an important service, still available, but the Association cannot compete with the professional expertise on health and safety that CLEAPSS and SSERC have developed. However, both CLEAPSS and SSERC keep the Committee informed about significant enquiries.

The more interesting and/or important queries were – and are – written up as an article for *EiS* or inspire a longer and more reflective piece in *SSR*. Between June 1978 and March 1993, *SSR* published a series of 12 safety articles on themes as diverse as hydrogen, science outdoors and radioactivity. However, it became apparent that many of the queries were from teachers or technicians who did not know about or have easy access to this series, or to the shorter notes in *EiS*. Accordingly, a decision was made to collect these together under particular themes: legislation, management, chemicals, etc. and publish them, in 1996, as a loose-leaf document, *Safety Reprints*. The intention was that members could copy articles in the Association's journals, as they appeared, and insert them into the correct place. In addition, updates would be published from time to time, allowing members to purchase just the new material and insert it as appropriate. Updates were published in 1998 and 2000 but, for reasons that are unclear, the whole pack was published in 2005 as a bound book (ASE, 1996, 1998, 2000, 2005). The current intention is not to produce any further paper copies of the book, but to make copies of those articles and notes that are still considered useful, available under a health and safety tab on the ASE website. Some are available just for members, others are publicly available, depending on the content.

Health and safety training for science teachers, technicians and others

In the 1970s, '80s and '90s, members of the Safeguards Committee were frequently asked to give talks or run workshops on aspects of health and safety. In his 1978 annual report, the Chair (a practising teacher at the time) noted that in the previous academic year he had spoken about health and safety issues at twelve meetings organised by Teachers' Centres or ASE Sections, and four other members of the Committee had also had extensive programmes. Most years, there was a session run by the Committee at the ASE Annual Meeting, often focused around a new publication, and that practice still continues. Although these talks, and the written advice to members contacting Headquarters, were seen as important services to members, the Committee decided that one of the reasons for so many requests was a lack of suitable health and safety training. Accordingly, over time, the Committee devised several packs of training materials, targeted at different audiences.

The first was a one-day training package for Heads of Science. After trials in 1991 and at the 1992 Annual Meeting, the course was published in 1992, entitled 'Management of Safety: a course for Heads of Science'. It contained discussion-type activities, card-sorting exercises, etc., with OHT masters for the presenter. Suggested answers were provided, the hope being that LEA science advisers or teacher trainers would be able to use the pack, in a cascade model. In practice, this rarely happened, because potential trainers lacked confidence in their own ability to handle what was seen as a difficult subject, even when they themselves had been on the training course. As a result, the course was usually delivered by members of the Safeguards Committee or by CLEAPSS and SSERC staff. The pack was updated in 1994 and again in 2000 (ASE, 1992, 1994, 2000). About 1700 copies of the most recent version were sold. CLEAPSS and SSERC adapted it further and both organisations still run related courses, although in recent years it has proved difficult for teachers to get time out of school for professional development.

A similar course was developed for technicians in 1995, with sponsorship from Esso UK plc. The writing team brought in a technician and an educational consultant (as well as members of the Safeguards Committee). Again, delivery was usually by members of the writing team, Safeguards Committee or CLEAPSS and SSERC staff. It was a much more popular course than the one for Heads of Science, as it proved much easier for technicians to be released from school. It was updated twice (ASE, 1999, 2004) and the 2004 edition alone sold 7400 copies, but demand for a specific ASE course declined, although CLEAPSS and SSERC now run their own courses derived from it.

Following their own course, Heads of Science were encouraged to provide some in-house training for members of their departments, because the pack that they took home included the overhead transparency masters, originals for the card-sorting exercise, etc. Gradually, however, it became clear that schools were not using the materials for departmental training and that materials more directly targeted at in-house and/or initial teacher training were needed. *Safe and Exciting Science* was published in 1999, with a second edition ten years later, now including a CDRom (ASE, 1999, 2009). The pack contained a range of activities that departments could dip into, as and when needed: awareness raising, emergency procedures, induction of new staff, etc. Some items were especially useful for initial teacher training or when working with newly-qualified teachers or recently-appointed teaching assistants. Some local authorities were setting up training programmes for teaching assistants working in science in secondary schools and the Safeguards Committee published a checklist to help them (*EiS*, 2004).

It was inevitable that, with the increasing prominence of primary science, there would be a demand for training materials around *Be Safe!* A start was made at the 1991 Annual Meeting. Initially there was a collection of artefacts intended to act as a focus for discussion. It was envisaged that these might be available for loan, but they were later replaced by a set of drawings. An INSET pack was developed comprising a number of discussion activities, aimed at helping teachers spot hazards, understand the principles of risk assessment, manage health and safety and teach children about hazards and risks in the world around them (ASE, 1994). The intention was that advisory teachers could use it to train science co-ordinators and that co-ordinators might use it for training staff in their school. It was also thought to be relevant to initial teacher training and the induction of newly-qualified teachers. A Scottish edition of the INSET pack, based on the Scottish edition of *Be Safe!*, was developed in partnership with SSERC (ASE, 1997). A Canadian version was also published. Following the arrival of the third edition of *Be Safe!*, a second edition of the INSET pack was published in 2002. With the publication of the fourth edition of *Be Safe!* in 2011, *Update Sheets* were made freely available on the ASE website and a few extra materials, exploiting the changes in *Be Safe!*, were made available to ASE members.

Other groups about which the Safeguards Committee became concerned were school governors and Headteachers for whom the Committee produced a short information leaflet. A copy was enclosed with *EiS* in 1999, with members being encouraged to pass it on to their Headteachers. It was revised in 2002 and 2007 and a slightly updated version was later placed on the public part of the ASE website.

Fighting back

As early as 1986, David Tawney (then Director of CLEAPSE) was warning about inaccurate and irresponsible newspaper reports about health and safety issues (ASE, 1986). By the 1990s, it was apparent that some teachers were avoiding large amounts of traditional practical work in response to what they regarded as official health and safety restrictions. The national press picked up on this and, throughout the 1990s and 2000s, articles appearing saying how boring science had become because teachers were no longer allowed to carry out exciting demonstrations or engage students in challenging practical work. On investigation, these complaints rarely, if ever, turned out to be justified. *Topics in Safety* had originated in an attempt to define national standards. In this it had succeeded – very few employers had unilaterally banned anything – but the press very rarely published replies from the Safeguards Committee and/or CLEAPSS or SSERC refuting such misinformation. This made matters worse, because it encouraged teachers to believe what they read in the papers and thus reinforced their belief in usually non-existent bans.

The Committee thus embarked on a long-term campaign of *'fighting back'*. The emphasis was on encouraging teachers to engage in good practical science. Better health and safety training of teachers was an important component, but a succession of articles and notes appeared in *SSR* and *EiS* with self-explanatory titles such as *'That's banned, isn't it? Some safety myths in science'*, *'It must be true, it was in the* Sunday Times*!'* and *'We don't do that – it's not safe any more'*. Most of these can now be found under the Health and Safety tab on the Resources part of the ASE website and, in the spirit of the *'fighting back'* campaign, are publicly available, not just accessible to members. That the campaign still continues after almost 20 years is perhaps an indication of its failure. In 2004, the Royal Society of Chemistry commissioned CLEAPSS to carry out a survey, published as *Surely that's banned?* (RSC, 2005), which confirmed that almost every alleged ban was indeed a myth. Even the HSE itself became alarmed that there were so many myths around and started its own campaign, with a monthly cartoon. The Chair of the HSE was photographed safely setting fire to methane bubbles on her hands. ASE adopted a robust policy statement, *Health and safety in good practical science*, vigorously refuting the argument that health and safety legislation was inhibiting exciting practical work. It was published on the ASE website.

In a similar way, there was concern that books for students were over-emphasising hazards, or simply getting them muddled up. The Safeguards Committee was therefore keen to co-operate in the work for the *New SATIS Project 14–16* (ASE, 1997). Of the 44 double-page spreads, five were specifically on health and safety and another seven had significant health and safety content. The Committee also published several ideas for teaching about safety (Borrows *et al.*, 1998; *EiS*, 2009).

In a further development of the *'fighting back'* theme, for several years from 2008, the Committee organised a demonstration lecture at the Annual Conference on 'Practical Work using Low-level Radioactive Materials available to the Public' and this was later published (Whitcher, 2011).

There was a small victory in 2011. Under the Animal By-Product Regulations 2004, animal materials that had been used in a laboratory had to be disposed of through a licensed waste disposal service in an incinerator. Thus sheep hearts dissected in science lessons had to be treated differently from kitchen waste, even though they could have been purchased at the same time from the same butcher. After several years of lobbying by ASE, CLEAPSS and SSERC, when the European legislation was amended, in 2011, all the governments in the UK took the opportunity to issue derogations excepting low-risk waste from educational establishments, subject only to the general duty of care. This is encouraging because, at the time of writing, European legislation, implemented in the UK as the REACH Regulations (Registration, Evaluation, Authorisation and restriction of Chemicals), is presenting further threats. In the Irish Republic, a number of commonly-used school chemicals have already been banned and there are concerns about what will happen in the UK. The Safeguards Committee is collaborating with the RSC, CLEAPSS and SSERC to try to mitigate the impact.

Part 2 Units and nomenclature: promoting national standards

One of the justifications for having a nationwide Association is the development and encouragement of national standards. This has already been referred to in the work leading to *Topics in Safety*. However, there were other areas needing standardisation, notably units and nomenclature. The Association played a key role not only in defining the relevant standards but also in persuading examination boards and publishers to adopt them.

In 1966, the ASE Executive decided that there should be an attempt to standardise symbols and nomenclature in *SSR* and across ASE generally. Those educated pre-1960 had to cope, particularly in physics, with calculations in both the British fps system (foot, pound, second and including such units as the poundal) and metric cgs (centimetre, gramme, second and including such units as the dyne) system. There were also advocates of the equally metric MKS (metre, kilogram, second) system and this eventually prevailed as the SI system (Système Internationale). A recipe for chaos arose not only from the proliferation of units but also from the fact that there were over 20 boards examining for GCE O- and A-level and CSE with little consistency between them, with much seeming to depend on the whim of a chief examiner. Textbook authors and their publishers were almost bound to be wrong, whatever they did. The Nuffield science teaching projects took a lead but to many science teachers much looked frighteningly unfamiliar. There was also a government push for metrication (and decimalisation of the currency). In 1968, the Royal Society convened a conference of interested parties and later published two short booklets (Royal Society, 1969). In 1969, *EiS* reported on the policies of the various examination boards in adopting SI units.

There was a similar problem with chemical nomenclature. Examination candidates would certainly recognise the formulae of cupric sulphate, ethyl alcohol, acetaldehyde or propionic acid, but was it reasonable to expect them to do the same for amyl alcohol, succinic acid or anisole?

In 1969, ASE convened a conference attended by representatives of the Royal Society, British Standards Institute (BSI) and examination boards. The morning session was devoted to units, the afternoon to chemical nomenclature, the aim being to achieve a consensus and to spur examination boards into coherent action These were controversial topics and there was lengthy and heated correspondence in most issues of *EiS* as well as a session at the 1969 Annual Meeting. It was a time of rapid change in thinking. The Association was much influenced by booklets from the Royal Institute of Chemistry (McGlashan, 1968) and the Royal Society (1969, 1971), but had to consider how to adapt the recommendations to suit the needs of children of different abilities and ages. ASE's Education (Research) Committee set up two working parties, one on units, the other on chemical nomenclature. The former published a report, *SI Units, Signs, Symbols and Abbreviations*, fairly quickly (ASE, 1969), although critical comments on some aspects were expressed by BSI and a page of amendments appeared in *EiS* a few months later. It was updated in second and third editions in 1974 and 1981 respectively. Recognising that this was heavily weighted towards O- and A-level physics, a simplified version was published in 1975. A paper in *EiS* (1986) discussed the question of symbols for logic circuits, on which the third edition had somewhat prevaricated.

The working party on chemical nomenclature faced more difficult issues and published some draft ideas for discussion. These presented quite radical proposals for a largely systematic approach to chemical nomenclature and provoked some lively debate in *EiS*. The report, *Chemical Nomenclature, Symbols and Terminology,* was finally published in 1972. As a direct result, the GCE boards issued a *Joint Statement*, which each board would use as the basis for setting examination papers. Although the CSE boards did not endorse the *Joint Statement*, generally they fell in line with the policies. A second edition, in 1979, took account of many of the comments received and included a copy of the *Joint Statement*. The third edition, in 1985, included a revised *Joint Statement* and was endorsed by the Royal Society of Chemistry Panel on Chemical Nomenclature.

One of the problems with changing nomenclature was that bottles of chemicals had names that would often be unrecognisable under the new system. Accordingly, ASE set up a further working party. This had some success in persuading the suppliers to include more systematic names on bottle labels. However, the working party realised that existing bottles would remain in use for a long time and decided to produce self-adhesive labels for the most commonly used chemicals. The opportunity was also taken to put emergency action information onto the labels, which required co-operation with the Safeguards Committee. Published in 1975, members could buy a set of 99 labels or 10 copies of any one label. Despite the long history, chemical nomenclature remains controversial in some quarters (*EiS*, 2001).

There were fewer problems with biological nomenclature but, in 1986, the (then) Institute of Biology (IoB) set up a committee to recommend agreed practice. The outcome was published in 1989 and, despite only limited ASE representation on the committee, the cover carried both ASE and IoB logos.

The ASE's guidance on nomenclature and units was united in the publication, *Signs, Symbols and Systematics, the ASE companion to 5–16 science*. For the first time, this also included biology and earth sciences

Figure 7.3: A selection of ASE publications about health and safety.

terminology. The title indicated an intention to cover primary science, but much of it was well beyond the needs of primary schools, so members of the Primary Science Committee extracted the most relevant parts, added some definitions and explanations, and published *Signs and Symbols in Primary Science* in 1998. This was followed by *Signs, Symbols and Systematics, the ASE companion to 16–19 science*. The introduction of the National Curriculum in England brought ideas into schools about how 'science works' and the processes of science and, with it, a whole new terminology. As with chemical nomenclature and units some 40 years earlier, there was growing evidence of inconsistencies between different awarding bodies and different authors about the terminology to be used in school science investigations. ASE initiated a joint project with the Nuffield Foundation, with support from the National Strategies (Science) and the awarding bodies for England and Wales. The outcome was a booklet, *The Language of Measurement*, published in 2010, intended to achieve a common understanding of important terms that arise from school practical work, consistent with the terminology used by professional scientists.

Part 3 Laboratory provision, design and equipment

ASE has long had an interest in science equipment and laboratory provision and design. In 1962, an SMA pamphlet reported on the number of laboratories in schools, especially commenting on the poor provision in girls' schools. In 1973, the Science Advisers' Group (SAG) was asked to write a series of articles for *SSR* and in 1975 there was a statement on the provision of temporary laboratory accommodation. In 1980, SAG carried out a survey of laboratory sizes and class sizes. In 1989, a sub-group of the National Science Advisers and Inspectors Group published *Building for Science*. The document made clear that it did not constitute Association policy, but it did discuss the number of laboratories needed, likely costs, issues around layout and services, the need for storage and preparation areas and the provision for children with special educational needs and for sixth form students. This booklet had a significant influence on later publications, both those of CLEAPSS and the DfES. A survey by science advisers in nine LEAs in 1992/3 concluded that almost all science teaching did take place in laboratories, but it did not investigate the quality of provision.

The Labour governments of 1997–2010 invested large sums of money in new school building and refurbishment. There was a growing body of evidence that, whilst this often resulted in magnificent buildings, some of the laboratory accommodation was not fit for purpose: science departments had been constructed without chemical stores, or even without prep rooms; prep rooms were without gas supplies; mobile fume cupboards were too large to fit through the doors.

Heads of Science were sometimes consulted, but for new schools a Head of Science might not yet have been appointed. 'Consultation' might simply involve the Headteacher giving the Head of Department the architect's plans on Friday afternoon with a request to return them on Monday. In rare cases, there was good consultation with science teachers and technicians and this did result in some good facilities. In 2003, Planet Science (see Chapter 8) and The Royal Society funded ASE to manage the Laboratory Design for Teaching and Learning (LDTL) project to help improve laboratory design. The outcome was a CD and website, which included guidance about various aspects of laboratory design (some specially written, others from standard CLEAPSS and DfES publications) and software that allowed users to try out different room layouts. Some 20,000 copies of the CD were distributed with *SSR* (see also Chapter 8). The project succeeded in gathering information in one place, initiated some useful contacts and resulted in a laboratory design course at the National Science Learning Centre, which continues to this day. It also inspired some work on the design of chemical stores and a critique of unsatisfactory prep room designs.

In 1967, the Association set up a Physical Sciences Apparatus Committee to replace the previous Modern Physical Sciences Committee. The latter had covered both pedagogy and equipment and had been influential in the movement that resulted in the Nuffield Science Teaching Project. Nuffield covered pedagogy adequately, but there was felt to be a need to provide continuing guidance on equipment for all syllabuses. There was particular interest in standardisation, e.g. of fuses, plugs and sockets. Reports published in *EiS* covered such matters as syringes, microscopes, top-pan balances, slide rules and the conversion of Bunsen burners to natural gas. These included an evaluation of what was on the market but, in the long run, CLEAPSE and SSSERC were much better placed to carry out these functions. Thirty years later, with support from Esso UK plc., ASE published a guide to the equipment needed for primary science (Feasey, 1998).

Over its 50 year history ASE has maintained fruitful relationships with the major commercial laboratory and science teaching equipment supply companies, whose scope has waxed and waned with economic and educational trends. Several of these companies joined ASE as corporate members, with key members of their staffs playing an active part in Association events. Various companies have sponsored ASE activities, for example Philip Harris Ltd. which sponsored meetings and conferences and TTS which has sponsored the Primary Room at Annual Conferences and supported the Primary Science Teaching Awards (see Chapter 8). Such collaboration, as that with publishers, further exemplifies ASE as the Association for all partners involved in science education.

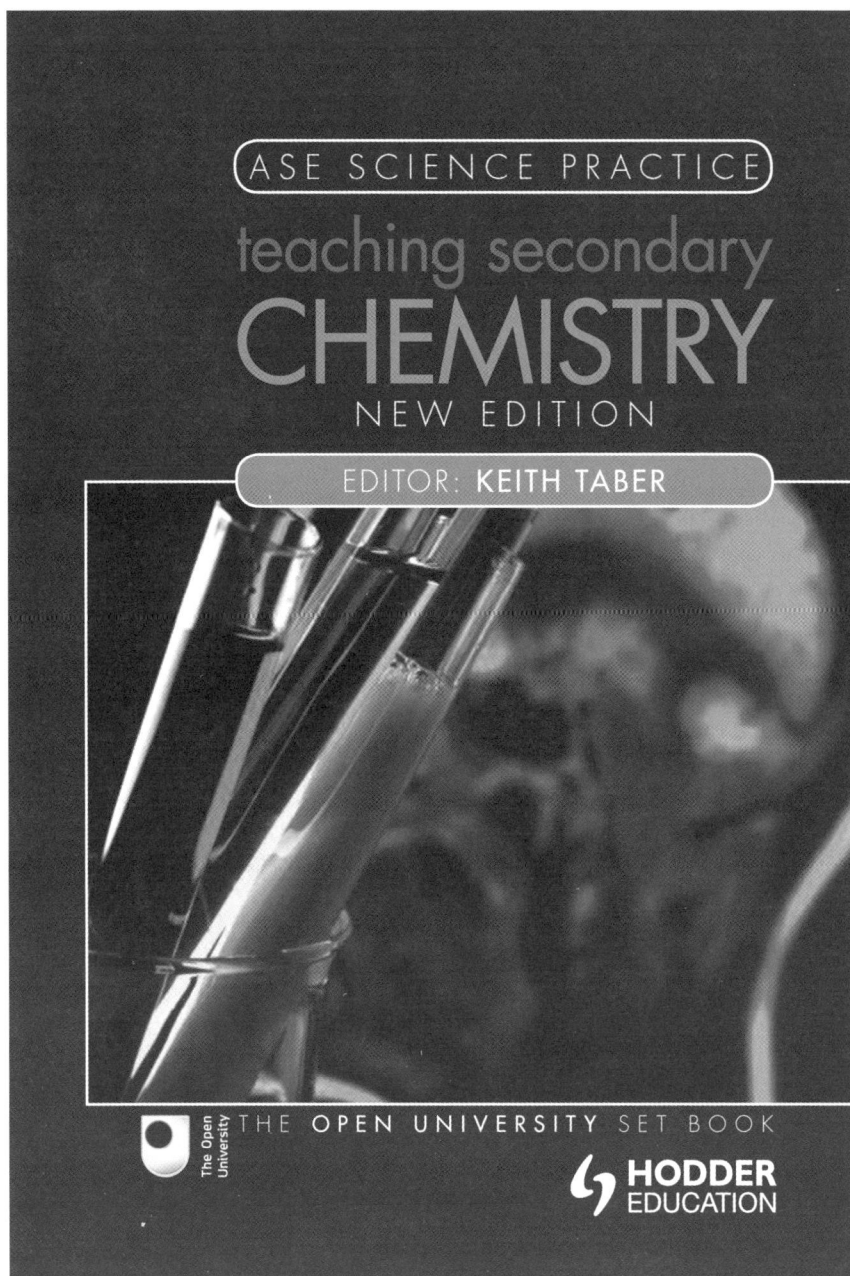

Figure 8.1: Publication, jointly with other bodies, is just one example of ASE collaborations.

8 The ASE working in partnership with others

Jane Hanrott and John Lawrence, with contributors

'In the early 1970s...the ASE turned...for external funding for curriculum projects...from bodies such as the Department of Energy, the Industry/ Education Unit of the Department of Industry and commercial and industrial organisations.' (Layton, 1984: 280)

The history of ASE working in collaboration with outside organisations spans the entire 50 years of its existence. Recognising that a 'do-it-yourself' approach, while successful, was limited in its scope for a self-funded association, the ASE leadership began to seek influential external support for the wider range of activities it wished to promote.

This chapter examines a number of those partnerships in which ASE was involved that were of direct benefit to individuals engaged in science education, rather than those, such as the Secondary Science Curriculum Review (SSCR) (see Chapter 3), which promoted science education in general. Partnerships from which the outcomes, whether published, award-giving, training- or event-based, were of direct benefit to the practising science teacher or technician, fall under a number of headings, listed here by the type of partner organisation:

○ government/national

○ industry/commerce

○ publisher

○ international

○ peer-supported

○ local authority and

○ university.

This chapter presents a number of case studies of ASE partnerships. Because eight case studies cannot do justice to the breadth and number of these partnerships over the years, we have also included many of the others for which detail can be found, with a brief explanation of each. We aim to outline the impact that the various partnerships have had on the Association (from the standpoints of membership, status and business development) and on the individual, whether member or non-member of ASE. We conclude by bringing the involvement of the Association in partnerships up-to-date and by looking to the future of what has proved to be a highly successful way of working.

Why work with others?

The first and obvious reason is that of financial support. ASE Headquarters took very seriously its responsibility as the keeper of its members' subscription income and was mindful that its priority had to be to support its members. To ensure that they had the best possible service and resources meant that funding for major projects, particularly those that would benefit all science practitioners, could be limited, and so outside support for such activities would be needed. External funding allowed for a greater choice of options for disseminating materials and, in most cases, a wider impact of whichever project was involved.

Collaborating with partners also allowed ASE to exert influence in a wider field of science education. By enjoying a relationship with, for example, the government of the time, or another significant educational organisation, the Association was able to bring the views of its members to bear in the corridors of power. However, this was not without its pitfalls. Layton, writing in 1984, commented that it was too early yet '...to evaluate the consequences of this closer association of the ASE with industry and with other bodies having a stake in science education. Important benefits have no doubt accrued, not least financial. At the same time effective partnerships require that both partners derive continuing satisfaction from the relationship without too great a loss of independence for each.

'In its multifarious relationships, one question for ASE concerns the extent to which it is 'an instrument being played' or 'a voice to be heeded'. Another is whether there is sufficient common ground between the aims and purposes of new partners to enable the Association to maintain a consistent point of view'. (Layton, 1984, 282–283)

These questions are as important today as they were then – a survey conducted by ASE of its members and non-members in 2011 raised the issue of whether the Association was at risk of being seen to be 'getting into bed' too readily with government and examination boards (ASE Survey, 2011).

Case Study 1
John Murray Publishers and ASE
Contributed by Katie Mackenzie Stuart

The link between John Murray Publishers and ASE goes back many years, to a time before ASE existed. The most obvious manifestation of this was the publication of the first issue of *The School Science Review* by John Murray in 1919, following a meeting between a committee member from The Association of Public School Science Masters (APSSM) and the firm in 1918. This relationship continued until 1976, by which time ASE's own publishing activities had become sufficiently well-developed for the Association to take responsibility for its principal journal. Another longstanding collaboration was the highly regarded *Safeguards in the (School) Laboratory,* which first appeared in 1947, having been compiled by the Science Master's Association (SMA) and the Association of Women Science Teachers (AWST) and continued as a joint publication with ASE until the 10th edition in 1996. (The word 'school' was inserted into the title with the 4th edition; see Chapter 7.)

However, not all links between publisher and Association resulted in published materials. Early on, it became a tradition for senior members of

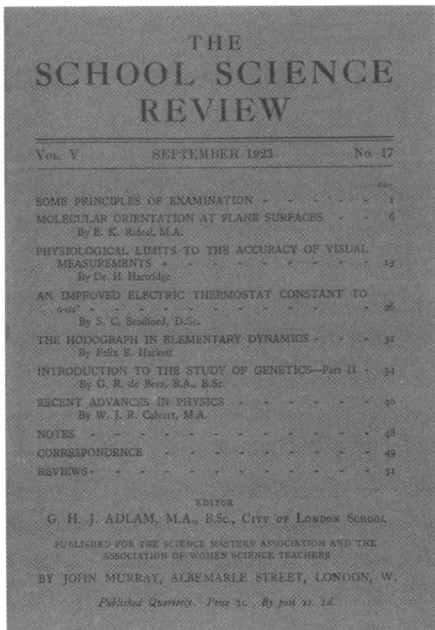

Figure 8.2: Cover from School Science Review, September 1923, published by John Murray for the SMA and the AWST.

staff from the company to take key members of staff from the Association out to dinner on the evening following the end of the ASE Annual Meeting, as a way of saying thank you for all their work. Over the years, this 'thank you' was extended to include a wider range of people and became a drinks reception following the Association Dinner, a tradition that many members today will have experienced. John Murray VI, a charismatic figure who worked for the company from the 1930s and was Chairman from 1967 to 1993, regularly attended the Dinner and reception and, on one memorable occasion, announced the arrival of the transport to the halls of residence by calling out 'the charabancs await!'.

Another key supporter was Kenneth Pinnock who joined the company in 1953, initially as Educational Manager, then as Editorial Director until he retired in 1984. He was instrumental in developing the educational side of the publishing firm and, as the person who spotted the potential of the authors D.G. Mackean and Tom Duncan, was keenly aware of the importance of science education and science textbooks. One of the many significant ASE publications during Kenneth Pinnock's tenure was *Interpreters of Science: the history of the Association for Science Education,* by David Layton in 1984.

Although ASE increasingly produced books and other resources under its own imprint, the organisation continued to work with John Murray and other publishers. In the early 1980s, the Association had set up the Science and Technology in Society (SATIS) project to develop a range of activities that reflected the increased emphasis on the applications of science. By the mid-1990s, there was concern that there was a new generation of teachers unaware of the potential benefits of the SATIS units, and so a collection of those judged most appropriate for the recently revised GCSEs was published by John Murray under the title *The World of Science.*

Following this collaboration, discussions took place about other joint ventures. As a result, the *ASE John Murray Science Practice* series was created, starting with *Teaching Secondary Biology, Teaching Secondary Chemistry* and *Teaching Secondary Physics.* The idea behind the series was that it should be a means by which ASE could promote best practice in science education. Far from being academic tomes, the books were written and edited to ensure that physics specialists, for example, could find ideas to help them teach genetics the following Monday morning. As well as being bought by existing teachers, the series is widely used in teacher training courses and so best practice is being spread to the next generation of teachers. New editions of the first three books have recently been published, though no longer with John Murray in the title. The publishing firm was acquired by Hodder Headline in 2002 and now publishes books under the Hodder Education imprint. However, the links with ASE remain as strong as ever.

Case Study 2

The Science in Society family

In the mid-1970s, there was concern to make school science and technology teaching more relevant to everyday life and thereby increase young people's interest in, and enthusiasm for, science. By the mid-1980s, this concern had translated into a wider measure of agreement that more needed to be done to relate school science to its social and technological contexts. It was reflected in the recommendations of reports such as *Science 5–16: a statement of policy* from the Department of Education and Science (1985) and *Education through Science* from ASE.

One important outcome of this concern was the group of ASE projects known affectionately as the SATIS family: Science and Society, Science in a Social Context (SISCON), Science and Technology in Society (SATIS) and, finally, Science with Technology (SWT). These projects were all supported, either financially or otherwise, by a range of external organisations, but it was the Association that commissioned and directed the projects and published the outcomes. The SATIS Steering Group of the time (1984 onwards) consisted entirely of key industrialists, mostly at Chief Executive level, each agreeing to put in an agreed amount of funding to support the project. Latterly, the Office of Science and Technology joined the supporters on a matched-funding basis. The 1976 project, Science and Society, started by John L. Lewis, resulted in a range of publications jointly published by ASE and Heinemann Educational Books in 1981.

A little later, materials from the Science in a Social Context (SISCON) project, run by Joan Solomon, were jointly published by ASE and Blackwell, as an additional resource for post-16 courses in this new field (Layton, 1984: 171).

SATIS itself started when ASE set up the project in 1984, under the directorship of John Holman, to continue to support teachers in relating school science to its social and technological contexts. The units were seen as a model for developing topical lessons to show some of the applications of science, and illustrate aspects of 'how science works'. The development of SATIS followed the recommendation of an Association working party, which had considered how teaching about the interactions of science, technology and society could be introduced into pre-16 science courses. The working party drew upon the experience of those who had pioneered the Science and Society and SISCON materials.

Initially, the SATIS project developed 120 units of lesson resources for teachers of 14–16 year-olds, published as ten booklets. The units were short, easy to use, cheap, and relevant to young learners and the curriculum. They typically required about two periods of class time (about 75 minutes). Teachers were encouraged to use the units flexibly – to tear them apart, rearrange and modify them. The units were intended to engage young learners as actively as possible and involved a variety of teaching and learning methods, including comprehension questions, directed activities related to text (DARTs), small-group discussion, problem-solving, surveys, simulations, decision-making exercises and role-plays (National STEM Centre eLibrary).

The next phase of ASE's science and society initiative was directed at the post-16 sector of education. The SATIS 16–19 project was set up in 1987 to build on the success of the 14–16 initiative. With Andrew Hunt as its Director, the project was a means of helping teachers to share good ideas and effective classroom practice. The flexible bank of resources aimed to support the general education of 16–19 year-old students and to enrich specialist science courses in academic and vocational programmes. The resources were published in four files, each with 25 units. They were designed to be used in general studies, in core/key skills programmes and in AS and GCSE courses. They could also enrich post-16 specialist courses, to cover both the nature of science and the applications and implications of science. Three short readers, *What is science?*, *What is technology?* and *How does society decide?* were also published as background information for teachers (National STEM Centre eLibrary).

The third SATIS project, SATIS 8–14, which commenced in 1990 under the leadership of John Stringer, focused attention on primary school science education. The materials were photocopiable and flexible. They were intended to enrich work in the English National Curricula for Science and for Technology. The units were designed to stimulate group work and co-operation and comprised several hundred units in booklet form grouped into three box files, covering ages 8 and 9, 10 and 11, and 11 to 14 respectively.

In 1991, ASE published *UPDATE 91*, providing information to update or supplement the hundred 14–16 units published between 1986 and 1988. A later title, *The World of Science: new SATIS 14–16,* was published by John Murray (Publisher) Ltd. in 1996 and included new and updated units (see Case Study 1, above).

In 2009, ASE revised several key SATIS units in order to provide further support for the implementation of the 'How science works' element of the science curricula for England and Wales. This material was published as *SATIS Revisited*, and is available free of charge on the ASE website.

The Science with Technology Project (SWT) was a joint initiative of ASE and the Design and Technology Association (DATA). It was developed in the mid-1990s to foster curriculum links between science and technology for students in the 14 to 19 age range. The project provided resource materials for students and support for teachers of both science and technology, which could be used with courses leading to GCSE, GNVQ and similar level qualifications. It was supplemented by a programme of in-service training run by ASE INSET Services (see Case Study 6 and Chapter 5). The programme was supported by a wide range of industrial partners, as well as by the Gatsby Charitable Foundation and the Royal Commission for the Exhibition of 1851. Two types of unit were produced: extended units providing in-depth coverage of a topic or area of the curriculum, and focused units concentrating on a particular aspect of a topic. Titles included *Managing Energy, Designing a Fermenter, Understanding the Science of Food, Making Use of Renewable Energy, Cars and the Environment* and *Evaluating Environmental Impact.*

The SATIS 'family' made an enormous impact. It may well be that these projects and their published and training outcomes represent one of the most significant influences that ASE has had over the last 50 years. Its influence was significant in the contexts of several chapters of this book, so, inevitably, references to SATIS recur throughout the volume.

Writing in 1998, Watts and McGrath (1998) explored the level of impact of the SATIS resources on the science curriculum. After examining a number of surveys conducted by ASE on the usage and impact of SATIS during the 1990s, they concluded that: *'SATIS has clearly been a valuable classroom resource and has had an impact on science education in the UK...the materials still emphasise the skills and issues outlined above. They cover "Science in everyday life" and tie directly into the new science curriculum as well as the revised GCSE exam syllabuses introduced in September 1996'.*

However, they pointed out that, within the UK, two categories of teacher were emerging: those who saw the National Curriculum as a 'hindrance', and those *'who find the same curriculum a welcome opportunity and necessary impetus to develop personal, social and technological relevance'.* They concluded that those in the first group found little use for SATIS material, but those in the second appeared to find SATIS resources useful and relevant.

The fact that there had been a call from a number of teachers for more, or updated, SATIS material in 2009 and up to the present day, prompted ASE to produce the online resource, *SATIS Revisited*, referred to above. This suggests that the units still offer teachers useful resources and that nothing else has ever come quite so close to meeting the need for science and technology in society materials.

The successful use of SATIS materials in overseas countries gave rise to Science across Europe and Science across the World (see later in this Chapter).

Case Study 3

Initiatives in Primary Science: An Evaluation (IPSE) Project

ASE was commissioned by the Department for Education and Science (DES) and the Welsh Office (WO) to carry out a national evaluation of the effectiveness of the Education Support Grant (ESG) (science) initiatives, and to disseminate successful strategies developed by the Local Education Authorities (LEAs). As a result, Initiatives in Primary Science: an Evaluation (IPSE) started in September 1985.

All the ESG projects were set up on the basis of the DES/WO policy document on science (HMSO, 1985). Within this context, the evaluation team stressed practical, hands-on experience of primary science, in the context of good primary school practice. The project was managed by ASE and was generously supported by ICI at whose Welwyn Garden City offices the project was housed. The Director was John Slade, then Science Adviser for Cleveland. The DES also appointed a steering group, which was chaired by Dennis Sutton from the College of St Paul and St Mary, Cheltenham. IPSE completed its work in August 1988, with the publication by ASE of a *Report, Building Bridges, The School in Focus,* and *Snapshots.*

Prior to 1985, there were very few advisory teachers for primary science; in 1985, there were suddenly 187 of them. So what had happened? The answer lies in funding that can be traced back to DES Circular No 6/84 and WO Circular No 39/84, which made ' *grants available to support expenditure of approximately £2m in 1985–1988, designed to improve the effectiveness and relevance of science teaching for pupils aged 5–11'* (DES, 1984). Some 52 English and 4 Welsh LEAs subsequently received funding through the ESG scheme for primary science. No two LEAs used the funding in exactly the same way. Different LEAs adopted a wide range of strategies for developing their primary schools' teaching of science, but all of them had appointed advisory teachers as a central part of this strategy. This is not surprising, because Authorities had been invited to put forward proposals for the appointment of advisory teachers, drawing on the successful work that had already been carried out in a number of different parts of the country. Other elements which could be supported included, for example, visits by teachers to schools which already had successful science provisions; the release costs of teachers to take part in suitable in-service training; and the purchase of materials and equipment (ASE, 1988a).

Many advisory teachers had been appointed directly from the classroom, a large number having been class teachers in primary schools just the term before. Many regarded this as a strength, since it gave the new advisory teachers credibility. In the words of one adviser, *'You have to be respected as a specialist primary teacher'*. The function of advisory teachers was to influence colleagues in schools to develop their practice in ways that would benefit the children they taught. The five important roles of these advisory teacher related to:

○ supporting the class teacher

○ collaborating with co-ordinators/postholders

○ working with Headteachers

○ running courses and workshops

○ contributing to school staff meetings.

Unlike advisory teachers for mathematics, for example, science advisory teachers often had to convince teachers of the legitimacy of science being in the primary curriculum at all. One teacher acknowledged that *'Previously, I really didn't think science had a place in the infant curriculum.'* The aim of many advisory teachers was therefore to change teachers' attitudes towards science. They stressed the importance of first-hand investigations, problem-solving and giving children responsibility for their own learning. Many wished to see science as just one aspect of good primary practice, with more practical work, a more process-based approach, a greater integration of science with other subjects, and a greater degree of continuity across a school. Achieving these goals was not a straightforward task and, as the evaluation report recognised, *'one of the keys to success was the quality of the advisory teacher'*.

The Project identified ways of recognising good practice. A list of statements was drawn up by the IPSE evaluation team early on in the project in order to indicate aspects of school- and classroom-based practice that were thought desirable. The purpose of this was to provide a means of indicating the nature and extent of the changes intended or occurring as a result of the ESG projects. The paper, *Good practice in primary science*, written by the four IPSE evaluators, contained the following key statement.

'The golden rule: The one absolute characteristic of good science is that it involves children doing things themselves. This is not to say that there is no place for demonstration by the teacher, for children consulting books, or even the occasional imparting of knowledge by the teacher. We must be careful not to leap to conclusions after a brief visit to a classroom.

We need to know what is the overall pattern of activity in a class. BUT, we believe that science must involve, to a large degree, children actively interacting with their environment, physically handling the materials they are investigating, and not watching someone else.' (ASE, 1988b)

In addition to considering the nature of the changes being promoted, IPSE also applied two other criteria to assess the value of the ESG work: the potential permanence of the changes, and the scale of operation within an LEA. The Project also identified features that enhanced long-term prospects for successful primary science. The conclusion was that systems that inspire confidence that progress may be sustained are similar in that:

○ the Headteacher understands what is involved in primary science, is committed to its development and continuance, and accepts responsibility for ensuring progress is maintained

○ there is at least one teacher with expertise in primary science

○ there are procedures within the school to help sustain science

○ adequate resources of equipment and materials are available throughout the school.

One outcome of the ESG initiative for ASE was that many of the polytechnics and colleges developed centre-based professional development courses for both teachers and co-ordinators of science in primary schools. These were developed in response to a government initiative, the LEA Training Grant Scheme. Many of these education establishments approached the Association to validate their programmes, a collaboration that prevailed until the institutions acquired their own powers of validation, and the ASE Validation Board was dissolved in 1995. More particularly, the award of a Certificate proved to be the first step on a validated professional development ladder, which previously had not been available. Many participants subsequently went on to gain further, higher-level qualifications. A second outcome for the Association was a greatly increased awareness of, and attention to, primary science education.

As part of ASE's aim to support the ESG advisory teachers, two committees were formed to provide a focus for these important ambassadors: the Primary Science Advisory Teacher Group (PSATG) and the Science Advisory Teacher Group (SATG). Both of these were extensively supported by Philip Harris Ltd., which sponsored meetings and conferences (and even provided monogrammed clipboards!). The two Groups organised and implemented national conferences for advisory teachers for science during at least two of the years of the scheme. These led to much staff development, through inputs by the Group members and others, and through the sharing of expertise and experiences among the advisory teachers themselves.

Case Study 4
The BT/ASE Teacher Fellowship Scheme

In 1997, ASE celebrated ten years of one of the longest running and most successful industry-education collaborative ventures, the BT/ASE Teacher Fellowship Scheme. The scheme was open to primary and secondary teachers and FE lecturers from all over the UK. It enabled interested teachers to gain experience of work practices in BT and industry in general, to investigate how, in the phraseology of the day, telecommunications and IT in industry could be related to science, technology and IT teaching, and to expand their ideas for curriculum development materials. The Fellowship took the form of a two-week placement with BT in July/August, it was supported locally by a BT Education Manager and attracted a bursary and travel expenses. In later years, it was also organised in collaboration with the Teacher Placement Service.

The scheme started as a pilot in 1987 as the brainchild of Peter Thomson, Deputy Head of the BT Community Partnership programme, also a former member of the ASE Education (Co-ordinating) Committee. It was, at the time, an integral part of BT's programme of activities in the community and the education sector. The scheme provided support for, and recognition of, what was seen as the important role of the teaching profession in the motivation and development of industry's future scientists and engineers.

With the scheme in place for a number of years, it allowed incremental improvements to be made. For example, in 1994, a pre-placement seminar lasting a whole day was introduced. This involved presentations from BT Education Managers and Fellows from previous years, interactive workshops and opportunities to explore the Internet, Campus World and other BT resources. This became an integral and much appreciated part of the scheme. One of the great values of the scheme was being able to address the needs of individual teachers through developing a personal programme: *'The introductory day was stimulating and gave everyone a taste of what to expect'* (BT Fellow).

Another change was to introduce the idea of Star Placements for all Fellows, which included visits to the Satellite Communications Centre at Madley, the research and development Laboratories at Martlesham, the Networks Management Centre at Oswestry and the BT Tower and BT Museum in London:

'*I discussed a lot of ideas with the other teachers during my placement*' (BT Fellow). In 1997, for example, there were some 28 successful applicants and the notion of Star Placements not only took the pressure off the individual BT Education Managers, but also gave an opportunity for teachers to network and share ideas over the course of the placement: '*I found the sessions I had with managers enlightening as much for the differences from education as for the similarities*' (BT Fellow).

Participants identified a number of objectives, notably around curriculum enrichment, personal/professional development, management skills, careers education, school/industry links and industrial applications of science. Experiences included: work shadowing engineers; visits to BT training and apprenticeship centres and learning about aspects of optical fibre technology; and BT visual services – outside broadcasting using cable and satellite links: '*I have found the placement refuelled my excitement of science…my teaching of physics will be greatly improved and I will be using my placement directly in the teaching of electricity, light and sound*' (BT Fellow).

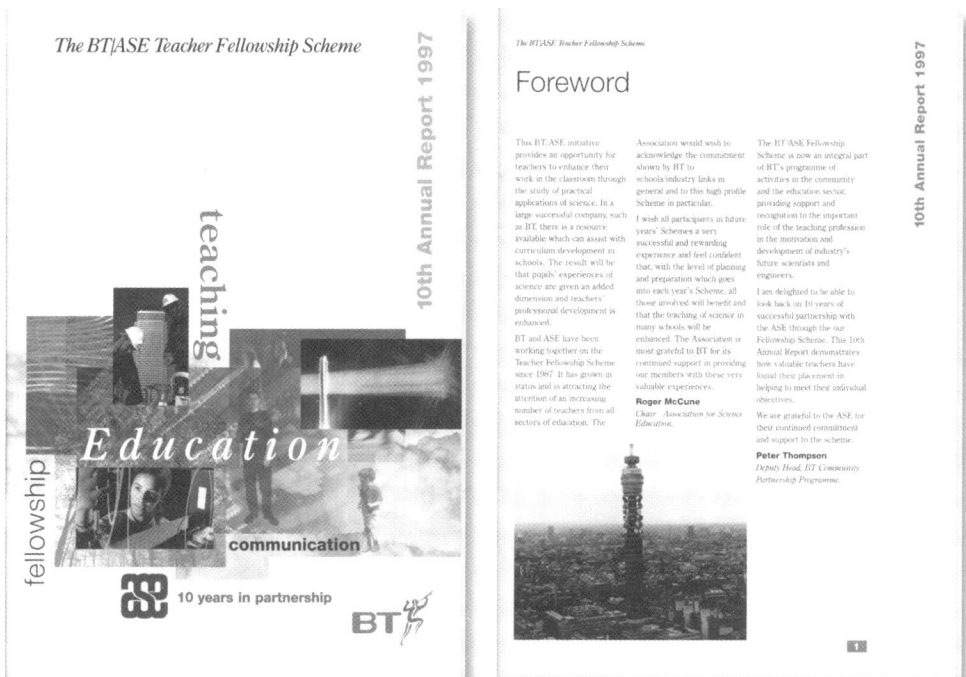

Figure 8.3: BT/ASE Teacher Fellowship Scheme report, 1997.

The teachers gained many new insights from their time at BT and returned to school with fresh perspectives, increased inspiration about aspects of science and ideas for developing their teaching and for sharing their experiences with their colleagues in both their own and other departments: *'I have had a wonderful time and enjoyed meeting the wide range of BT employees who gave of their time and expertise to enable me to broaden my understanding of telecommunications. I will return to school with renewed enthusiasm to teach the topic of communication in a more structured and relevant manner, enabling my pupils who have learning difficulties to have a broader and more balanced curriculum'* (BT Fellow).

Many of the Fellows felt that their knowledge of IT and its applications had been greatly improved. Teachers from the primary sector found that their experiences would benefit the whole curriculum – using drama and storytelling to explain how a telephone call works and setting up hands-on displays using samples of wires and pipes and posters. People management, appraisals, linking local BT centres and developing education-industry partnerships were also explored as part of the Fellowship: *'If I have been the first technician ever to have taken part in this Scheme, I can only encourage others to use some of their holidays and apply to future Schemes. There is a big opportunity to develop your profession…'* (BT Fellow).

One tertiary college lecturer wanted to use his fellowship to produce industry-related resources for a BTEC course he was developing: *'I am delighted about this programme, because it provides a new route into engineering for students who have the ability to do a vocational course but not the academic qualifications to get started. This will give them an opportunity to use their skills to gain a qualification which could lead on either to a GNVQ course or to a modern apprenticeship'* (BT fellow).

Support for the scheme was deeply embedded within BT, which is a key factor: *'It featured prominently on my CV – it was a contributing factor towards my promotions'* (BT employee).

In 1997, there were nine full-time education managers co-ordinating a wide range of local activities, which complemented BT's national programmes. They also made the scheme a success by supporting teachers locally. In the 10 years or so of the scheme, some 300 teachers were awarded a Fellowship. *'It far surpassed my wildest expectations. I feel as though it has given me a whole new insight into the way technology is being developed and how it is going to affect future generations'* (BT Fellow).

The scheme ended a year later when funding was withdrawn.

Case Study 5
Science Year and ASE: 2001–02

'...what will make Science Year work are the things you do in your classroom – one lesson that you try a different way; one exciting contemporary idea that you build a lesson around and pupils remind you of for years to come; a Science Fair that children and parents talk about long after it's all finished... above all, enjoy doing it – because, on this occasion, you don't have to!' (Burden, 2001)

Science Year was a 12-month calendar packed full with events, projects and resources, designed to stimulate the imagination about science and technology. It was for everyone, but was focused particularly on people between the ages of 10 and 19 and the adults around them – especially their teachers. Science Year was not about test tubes and Bunsen burners; it was about raising awareness of the wide and wonderful world of subjects and careers that are underpinned by science and technology (SYCD website).

    In the late 1990s and early 2000s, there was mounting concern about the declining numbers of school students taking up science subjects beyond compulsory schooling. Following on from the World Mathematical Year 2000, and following a suggestion to the Department for Education (DfE) by the Chair of ASE, government decided to fund a Year of Science and invited bids to manage the project. The Association responded by putting together a bid in partnership with the British Association for the Advancement of Science (BA, now the British Science Association). Although this bid was unsuccessful, the winning organisation, the National Endowment for Science, Technology and the Arts (NESTA) gained the contract on the condition that it involved ASE, the BA and other key bodies. This resulted in £500,000 being awarded jointly to ASE and the BA to fund a project team and underwrite the provision of resources for schools and teachers. Other bodies, including the DfE, the Wellcome Trust, PPARC, BNFL, BP, INTEL, Health and Safety Executive and others, also provided support for Science Year activities.

Science Year was set up with the following goals:
- to increase engagement of young people in science
- to increase parent engagement in science
- to strengthen links between schools and Higher Education Institutions
- to increase the take-up rate of science in further study and career options, particularly teaching

○ to raise the profile of science, and

○ to celebrate achievements in science and identify role models (Burden, Sherborne and Heslop, 2001).

ASE worked with NESTA to ensure that science education benefited from Science Year, with a key concern being to generate excitement and interest amongst children upon which teachers could capitalise. Resources designed to be used in science lessons during Science Year were made available free of charge to all state-funded secondary schools in England. These resources, in CDRom format, not only provided lesson ideas but also materials to enable schools to run events and schemes themselves, long after Science Year had finished.

Another innovation was that, as part of its commitment to Science Year, ASE was expected to make a range of other resources (not just its own) available

Figure 8.4: SSR article promoting the Science Year CDRoms in 2001.

to schools, including free resources via the Kitpot scheme. The registration of schools to enable the free distribution of the CDRoms provided a portal through which publicity about other resources could be disseminated.

The ASE Science Year team was appointed in early 2001: Jenifer Burden (Project Director), Nigel Heslop (Head of Training), and Tony Sherborne (Head of Development). Daniel Sandford Smith, Director of Curriculum Support at ASE, was instrumental in the initial bidding and interviewing process for the project, and worked closely with the team once established.

A group of teachers was brought together to come up with initial ideas of themes and the team then worked with them, and others, to generate ideas for activities relevant to those themes. Tony was particularly keen to push the interactive element, not a common style or format in classrooms at that time. Nigel acted as an ambassador for the Project, in particular with the Science Passport idea. Jenifer managed the creative team, acting as an interpreter of the ideas, and Daniel provided a sounding board for the team's plans whilst managing the project. All team members helped with the writing of the materials and it clearly was a close-knit group.

During the Year, five CDRoms were produced for secondary school students. A little later, a primary school CDRom was also published. Each CDRom was intended to include something for *every* teacher, and each contained activities for individuals, classes and whole school events.

Early discussion produced the template for each CDRom, which was in the form of a magazine with major features (such as Planet 10, Science Passport, Sci-files, and so on) and regular features – the five 'Es'.

○ **Excite:** Assemblies; Events; Newsletters; Grants

○ **Everywhere:** Cross-curricular; Literacy; Citizenship; Drama; Quizzes

○ **Explore:** Fun-size (short lesson-enlivening activities); Modelling; Mini-projects; Other Resources; Weblinks

○ **Engage:** Scientist (linking a real scientist with schools via email); Careers; Science Across (the ASE/GlaxoSmithKline international flagship project)

○ **Energise:** Science Challenge (sponsored investigations run with the BA); Competitions (series of sponsored competitions for students)

The project produced five CDRoms:

○ **Who am I?** (diet; health; DNA; sex)

○ **Is there life?** (in space; in the Earth; robots; consciousness)

○ **Can we, should we?** (ethics; gene therapy; sustainability; risk)

○ **Only connect?** (mobile phones; transport; brain and learning; communication science)

○ **AKA science** (science and art; proof and truth; science fiction; attitudes to science)

One copy of the first CDRom was sent to all secondary ASE members with their copy of *SSR*. Schools were invited to register, via ASE, for a free copy of the four subsequent resources. Schools could also purchase additional individual, or series of, CDRoms through ASE Booksales.

In addition, the following schemes were initiated by Science Year.

Passport into science
A template for successful bridging projects between primary and secondary schools, *Passport* was available for issue to all Year 6 (age 11) students in England. It was an ICT-based booklet containing activities to select from, related to the Key Stage 2 (age 7–11) curriculum, completed by the student and then taken with them into secondary school to inform the Key Stage 3 (age 11–14) teacher(s) about their scientific achievements. This scheme is still being used today.

Science Year Grants Scheme
Funding was supplied by both ASE and the BA to award up to £750 to successful schools and individuals to run exciting and stimulating science activities for pupils, parents, governors and local communities.

Kitpot
Thanks to generous sponsorship totalling over £4 million, Kitpot provided a range of free equipment to teachers throughout Science Year, commencing with the issue of a free INTEL microscope. Kitpot expanded into ScienceOneStop in subsequent years, which itself became the successful www.schoolscience.co.uk website of today.

upd8
Secondary *upd8* was partly funded initially by Science Year money. The original idea was to produce up-to-date science that teachers could use in lessons via mobile phone text messages and supported by pdfs of possible lesson activities. These pdfs proved much more popular than the text message idea and out of these grew *upd8,* still running today.

Planet Science

The new name for Science Year, once the Project had been extended in mid-2002, Planet Science continued for a further year, and welcomed additional partners, the Royal Society and the National Confederation of Parent Teacher Associations. More activities, competitions and schemes, plus an outreach programme, continued the legacy of Science Year, until it ceased, in that form and associated with ASE, in 2003. (The name Planet Science has persisted for a series of projects, and is currently under the ownership and guidance of Tinopolis Interactive.)

A key factor in the success of Science Year was the strength that came from involving classroom teachers in the development of relevant materials that they could use in their lessons, and this element was delivered by ASE. With its history of working with teachers and so understanding their needs, the Association was able to deliver, through Science Year, professional resources that met those needs.

Much remains to this day of the Science Year legacy – many current projects and schemes are based on, or mirror, the activities that this exciting project introduced. The reason that so many are still used is that they were starters and ideas, ripe for individual adaptation, bringing together materials from a range of bodies in one place, but in different ways – adaptable then, and adaptable to the modern day.

Case Study 6
ASE INSET Services 1991–2007
Contributed by Malcolm Oakes

By 1991, the National Curriculum had been operating in England and Wales for two years and the Government was beginning to respond to its impact. One response was to move funding for teacher support from LEAs into schools, with the result that LEAs began to restructure their support services and reduce their provision of professional development opportunities for teachers. This was a situation to which ASE felt it should respond and so ASE INSET Services was created.

Based at the University of Warwick Science Park, the team initially comprised Director Malcolm Oakes and Administrator Polly Fenn but, by the time INSET Services finished, there was a team of six working with numerous associates around the country.

From the outset, INSET Services was very active in exploring ways in which it could support the science teaching community. Its aims were:

○ to provide a lead role in the identification and provision of INSET

○ to provide a service available throughout the UK

○ to provide a range of INSET recognised to be of high quality

○ to provide a range of INSET of benefit to ASE members.

Underpinning these aims was an understanding that the work of ASE INSET Services would offer leadership, aid recruitment to ASE and facilitate ASE policy, be complementary to other INSET provision in the country, and cover costs. The last point was crucial – after the initial pump-priming, ASE was not in the position to provide more, so it was necessary that the business was financially sound. This was achieved after the first year and surpluses for ASE were produced over the years.

At the start, there was little mention of what was to become an important aspect of INSET Services activities over the years, namely project management for third parties. Working with organisations as diverse in background as the Institute of Electrical Engineers, Association of the British Pharmaceutical Industry, Northern Foods, British Nuclear Fuels and government bodies added greatly to the successful range of professional development work over the years. These included such projects as: the creation of INSET outlines for National Curriculum Council publications; a report for British Nuclear Fuels on the teaching of controversial issues in primary and secondary schools; the production of teaching materials and INSET workshops for local authorities, government

Figure 8.5: ASE INSET Services: Malcolm Oakes, Polly Fenn and a programme of courses, 2006.

departments and industry; and the management of the ASE Certificate of Continuing Professional Development.

Throughout its lifetime INSET Services operated in all parts of the UK, in spite of the challenges presented by different educational systems. One indication of coverage is that INSET Services was invited to work in more than half of the LEAS by their advisory services and close links were maintained at all times through the NAIGS network and the wider ASE networks, enabling INSET Services to work with and for a wide range of members and interest groups of ASE.

Courses and conferences

Courses and conferences are a most popular form of INSET and a good means of conveying information. Throughout the lifetime of INSET Services they were a constant presence, both as formal programmes and as part of many of the projects that were undertaken. Around 1993, the formal course programmes began, with workshops on Health and Safety for both teachers and technicians, an annual programme of one-day courses on all aspects of science education and the weekend residential course, Developing People and Departments.

There were also one-off conferences on behalf of groups such as the West Midlands NAIGS Group and the Primary Subject Associations. One particularly challenging event was the request in September 1995 to organise the Kick-Off Conference to launch, just three weeks later, the Department of Trade and Industry/industry-sponsored Schools Online Project. This was a project to encourage schools to access and use the internet and the conference was to be residential for 250 participants, during which time there had to be constant online connections available, at a time when such connections were neither common nor reliable!

University links

University links were important throughout the life of INSET Services, leading to a number of collaborations, some lasting for many years. Key university partners included Sheffleld Hallam, the University of Bath, the Roehampton Institute, King's College London, and the Universities of Wolverhampton, York and Loughborough, to name but a few. A variety of CPD projects, too numerous to mention here, came out of these collaborations, informing policy makers and assisting teachers, trainees and tutors alike.

Other collaborations included an early input into the Researchers in Residence project, in which INSET Services developed a biological equivalent to that being run in the physical sciences and supported by some of the

Research Councils and the Wellcome Trust. In the first decade of the 21st century, assessment for learning became an important element of educational policy and one of the earliest products to promote the philosophy was a set of teacher materials called *Assessing Progress in Science* written by CRIPSAT and published by QCA. CRIPSAT and QCA perceived a need for training materials that would introduce teachers purposefully to the units and, in 2004, INSET Services was invited by QCA to manage the project on its behalf in collaboration with CRIPSAT. This resulted in sets of professional development activities using the latest technology and, by the day of publication, all 9000 copies had been pre-sold.

Embedding ICT in science teaching

From the end of the 1970s and through the 1980s, ICT in schools was a minority, but developing, activity. By the early 1990s, simple software was being replaced by more complex multimedia programmes and, given the potential uses of data logging in practical work and other aspects of ICT in support of all aspects of science teaching, it was not surprising that promotion of the use of ICT became a major thread of activity for INSET Services, including:

○ 1993–98: IT in Science

○ 1995–96: Schools Online Project

○ 1998–2005: The Science Consortium. This was a partnership of key individuals who created teaching and training materials funded by the government's New Opportunities Fund (NOF) programme, and whose materials INSET Services promoted, recruiting the teachers and managing the training programme. The Science Consortium trained 8000 teachers from 976 schools, with a completion rate of over 80%. This compared very favourably with other providers.

○ 2002-04: Online CPD in science at Key Stage 3 (age 11–14)

○ 2003: Exemplar materials for ICT – on behalf of DfES

○ 2003–2009: ICT projects (for DfES/Becta)

○ 2004–05: Improving performance at Key Stage 4 (age 14–16) through use of ICT

○ 2004: Online INSET event.

From 2004 onwards, INSET Services, with a team of associates, managed 12 science-based projects for Becta, the final one finishing in 2009. The projects covered many aspects of science education, two examples being 'Tailored Outcomes' (2005–07) and 'Hard to Teach Topics in Science' (2007–09).

The Certificate of Continuing Professional Development

From its creation, ASE INSET Services placed a high priority on making a difference to the working lives of science teachers and constantly sought ways both to identify means by which professional development was truly effective in making that difference and to recognise what had been achieved.

In 1997, INSET Services was invited to explore ways in which ASE could establish a professional development qualification. The resulting programme was designed for teachers in the early years of their career, but not for NQTs who had their own in-school programmes to follow. Participants were asked to provide evidence of progress in all areas over a two-year period by writing up teaching activities that targeted one or more of the selected areas. In doing this, they were provided with support from a mentor based in their own school, the INSET Services central team and an online tutor. Success was judged at two levels – Good or Satisfactory. One development that was seen as important was to associate the Certificate with a Masters qualification and consequently universities were invited to consider collaboration. The outcome of this was an agreement with the Open University to develop the qualification jointly on the basis that the Certificate programme would continue much as it had been developed, and would be complemented at the end by a further programme that would enable participants to gain an Open University MEd. The Certificate programme ran until 2008.

The creation of ASE INSET Services was a bold step into the unknown. No subject association had attempted such a venture before. This period of 16 years was 30% of the lifetime of the ASE and a time of great change in British education, and also a period through which there was increasing government involvement in the direction of professional development.

For ASE, there were many benefits from the work of its creation. Sufficient income was generated to be able to cover costs and make contributions to the finances of the parent body. A major feature of operations was the need to publicise and promote products, which meant that there was a constant flow of advertising materials to schools and teachers informing them of courses and projects. This placed the name of ASE repeatedly in front of teachers nationwide and frequently the envelopes contained publicity materials for ASE membership, publications, products and conferences. For ASE members, and to encourage potential members, there was always a cost benefit in attending INSET Services courses and conferences. Furthermore, the high regard in which the work of

INSET Services was held also enhanced the reputation of ASE.

At its conclusion, all those involved could claim with confidence that ASE INSET Services had made a difference.

Case Study 7
Five for Sydney – honouring excellence

'The phrase "Five for Sydney" is well known to the majority of ASE members, but not all will know about the magnitude, importance and impact of the scheme itself. Every two years, ASE is involved in selecting five scholars from all the outstanding scholars nominated by the Regions, to attend the International Science School held at the University of Sydney. The Science Schools have been running for over 30 years and the same man, Professor Harry Messel, has been involved for the whole of that time.'

(Broadbridge and Wilkinson, 1997)

Figure 8.6: Five for Sydney scholars from various years with respectively, a) HRH The Princess Royal, b) HRH The Duke of Edinburgh, c) Prime Minister Margaret Thatcher, d) ASE President, Wynne Harlen, Chief Executive Annette Smith and Chair, Carolyn Yates.

This long association between ASE and the Australian Science School, now known as the Professor Harry Messel International Science School, is rapidly approaching its half-century. This partnership is the only one in the ASE's history to directly involve school pupils, but it is an indication of the dedication of all the inspirational teachers involved as well as of the commitment of the Association and its Regions to the cause of science education.

The Science Foundation for Physics, set up by Professor Harry Messel within the University of Sydney, consists of representatives of business who provide funds for outstanding research programmes and aims to improve the flow of science graduates into the University. The Foundation actively supports initiatives to bring science to the public and to raise the level of science awareness among the school population.

In 1967, ASE became involved in helping to find 'Five for Sydney' from Great Britain, although a short report in the September 1967 edition of *Education in Science* mentions the selection of *'about six outstanding pupils'*, with the initial selection being made by ASE Branches (*EiS*, 1967). In these early days, and to match the process adopted by the newly-enrolled American contingent to the Summer Science School in which the US President *'gave a good send-off'* to the American scholars, the Patron of ASE, HRH The Duke of Edinburgh, agreed to do the same. The cost of air fares, accommodation and some pocket money (for the students, not the adult escort) was met by the Australian Science Foundation. For the first decade, the scheme was run annually, changing to every two years in the late 1970s.

The principles governing selection included 'high intelligence', 'personality and character', and 'knowledge' – in that order. The selection of at least one girl was preferred, along with a good geographical spread and perhaps one scholar from an independent school. The age required was that of pupils about to commence their second year in the sixth form. Scientists were preferred, but mathematicians and possibly one non-scientist were not ruled out (*EiS*, 1967). In later years, the students were often referred to as 'young ambassadors for Britain', making the non-academic attributes required even more important.

With the first year of selection, close ties were formed with the Royal Institution (RI) and these continue up to the present day. This support has variously taken the form of hosting the selection days in some years, financial support, and providing a venue for a prestigious awards day for the successful candidates. The RI and the Australian Science Foundation are just two of the organisations that have supported Five for Sydney over the years. Sponsors such as Qantas Airlines, the Comino Foundation, the Royal Society, the Ogden Trust and British Airways have also made it possible not only to give more than

135 gifted UK youngsters over the years the chance to launch their no doubt glittering scientific careers, but also to present the best of young British talent as ambassadors for UK science education.

It appears that little has changed in the selection procedure over the years, although online nominations and e-consultations with ASE regions prior to the final interview selection now replace the old postal and face-to-face methods. Until 2011, ASE members were invited to send in nominations of outstanding pupils in their areas to ASE Region secretaries, and regional interviews took place, often using regional panels. Applications as a result of this first sift were then sent into ASE Headquarters, at which point a final selection was made, using a panel of judges comprising officers from, until recently, the RI and ASE. This final selection procedure still involves interviews with the shortlisted candidates and, at the end of the proceedings, the top five are chosen.

From the outset, it was deemed sensible to send an adult escort to the Summer Science Schools to accompany the scholars. These escorts have tended to be key ASE members who have shown commitment to ASE activities, particularly regionally. Apart from the obvious role of acting as a responsible figure *in loco parentis,* the escorts traditionally wrote about the Summer Science School experience in subsequent issues of *Education in Science.* Some of these articles demonstrate the extent of their pastoral commitment, with several instances of the scholars being invited to stay at the home of their particular escort prior to the trip, *'so that they could get to know each other'* (Wilkinson, 1984). On several occasions, the spouse of the escort accompanied the group (self-funded) to add to the depth of care offered to the young people.

Over the years, the Five for Sydney scholars have enjoyed many high-profile experiences before the Sydney trip actually started. These included lavish full days spent at the RI, during which they would receive their certificates, variously presented by such eminent persons as the then Prime Ministers, Mr Edward Heath and Mrs Margaret Thatcher, HRH The Duke of Edinburgh and HRH The Princess Royal, amongst others, in front of an audience that included teachers, parents, ASE Region representatives and members of the press. Quite often, this would be followed by attendance at a Royal Garden Party and, in earlier days, trips to other countries to meet with fellow scholars from around the world, including at least one trip to the White House to witness the US scholars receiving their medals. Visits to famous scientific venues, field trips at home and abroad and the Australian Embassy were other highlights of the pre-Sydney experience.

Some years, the Summer Science School focused on a particular theme; others took a more general form. The scholars and their escort would fly to Sydney, sometimes directly, sometimes via other countries with excursions included. Often a few days' sightseeing in Australia were built in, allowing the scholars to relax after the flight and explore the city. A typical schedule for the two-week Science School would comprise days split into 90-minute sessions, the majority of which were lectures from the world's leading scientists on subjects ranging from pure physics to science fiction in films. Tours of the University and various research facilities were included, as were many practical workshops where the scholars often worked in teams. A wide range of social activities accompanied the academic schedule, thereby reinforcing the bonding experience for both the 'home team' and those from other countries. In recent years, the scholars themselves have written about their experiences in *Education in Science,* and readers are urged to find these inspirational articles and enjoy them!

Case Study 8

Collaborating for Health and Safety: ASE, CLEAPSS and SSERC (see also Chapter 7)
Contributed by Peter Borrows

ASE has a lifelong partnership with the organisations now known as CLEAPSS and SSERC. A few members of the SMA, in 1959, wrote to HMI as they were concerned to find ways of improving the quality of equipment for teaching science. As a direct result, C.L.E.A.P.S.E. (strictly, the Development Group of the Consortium of Local Education Authorities for the Provision of Science Equipment) was born almost contemporaneously with ASE in 1963, as was S.S.S.E.R.C. (the Scottish Schools Science Equipment Research Centre). Both subsequently changed their names, C.L.E.A.P.S.E. becoming the School Science Service of the Consortium of Local Education Authorities for the Provision of Science Services and later just CLEAPSS. S.S.S.E.R.C. became SSERC, dropping Science from its title. These changes reflected a move away from the original focus on equipment to an emphasis in the 1980s on health and safety. Later, both came to realise that in-service training of teachers and technicians was crucial to promoting better practical science. It is important to realise that, whilst ASE is a membership organisation for employees, CLEAPSS and SSERC are membership organisations for employers, mainly Local Authorities, schools and colleges. However, rather than creating the confrontation that might be anticipated in some industries, this collaboration is viewed by the HSE as a model of industry self-regulation. CLEAPSS has had ASE representation on its Governing Body and its Steering Committee since 1964. CLEAPSE and

SSSERC both took part in the original conference that gave rise to *Topics in Safety*. Since 1977, CLEAPSE and, since 1993, SSERC, have been represented on the ASE Safeguards Committee. Indeed, their presence is now seen as crucial to the work of the Committee, which provides a unique health and safety forum across the UK.

ASE, CLEAPSS and SSERC were set up at the same time as the Nuffield science teaching projects (see Chapter 3), which advocated practical work involving the use of radioactive sources. Such use was tightly controlled by the Ministry of Education. Almost all members of the SMA's Radioactive Substances Sub-committee had said that the new license conditions were so onerous that in future they would confine work to naturally occurring radioactive materials and luminous artifacts. The Ministry asked for detailed evidence of problems. John Lewis (a future Chair of ASE) commented, in 1961, following discussions with the Radiochemical Centre, Amersham, the Radiation Protection Service, the Ministries of Education and of Health, that *'I do not think this will present any difficulty'*. Although the exact role of ASE is unclear, in 1965 the *ASE Bulletin* reported: *'As a result of prolonged negotiations and discussion, the DES has introduced a simplified procedure for authorising the purchase and use of radioactive sources... to apply to the experiments recommended in the Modern Physical Science Report'*.

The 'simplified procedure' was published by the DES as *Administrative Memorandum AM 1/65*. Given the tight control, it is ironic that, 40 years later, the DfES reviewed its policy of approving radiation products for school use and concluded that administrative memoranda were purely advisory, that such approval was inappropriate and could be replaced by advice from those with suitable expertise, and commissioned CLEAPSS to do just that.

The Nuffield science teaching projects also specified the use of low-voltage power supplies. In the 1970s, this caused several LEAs to install highly sensitive electrical protection units (Blakley units), which did not use ordinary 13 A plugs, so equipment could not be moved to parts of the school with standard power supplies. In 1978, ASE re-published a CLEAPSE guide on electrical safety (ASE, 1978). Then, in 1981, the MP for Cambridge asked a question in Parliament on the need or otherwise for non-standard mains supplies in school laboratories. As a result, the DES called a meeting attended by representatives of ASE, CLEAPSE, teachers' unions, LEA bodies, HMI and the HSE, the outcome being the publication, in 1983, of *Guidance Note 23* (HSE, 1983) identifying a sensible approach including regular portable appliance testing, together with improved maintenance. It appears that the combined influence of ASE and CLEAPSE was instrumental in achieving this.

ASE and CLEAPSS have also provided mutual support on committees of the British Standards Institution, particularly with respect to fume cupboards. It was easy for one person to be ignored by committee members who wanted all fume cupboards to be of the same high, expensive standard. This was not so easy with two voices!

In the early 1990s, ASE and CLEAPSS became increasingly concerned about health and safety errors in science textbooks and teaching schemes. In many cases there was wild over-reaction, with dire warnings of the toxicity of harmless materials. Conversely, there was sometimes a complete disregard for necessary precautions. As these documents were, presumably, written by practising teachers, the level of ignorance was – and continues to be – a matter of concern. In 1991, CLEAPSS and ASE convened a conference for publishers and outlined the problems. As a result, joint guidance was published in 1991 as *Health and Safety Checks on Science Texts: Guidance for publishers, authors, editors and readers*. This was updated several times with SSERC also involved, and placed on the websites of all three organisations.

Another example of joint action of ASE and CLEAPSS arose from the government reaction to alarm about AIDS. In 1987, the government issued *AIDS: Some Questions and Answers*, advising that neither of the widely used activities of blood sampling nor cheek-cell sampling should take place in schools. Although this was simply advice, most Local Authorities acted on it and, as employers, banned these activities in their schools. Most independent schools ignored it. Many teachers felt the bans were unfortunate (and there was correspondence to this effect in *EiS*) because these were motivational activities that allowed children to explore the biology of their own bodies. The Institute of Biology (IoB) opposed the bans, and suggested safe protocols for cheek-cell sampling, but both ASE and CLEAPSS took the view that it was difficult to argue against official government policy, however misguided.

By 1991, the DES (1978) booklet *Safety in Science Laboratories* was looking very dated and the DfEE decided that it should be replaced by a completely new publication. CLEAPSS and ASE argued that this was unnecessary because the issues were already adequately covered, but the Department persisted. After approaches to both organisations separately, ASE agreed to do it, sub-contracting about half of the work to CLEAPSS. A weekend conference was held in 1991 to plan the book. After several delays and problems, including the introduction of a number of scientific errors, especially in the microbiology section (as a result of the Department's attempt to reduce the length), *Safety in Science Education* was finally published by the DfEE in 1996. The book went out of print *ca.* 2001, but ASE was given permission to make it available on its website and to update it, especially the tables in *Part B, Safety in Science Teaching*. As a DfEE publication, it applied only in England and Wales, and hence SSERC was not involved but, when the Safeguards Committee modified the tables for the website, Scottish members were fully involved. Despite the initial errors, in many ways this was a seminal publication, which served as something of a successor to *Topics in Safety* because it was a document (from a government department) spelling out what was acceptable in school science. Both the first and second editions of *Topics in Safety* had included a long table listing chemicals and their suitability for teacher use only or for various ages of students. *Safety in Science Education* had a far superior table, covering many more chemicals and giving much more detailed advice. As a result, when the third edition of *Topics in Safety* was published in 2001, the table of chemicals was omitted.

However, perhaps more significant than the chemicals issue, the work on producing *Safety in Science Education* led the authors to rethink the advice on blood and cheek-cell sampling. Since the original advice had been issued in 1987, regulations introduced under the *HSW Act* had introduced the concept of 'risk assessment'. The authors took the view that blood and cheek-cell sampling should be acceptable, providing there was an adequate risk assessment. When this appeared in print in *Safety in Science Education*, CLEAPSS adapted the Institute of Biology protocol for cheek-cell sampling and the original procedure for blood sampling from *Topics in Safety* and most Local Authorities rescinded their previous bans. However, such is the power of myths that many teachers, years later, still believed that cheek-cell sampling was banned. In 1994, ASE convened a one-day conference on genetic engineering and, partly because of the errors in *Safety in Science Education,* a further conference on microbiology and biotechnology in 1997, with major contributions from MISAC (the Microbiology in Schools Advisory Committee). A joint statement was produced and made widely available via ASE, CLEAPSS, MISAC and SSERC. It later formed one *Topic* in the third edition of *Topics in Safety.* The most recent joint victory has occurred, after several years of lobbying by ASE, CLEAPSS and SSERC, about the disposal of animal waste from dissection in schools, under European regulations (see Chapter 7).

In the 1990s, the Safeguards Committee began receiving complaints about how health and safety issues were handled in Ofsted inspections in England, with inspectors sometimes unduly criticising relatively trivial matters and sometimes simply being wrong. Accordingly, in collaboration with CLEAPSS and the Science Advisers' Group, two guides were produced, for the use of inspectors of secondary and primary schools respectively, and made freely available (CLEAPSS, 1996).

Other collaborative publications include *Be Safe! Some aspects of health and safety in the Scottish Curriculum Environmental Studies,* which ASE published with editorial support from SSERC, in 1995. This was a Scottish edition of the primary health and safety booklet, *Be Safe!,* including extracts from the Scottish curriculum guidelines. A Scottish edition of the INSET pack, based on the Scottish edition of *Be Safe!,* was developed in partnership with SSERC. The fourth edition of *Be Safe!,* published in 2011, was sponsored jointly by CLEAPSS and SSERC, who paid for a writing weekend near the start of the process of production.

In 1996 CLEAPSS publicised its *Helpline.* Teachers and technicians in CLEAPSS member establishments or officers in member LEAs had always been able to telephone or write for advice, but this was not widely known. Publicity resulted in a rapid increase in the number of calls to CLEAPSS and a corresponding decline in the calls to ASE, which cannot compete with the professional expertise on health and safety that CLEAPSS and SSERC have developed. However, both CLEAPSS and SSERC keep the Safeguards Committee informed about significant enquiries and all three organisations continue to collaborate in the field of health and safety.

Some other partnerships over the past 50 years

School Natural Science Society, late 1960s to mid-1970s
A small society taken over by the ASE in the 1970s, after years of support in which ASE sold the Society's publications through its bookselling arm.

Studies in Decision Making in Science Education, 1978
A project funded by the Schools Council, which resulted in the widely acclaimed report, *Decisions in the Science Department,* published in 1981.

Teachers into Industry, mid-1980s
This project was run by ASE on behalf of the Standing Conference on Schools' Science and Technology (SCSST), a body established in 1971 to promote and encourage the development of science and technology in schools, 'in the public interest'. SCSST was supported by the then DES, the Department of Trade and Industry, the engineering professions, industrial companies and others. Based on the work of experienced teachers who, in 1984, were linked to various industrial companies as part of this project, *Experimenting with Industry,* a series of 13 booklets, featured experiments drawn from industrial processes, exploring

scientific concepts and showing how they were applied in industry. They were designed to replace some of the practical work being done in schools pre-National Curriculum. The booklets covered such topics as *Electrical Testing, Extracting Metals from Scrap, Physics of Fluid Flow, Safety in Gas Appliances* and *Sugar Challenge,* to name but a few. Each of the booklets was sponsored by a different company: GEC, Nipa, Square D, British Sugar, ICI, Shell Chemicals, British Gas, Elkington Copper Refiners, British Aerospace, Marconi, Ciba-Geigy, Dowty Services and Unilever, and there was additional support from Lloyd's Register of Shipping. The impact of these booklets is best summed up by the following quote about the *Plant Tissue Culture* booklet, reprinted in 2002 by the National Centre for Biotechnology Education (at the University of Reading): *'This booklet remains the only introduction to practical plant tissue culture for schools ever published in the United Kingdom. Its influence during the late 1980s, before the introduction of the National Curriculum in England and Wales, was considerable.'*

(National Centre for Biotechnology Education,
The University of Reading, 2002)

ASE/British Gas, 1981–1995
Gas Applications in School Science (GASS) was a project organised jointly by British Gas and ASE. The two organisations had had contact over a number of years but, in 1981, the link became more formal when the Chairman of British Gas, Sir Dennis Rooke, was elected President of ASE. GASS 81 involved collaboration between 27 science teachers (all members of ASE) and an equal number of scientists working at five British Gas research establishments. The project was officially launched at the ASE Annual Meeting at the University of Warwick in January 1981. Each of the selected teachers spent four days at their chosen research station. *The GASS Book* comprises materials produced by the GASS 81 participants and each unit is self-contained.

In 1984, British Gas and ASE produced a series of learning packages, *Management in School Science Departments*, which were developed in response to needs identified by members of a joint workshop representing British Gas and ASE at the British Gas National Management Centre in November 1981. Modules included: *Time Management; Meetings as Vehicles of Communication; Staff Development – Selection & Appraisal* and *Understanding Managerial Roles.*

Between 1991 and 1995, British Gas ran the British Gas Bursary Scheme, similar in scope to the BT scheme but based in one of its research centres.

223

In 1991, the structure of ASE was under review, with the aim of making it more responsive to members' needs. British Gas sponsored the Codicote Conference, which eventually led to a new structure for the Association.

The Science Challenge, and Health Matters, 1992–2003

Originating in 1992, this long-running partnership between ASE and industry resulted in many young children being inspired and enthused by science. The Chief Executive of the then Nuclear Electric Company (later to become BNFL) witnessed his four sons all entering into science careers having been 'turned on' to science at primary school. He asked ASE to collaborate in a competition that would inspire younger children (at the time, much corporate funding was being poured into the secondary sector) and the *Science Challenge* was born. It was rejuvenated several years later when it ran alongside Science Year, being a project that was a science investigation activity aimed at pupils aged 9–13 years. The Science Challenge encouraged pupils to carry out investigations and experiments at school and then present their findings to teachers or governors, or at a school assembly. A summary of what they had found out was sent to ASE for judging and the winning schools were invited to the Fun Day Finals, a unique experience in which the pupils took part in a drama with a science theme and in a quiz, and were introduced to a TV celebrity. The Science Challenge prided itself on enhancing National Curriculum science, encouraging scientific enquiry, promoting teamwork and developing communication skills. The Science Challenge was sponsored by BNFL and run in conjunction with the British Association for the Advancement of Science.

Another key collaboration of the time was Health Matters, run by ASE and SmithKlineBeecham, until the latter became GlaxoSmithKline (GSK) and when its focus was transferred to Science across the World.

Science across Europe (SAE) and Science across the World (SAW), 1992–2011

The origin of these projects is recorded in Chapters 2 and 3. Starting in 1992, Science across Europe was a project that linked secondary schools across Europe through the science curriculum. The project selected science, technology and society topics with a European dimension and participating students were encouraged to gather information, reflect on their opinions and compare them with those of students in other countries. As well as enhancing science understanding and providing a global dimension to science learning, the project provided opportunities for using foreign languages and, at the time, exciting new communications technologies. The scale of the international collaboration was extraordinary, with Science across Europe spreading to Science across Asia-Pacific, Southern Africa, and the Americas, ultimately merging to become Science across the World.

Over the last 20 years, many thousands of school students from 150 countries have been *'exploring science locally and exchanging their insights globally'* in many languages from French to Farsi. The publication of the topic support materials in many languages has been an unique feature of the project. From the start, the projects were supported by a team of volunteer country co-ordinators such as Lida Schoen (The Netherlands), Keith Kelly (Bulgaria), Xavier Juan Pons (Spain), Egbert Weisheit (Germany), Khar Thoe Ng (Malaysia), Nigel Heslop (UK) and Andrew Hunt (UK) who continue to promote the programme with enthusiasm today. In the early days, the exchanges were by post, then increasingly by fax, email and finally via the Science across the World website as communications technology developed. These days, teachers have made more use of modern technologies such as social networking sites and virtual learning

Figure 8.7: Some past and present Science Across the World (SAW) co-ordinators at their annual writing team meeting in Lisbon, Portugal, May 2000.

environments (VLEs). The project has benefited from significant EU Comenius funding to provide teacher training workshops for hundreds of teachers from across Europe.

Science across the World has gained global recognition through major international awards – Global Best Award for Business–Education Partnerships in 1996 and 2000, and European Award for Languages in 2004. These projects were the most wide-ranging and influential of all ASE international activities and were run in collaboration with, first, BP and later GSK.

Researchers in Residence, 1994–2012

Originally introduced in the mid-1990s, the Researchers in Residence scheme was funded by Research Councils UK (RCUK) and supported by the Wellcome Trust, with the aim of motivating and inspiring school pupils by bringing 'real life' researchers into the classroom. Over the following 17 years, 3000 researchers were placed in UK schools and evaluations illustrate that the scheme was successful in its aim to inspire school-age students about the world of science and scientific research. ASE became part of the delivery team for the scheme, with a dedicated member of staff operating from ASE Headquarters, and it continued to support the initiative until its closure in January 2012.

techcen 2005–2008 (see also Chapter 6)

The aim of the techcen project was to improve the support available for school science and design and technology by developing a comprehensive framework for the professional development of school technicians, including the delivery of revised National Vocational Qualifications (NVQs) that underpinned a new career structure. In partnership with DATA (the Design and Technology Association) and supported by a grant from the Gatsby Charitable Foundation, an NVQ virtual centre, known as techcen, was set up in 2005–6 to provide access to the Laboratory and Associated Technical Activities (LATA) NVQ for technicians in schools and colleges. Through techcen, technicians developed an e-portfolio, which could be accessed at any time by assessors who could also assess and verify online. All communication between candidates and assessors was logged and evidence within the e-portfolio automatically cross-referenced. As stated by John Lawrence in 2007, '[this]…allows educational assessment support to technicians who want to engage with further qualifications, but are limited by their location. Prior to techcen, access was only possible if a sufficient number of colleagues in their area wanted to embark on the programme. With the techcen virtual centre, location is not an issue.'

(Lawrence, in Bell, 2007)

The website was shortlisted for the BETT 2008 Awards and was showcased at a Best Practice PAAVQSET conference. Some 234 technicians were recruited into the first two cohorts, with a success rate of 53%. An evaluation of techcen by Gatsby, in 2007, estimated that the full costs (£850 at Level 2) were about half that of an industrially-based LATA NVQ. techcen was believed to be unique in that it was written in open source code, meaning that it could be transferable to other NVQs. The pilot had been subsidised by the Gatsby Foundation and it was believed schools were unlikely to pay more than £350. In spite of massive support from many parties, further funding to continue the project beyond 2008 was not forthcoming and the project came to an end later that year.

Laboratory Design for Teaching and Learning, 2004 (see also Chapters 5 and 7)

Laboratory Design for Teaching & Learning was developed by ASE in partnership with NESTA and the Royal Society. It aimed to encourage school staff and LEAs to have a more influential role in the design and refurbishment of school science laboratories and to place the emphasis of any design on teaching and learning. The resource was distributed to Heads of Science and ASE members. In promoting ownership of science laboratory building and refurbishment plans by school staff, the aim of the resource was to facilitate interactions with architects and contractors, so producing an optimum laboratory for teaching and learning. The software will no longer run on modern computers, but the documents associated with the project are still relevant and available on the ASE website. In addition, ASE, with others, had an input into the revision of *Building Bulletin 80* published in 1999 and was involved in *Project Faraday – exemplar designs for science* as part of the DCSF Steering Group, which was published in 2008.

Improving Practical Work in Science: Getting Practical, 2008–2011

This project, although now completed, is still very much in evidence and was the result of a multiple partnership on several levels. It was funded by the Department for Education and had co-ordinating partners (ASE, CLEAPSS, national network of SLCs, CSE at Sheffield Hallam University) and contributing partners (the SSAT, Institute of Physics, Society of Biology, Royal Society of Chemistry, Gatsby SEP, the National STEM Centre and the University of York). It was also supported by SCORE, the Royal Society, Gatsby SAPS, the National Strategies, LSIS, The Wellcome Trust, the Nuffield Foundation and the YSC at the Royal Institution.

In short, Getting Practical aimed to improve the clarity of the learning outcomes associated with practical work; the effectiveness and impact of practical work; the sustainability of this approach for ongoing improvements; and quality rather than the quantity of practical work used in schools.

At the time of writing, the formal evaluation is still being carried out by the Institute of Education at the University of London. However, there is already evidence that the project has had a wide impact on schools, with many teachers now trained well enough in the principles espoused by the project to be able to train others.

Partnerships with educational publishers

During the past 50 years, a large number of titles has been produced; some published by ASE alone, some jointly published and some by others with key collaboration from the Association. These publishing partners included commercial publishers, fellow subject associations, industrial companies, Examination boards, professional institutes and Local Authorities. As well as the obvious financial benefits to the Association of such co-publishing ventures, the expansion of the profile-raising potential for ASE was significant. Most of these co-publications were publicised by the partners, so reaching a far wider audience than just ASE membership. Examination Boards were able to include many of the titles in required reading lists and some commercial publishers carried the titles in their catalogues and through their school representatives.

The long-standing co-operation between ASE and John Murray is summarised in Case Study 1.

Another key group of collaborations resulted in the important *Science Teacher Handbook/ASE Guides* series, commencing in 1986 and continuing to the present day. A simple case of co-publication was started in 1986 with the first *ASE Science Teacher's Handbook*, published by Hutchinson in collaboration with ASE. Over the ensuing years, several new versions of this key guide for science teachers were published with a series of publishing partners, including Hutchinson, Stanley Thornes and Simon & Schuster. With chapters authored by key personnel from the world of science education, the handbooks/guides aimed to provide important reference information to allow both new and experienced teachers to develop a philosophical platform upon which to build and enhance their pedagogical skills, rather than subject knowledge. For many of those years, these were the only books of their kind and were widely used by trainee teachers in the UK. In 1993, the single Handbook was replaced by volumes specifically aimed at primary and secondary science education respectively. From 2006, ASE took over as sole publisher of the Guides. In 2012, a new Guide, the *ASE Guide to Research in Science Education* was published, to add to the already updated (2011) guides to primary and secondary science education.

Partnerships between subject associations

'Subject teaching associations are normally membership organisations, often registered charities, whose mission is to further the teaching and learning of a specific subject in schools, colleges and universities. They are independent of government and believe very strongly in supporting teachers in their subject specialism.' (Council for Subject Associations website)

In 1971, ASE invited a grouping of 20 subject teaching associations to form COSTA (the Council of Subject Teaching Associations), as a result of which the Association was given responsibility for administering the Council for several years (see Chapter 2).

In the late 1980s, an attempt was made to draw together as many of the subject teaching associations as possible to collaborate in providing help for primary teachers facing the challenges of the National Curriculum for England and Wales. The organisations involved included the Mathematical Association, the Association of Teachers of Mathematics, the National Association for the Teaching of English, and ASE. Numerous meetings were held, with varying degrees of success and some controversy, and the most achievable outcomes were seen to be published resources to help primary teachers facing this innovation, many of whom had never had to teach 'real' science. In 1989, the same year that saw the introduction of the National Curriculum for England and Wales, ASE and its partner subject associations, working as the Core Subjects Development Group, published *National Curriculum: making it work for the primary school* and, a little later, *Teacher Assessment: making it work for the primary school*. In 1991, the first and only issue of a joint journal, *Primary Associations*, was published. Due to insurmountable difficulties, the multi-partnership ceased shortly afterwards (see Chapter 4).

Following this less than successful joint venture, a group of publishing managers from a number of subject teaching associations got together in 2002–2003 to discuss future collaborations and from this emerged The Curriculum Partnership. The aim of this group was to produce cross-curricular materials for the pre-secondary market and make use of the shared expertise from each participating association. The first title to be produced, in 2004, was *The Early Years Handbook – support for practitioners in the foundation stage,* and involved ASE, the Geographical Association, the Mathematical Association, the National Association for the Teaching of English and the Design and Technology Association. Later, in 2007, the *Primary Project Box,* containing five themed cross-curricular teaching units for use with 5–7 year-olds, was published. All participating associations were able to market these titles, so widening the potential readership and resulting in impressively high sales. What made this particular collaboration so special was the ability, through a shared sense of purpose and a specific focus, to work together as fellow associations to produce material of mutual benefit.

In 2006, the then Department for Education and Skills (later to become the Department for Children, Schools and Families (DCSF)) asked the Subject Associations Steering Group (SASG) to consider a single organisation to support the subject association community and, in September 2007, the Council for Subject Associations (CfSA) was born. It was a membership organisation, recognised as a charitable company limited by guarantee and independent of government.

At its peak, the CfSA had a membership of over 30 associations, including ASE. As well as a website, the CfSA also published *Primary Subjects,* a series of seven published folders for teachers, particularly subject leaders, and whose early issues were sponsored by the DCSF. Each folder focused on a different theme, and contained a set of four-page leaflets, each written by a one of the subject associations, providing information and guidance, ideas and activities, and news and comment from that subject on the common theme. Folder 1, published in the summer of 2008, contained leaflets on *Art, Craft and Design, Citizenship, Dance, Design and Technology, Drama, English, Geography, History, ICT, Mathematics, Music, PE, Primary Languages, PSHE, RE and Science.* The subsequent six folders, published termly, followed the same format. Initially, one copy of each folder was sent free of charge to each primary school in England; after four issues, the external sponsorship was scaled down and a subscription charge was levied. In summer 2010, the seventh and final folder was published.

Then and now

With such a wide range of partnerships over the years, it is difficult to gauge how today's collaborations differ, if at all, from those in days gone by. From a practical point of view, it was certainly the case that, in the heady days of the 1970s and 1980s, teachers were more free to take active roles in ASE activities, with some standing committees being able to meet on a weekday as schools and Local Authorities were prepared to fund supply cover. Also, until the advent of the National Curriculum and national testing from the late 1980s, teachers seemed to feel more able to experiment with different teaching and learning styles, particularly in the primary sector, than they were after 1989.

The immediate post-National Curriculum years saw a rapid growth in membership of ASE, particularly in the primary area, and the resulting increased income allowed a greater range of activity. There was more money available, both in government and in industry, and so more possibilities for external funding and sponsorship. Many major companies had dedicated education teams, whose job it was to fund educational activities and resources and so were actively looking for partners for these. In the current economic climate, such educational provision in industry has been substantially reduced.

With the advent, too, of a number of key bodies carrying out, in part, similar activities to ASE, it is clear that the Association is no longer alone in doing what it used to do on a sole basis. The national network of Science Learning Centres, the National Strategies (now discontinued), the National STEM Centre and eLibrary, along with a tendency for the learned scientific societies to focus more on school education than before, have all led to a very much more crowded landscape in which ASE can operate. Add to this the fact that a growing number of educational publishers are now aiming at the teacher, rather than exclusively at the textbook market, and the introduction of so much free material via the internet, and the Association's future is a challenging one.

It is appropriate to conclude this survey with reference to some ongoing and recent initiatives.

Chartered Science Teacher, Registered Scientist, and Registered Science Technician

As described by Derek Bell in Chapter 2 of this book, establishing CSciTeach is just one example of working with the science professional bodies: the Royal Society of Chemistry, the Institute of Physics, the Society of Biology (formerly Institute of Biology), the Royal Society and the Science Council.

Following the granting of the Royal Charter, ASE set up a Registration Board and, in 2005, became a licenced body of the Science Council for the award of Chartered Science Teacher status (CSciTeach), equivalent to CSci. In 2006, the first five teachers were awarded CSciTeach designations. In April 2010, the Registration Authority of the Science Council awarded ASE a full license for this status.

CSciTeach is a chartered designation, which recognises the unique combination of skills, knowledge, understanding and expertise that is required by individuals involved in the specific practice and advancement of science teaching and learning. This is underpinned by an annual commitment to Continuing Professional Development (CPD). ASE, via its Registration Board, assesses the applicants' evidence, and the number of successful applications is rising steadily. Continuing efforts are being made to publicise the award and encourage more employers to recognise and value the CSciTeach post-nominal.

In January 2012, the Science Council approved the grant of a license to the Association to award Registered Science Technician (RSciTech) status to technicians, and Registered Scientist (RSci) status to teachers and, in April 2012, the first such designations were awarded. The Science Council is committed to raising the professional standing of all those working to advance science and its applications, and ensuring opportunities for further training and professional development at every level. Being licensed in this way, ASE is able to co-operate with the Science Council to build a framework of professional standards and recognition across the science education workforce.

Primary Science Quality Mark (PSQM)

A joint project led by ASE, the national network of Science Learning Centres, and Barnet Local Authority, PSQM is an award scheme to develop and celebrate the quality of science teaching and learning in primary schools. The scheme is supported by The Wellcome Trust. The principal process of the PSQM is school self-evaluation against the criteria established by the project team. With the support of a local hub leader, subject leaders in each school audit the quality of their school's science provision. They identify what is needed to improve their provision, and complete an action plan of professional development. Following relevant CPD, the subject leaders submit evidence to show that the school has met the criteria at one of three levels: bronze, silver or gold. The aims of PSQM are: to raise the profile of science in primary schools; to encourage primary schools to increase the range and quality of teaching and learning in science; to recognise, promote and spread good practice in science teaching and learning; to provide a framework for evaluating, planning and developing the quality of science teaching and learning in primary schools; and to celebrate a commitment to excellence in science in primary schools. To date, over 500 schools have achieved the Award, at one or other of the levels, and more are registering each year.

As part of the requirement for attaining the Award involves belonging to ASE, one positive impact has been a steady increase in primary school membership of the Association.

Science/Primary Science Teacher of the Year Awards

The TES/ASE Science Teachers of the Year awards were set up in 1993 to promote science teaching in schools. Sponsorship for the secondary award came from the Association of the British Pharmaceutical Industry (ABPI) and the primary award from Pfizer, until 2003/04, when the AstraZeneca Science Teaching Trust (AZSTT) took over support for the primary award, renaming it the AstraZeneca Science Teaching Trust Primary Science Teaching Awards.

Awards are given to a teacher showing outstanding classroom ability and an infectious enthusiasm for the subject, with skills in communicating and an ability to motivate students of all abilities. Thousands of pounds in prizes have been handed to individual teachers and their schools during the 20 years of the scheme. Declining numbers of entrants to the secondary category led ABPI to withdraw from the scheme in 1997/98, but the primary award survives under the auspices of AZSTT, in collaboration with ASE and with the support of educational supplier, TTS.

In 2010, the AZSTT Primary Science College was established, which all winners, past and present, of the AZSTT Primary Science Awards are invited to join. To support these outstanding teachers, AZSTT has made available large sums of funding to College members each year, to allow any projects and activities in which they are engaged to move forward.

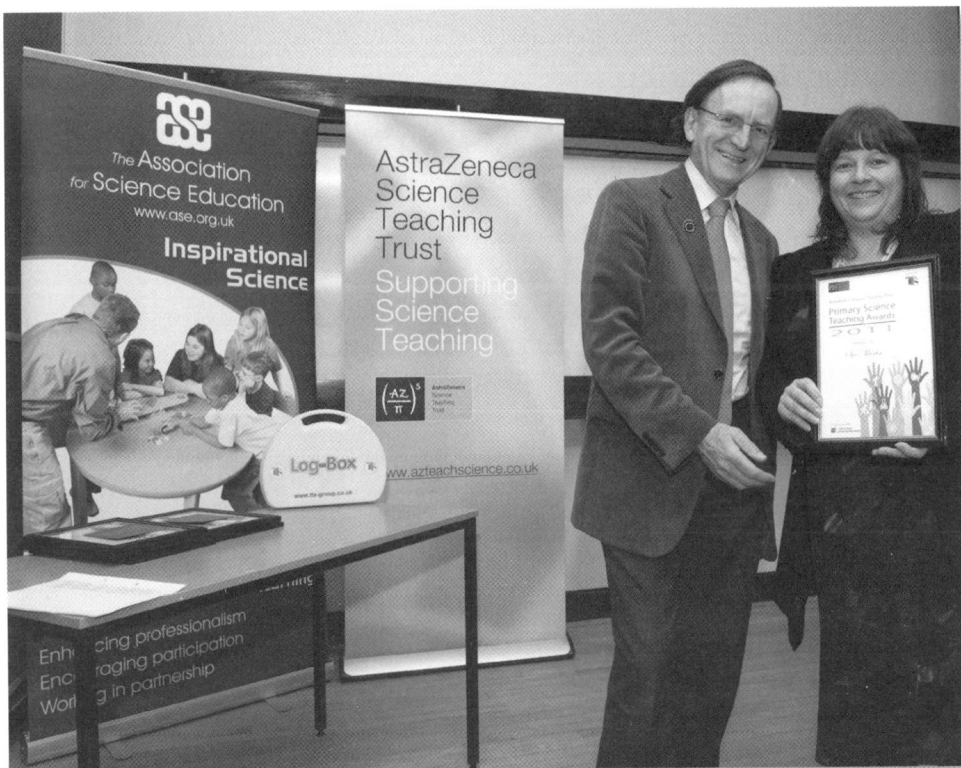

Figure 8.8: Martin Hollins presenting Sue Martin, AZSTT Primary Science Teacher of the Year, 2011, with her award.

schoolscience.co.uk

Originating in 2004 as a showcase for educational resources named ScienceOneStop, schoolscience.co.uk has evolved into a unique website, administered by ASE and supported by a host of industrial and educational organisations. It provides an educational news service, a research focus, and a comprehensive directory of resources, information and contacts for teachers and learners of science in the UK and abroad. Revamped and relaunched in November 2011, the site features competitions, awards, a range of free resources and 'giveaway' equipment, as well as articles on cutting edge science developments from experts in the field.

A central point of reference for all primary and secondary school science teachers and technicians, as well as students and researchers, the site offers a unique opportunity for practitioners to enhance their knowledge and experience of science and science education and for specialist organisations to raise their profile.

At time of writing schoolscience.co.uk supporters include Research Councils UK, The Association of the British Pharmaceutical Industry, The British Aerosol Manufacturers Association, The Copper Development Association, Earth Science Education Unit, ExxonMobil, IET Faraday, Institute of Physics, Institution of Chemical Engineers, Johnson Matthey Catalysts, Millgate House Education, Nirex, Salters' Institute, Society of General Microbiology, Society for Petroleum Engineers, Tata Steel, Texas Instruments, Unilever and Total.

The *upd8* family

upd8 is the principal ASE resources project and comes from a partnership between the Centre for Science Education at Sheffield Hallam University and the Association. *Primary upd8* is a series of high quality, engaging science activities for 5–11 year-olds. Each activity is based on a current event or an everyday life context to help make science lessons in the primary school more enjoyable and relevant. The secondary part of the family comprises a group of four resources: *Crucial, Topicals, Wikid* and *Segue. Crucial for GCSE* was developed to help teachers cope with increasingly demanding assessment at GCSE level and to provide affordable preparation for success. *Topicals* are a series of context-based secondary science activities, written in a punchy and innovative way to engage right across the ability range, for which 45,000 science teachers have registered. *Wikid* is a scheme of work for 14–16 science, which over 800 schools are already using. *Segue* is a complete teaching programme for Year 9 (age 14) science and is designed to provide a smooth transition from Key Stage 3 (age 11–14) to Key Stage 4 (age 14–16).

The overarching aim of these curriculum resources has always been to bring school science into the modern day and to engage and inspire students and teachers alike. Due to support from the DCSF, the AstraZeneca Science Teaching Trust and, in the future, the Comino Foundation, the *Topicals* activities are free to users and some of the *Wikid* development has been funded externally.

These recent initiatives demonstrate that, as throughout the past half century, the Association is responding to the challenges it faces.

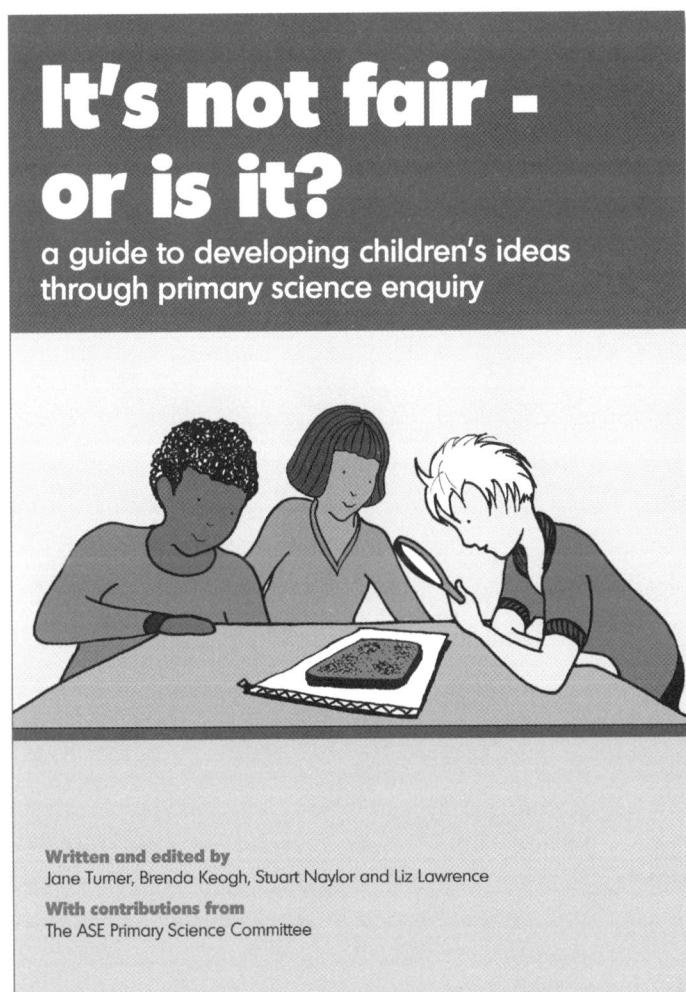

It's not fair - or is it?
a guide to developing children's ideas through primary science enquiry

Written and edited by
Jane Turner, Brenda Keogh, Stuart Naylor and Liz Lawrence

With contributions from
The ASE Primary Science Committee

Figure 8.9: ASE's most recent publishing collaboration has produced It's not fair... or is it? *Originating from development work by the Primary Committee, the book was collaboratively published by Millgate House Education, a company established by innovative ASE members Stuart Naylor and Brenda Keogh.*

Postscript: Looking forward

From Annette Smith, CEO of ASE

From the point of view of the Chief Executive, looking at the previous chapters, there is a lot to be proud of. ASE's engagement with all of the major developments in science education, acting as a leader or leading contributor for the subject association networks and maintaining a respected international presence are all causes for considerable pride. Looking forward, the only firm prediction I can make is that the next 50 years will be different from the past 50 years. This is because, towards the end of 2012, we find ourselves in a position of flux. In England we are anticipating a new National Curriculum and radical reform of the examination system, and there is a growing divergence in the nature of schools. In Scotland, the Curriculum for Excellence is being embedded in schools, but not without challenges, and there are curriculum and examination changes taking place also in Wales and Northern Ireland, leading to increased divergence across the UK. In all of the home countries, radical re-imagining of the examination systems is under way. These changes are all taking place in an environment of budget cuts and recession – not unknown in the past 50 years, but currently on a global scale. However, ASE has 50 years of experience in a variety of prevailing environments. Those who are committed to excellence in the teaching and learning of science will continue to band together in school staff rooms out of hours, at ASE Headquarters, in hotel foyers and in our partners' offices to discuss, develop, debate and produce the support for our members and for the community that has always been our strength.

This book is part of a year of celebration. We will begin by observing the fiftieth anniversary of the date of formation of ASE on 5 January 1963. A number of events at the Annual Conference, including the Annual General Meeting and the launch of this book will mark the anniversary. Following this, the Scottish Conference and Regional conferences will join the celebration and the proposed Summer Celebration Conference will form the focus of the year. Additional opportunities to look back as well as forward will be taken in the journals throughout the year and there is a plan, dependent on the success of the Anniversary Appeal, to use the occasion to refresh ASE's electronic presence and to thoroughly evaluate the major conferences.

Planning for the future is not a trivial task. The past three years during which I have been in the fortunate position of leading ASE have been wildly unpredictable. We have, however, made changes to our structure and our functions which fit us well for the future. I had the vision at the start of my tenure of a small, flexible and efficient HQ operation, able to react quickly to external circumstances and well connected with the membership and with our stakeholders. This vision is on the way to reality in 2012. I hope that in 2013 we will be reflective but not regressive and will use our distinguished past to inform a vibrant future.

I do have some firm predictions, however. Following the Annual Conference in January 2013 and the experiment that is the Summer Celebration Conference, the enormous gathering by which we are so well known will emerge stronger and more relevant. Our successful presence on social media will be consolidated and we will have further success with new, as yet unimagined, forms of electronic communication. Our careful work in researching membership will be translated into actions that will see an increase in membership in some categories and a halt to the decline in others. Our Regions will find themselves in demand for informal professional development events and networking opportunities as the traditional programmes may fall away. In terms of publications, there will be a series of thoughtful monographs and booklets, quickly written to respond to classroom issues. These will move swiftly from writer to reader and will largely be distributed online. Not only will new publications appear online, but considering ASE's roots, I am delighted that the early editions of *School Science Review* are to be digitised and made available on the National STEM Centre elibrary.

You may say that this is all remarkably positive, considering the gloomy current environment. My reasoning is as follows. Chief Executives are by the nature of their position optimists – we have to look to the future and perceive the opportunities ahead. I am sure that this was the stance of my predecessors and I follow them with great hope for the future of the Association for Science Education. I wonder if in 2063 my successors will take time off from travelling around via jetpack to download their memories and hopes for the future so that they can be absorbed directly into the brains of the next generation of science teachers. If so, I hope that they do so with the same pride in the organisation that I feel.

From Liz Lawrence, Chair of ASE for 2013

Although in this postscript we are looking forward to the future it is inevitable that my view of the next 50 years of ASE is shaped by my personal experiences of ASE past and present and its influence on my professional life. ASE has provided many of the learning experiences and personal encounters that have shaped my views of science education and built my capabilities. It is no coincidence that I was appointed to my first post of responsibility, Science and ICT Coordinator, shortly after my first Annual Meeting. At roughly the same time I attended my first section AGM and found myself propelled onto the committee. Opportunities to be involved in consultations, writing groups for ASE publications and the organising group for the local conference followed, along with encouragement to present workshops and become a Region Officer. This experience of receiving and providing CPD and being mentored and challenged was perfect preparation for senior leadership and then an advisory teacher position. Primary Science Committee and the chance to present at national events and work with some of the people who shaped my earlier development as a science teacher perfectly complemented this advisory role and brought me to where I am now, Chair of the Association and looking forward to ASE's Anniversary year.

One of the most exciting changes of recent years is the relatively new facility to have all the professional development that comes with active ASE membership accredited, first through CSciTeach and more recently with the RSci and RSciTech designations. These provide a pathway of professional recognition accessible to different categories of members at different stages in their careers. As numbers grow and they become an expected standard for science education professionals ASE will be able to demonstrate even more clearly its value to members and its contribution to science education in the UK and beyond.

ASE (and education in general) faces many challenges in the next few years. School structures and curriculum and examinations are changing in England and, as noted above, there is an increasing diversity of approach across the nations of the UK. ASE itself is still embedding structural changes, with the new Council and Assembly developing their complementary roles and National and Region Committees evolving alongside them. There are concerns that some things of value may be lost or diluted, but also optimism that the new structures and systems will lead to improvements. It is easy to become inward looking but the Association has always managed to change without losing sight of its core purpose of promoting excellence in science education.

Services to members are also changing and developing. The ASE continues to publish thought-provoking journals and must-have books for science educators but the future also holds an increasing number of e-books and web-based resources and maybe some apps and video clips. In addition to the face-to-face contacts which add such value to membership, meetings happen by conference call and discussions via forums. Members expect to interact with each other, their elected officers and HQ staff in an increasing variety of ways. Website developments and social media enable rapid communication but also create greater pressures to respond and can give excess weight to the opinions of the media savvy and quick-fingered. Compared to the past, the ASE's voice is now one among many making recommendations and debating the issues of science education. Although partnerships provide opportunities to influence and innovate, we still require effective internal communication to ensure that our one voice has the authority of being the collective voice of the membership. More than ever, ASE needs to reach out to all its existing members, draw in new ones and keep the two-way conversation going.

Although this anniversary celebrates the coming together of two organisations to form one, I was recently made aware that our single Association can be viewed as two symbiotic entities: The Association for Science Education, a professionally staffed business and charity, and ASE, a body of members, volunteers, passionate about science education and still drawn together to provide 'opportunities for intercourse and co-operation among those interested in the teaching of science'. The success of the next 50 years will be determined by the strength of both elements and their continuing ability to become more than the sum of their separate parts.

From Edgar Jenkins and Valerie Wood-Robinson, the Editors

When the ASE was formed in 1963, no one could have predicted the profound changes that would take place in schooling in the following half century or anticipate the challenges that these changes would present for the Association and for its members. Science, too, has been transformed. New fields of research and development have emerged, such as molecular biology, nanotechnology and space exploration, and the relationship of science to its public has risen on the political and educational agenda. Although predicting the future is a fruitless undertaking, the challenges facing the ASE in the past 50 years and its responses to them perhaps offer some pointers for the years beyond 2013.

As the preceding chapters make clear, it is the Regions and Sections of the ASE that provide opportunities for the professional development of members and their guests throughout the school year. The continuation of such opportunities will depend not only upon the willingness of relatively few members to devote time and effort to their organisation but also upon the size and support of the membership as a whole. Unlike1963, ASE is now open to all those interested in science education and if it is to speak with authority on behalf of its members, it must ensure that this is adequately reflected in the size and diversity of its membership. From this perspective, the award of Chartered status is an important development that deserves to be more widely recognised.

While the diversification of membership of ASE can be welcomed, it is not without risk. An over-riding interest in science education may well mask the more particular professional or other concerns of different groups of members.

It will be important, therefore, for the Association both to acknowledge this and to respond in appropriate organisational and managerial terms and in the services it offers. Increasingly much of that response will rely upon electronic means of communication, although interactive websites, however well-designed, clearly have limitations as agents of the professional development of teachers of practical science.

This articulation of the needs of different groups of members within the Association gains an added importance in the context within which ASE is now required to operate. Still a major provider of professional activities and support, it is now only one of many organisations active in this field, most of them operating on a commercial basis. While the voluntary work done by, and on behalf of members, is likely to remain fundamental to the effectiveness and credibility of the Association, commercial considerations are likely to increasingly intrude. This has important implications for the contribution that the ASE should seek to make and for the management of the organisation.

The same wider context also requires ASE to collaborate with others in the cause of science education, as, for example, in the work of the Science Community Representing Education (SCORE). Here, too, a clear policy position by the Association can only serve the interests of its members if its voice is not lost among that of many others with an interest in science education. Fortunately, the Association has been well able to retain its independence while working collaboratively and successfully with a range of partners including publishers, learned scientific societies and grant-awarding bodies.

For half a century, ASE has sought to advance science education in ways that range from the Annual Meeting/Conference and an impressive range of publications, to submitting evidence to government committees and the programmes of local and regional activities. However, as this book makes clear, its influence has extended far beyond that stemming from its own initiatives. Leading members of the Association have played seminal individual roles in all the significant school science curriculum developments of the past 50 years, from the Nuffield and Schools Council curriculum projects of the 1960s and 1970s to the working parties set up to advise the Secretaries of State about the content and assessment of the National Curriculum in England and Wales, and in parallel developments in Scotland. That they have been able to do so owes much to the organisation to which they belonged.

ASE has many international contacts, both personal and organisational, beyond the UK. These contacts are likely to become more important as school science curricula acquire a more global character, partly in response to international comparative studies such as PISA and TIMSS. At the same time, increased divergence of the education systems of the four home nations will require co-operation to compare and share good practice outside of specific curriculum frameworks.

In 2013, it is impossible to ignore the extraordinary degree of direct control that central government has secured over science education in recent years. There is little doubt that the issues surrounding standards of achievement, notably pedagogy, assessment and teacher education, will remain firmly on the political agenda, as current plans for radical reform of the examination system in England exemplify. If ASE is to influence these and other issues relating to science education more generally, there will need to be in place adequate structures to allow the Association both to formulate and to respond to policy initiatives that are well-grounded in research and the professional expertise of its members.

Finally, it is worth reminding ourselves that the strength of any organisation stems from the size, engagement and commitment of its members. The chapters in this book reflect those qualities in abundance and they serve, as well as anything can, as a firm pointer to the way forward. It has been a privilege to edit this anniversary book, particularly in the light of its very distinguished antecedent book of the history of ASE. We hope that the succeeding history of the Association, whenever it is produced and in whatever unforetold format, will document further years of continued but developing success.

Appendix: Presidents, Honorary Members, Chairs and Annual Meeting/ Conference venues

Year	Presidents	Honorary Members	Association Chair	Conference Venue
2012	Professor Robin Millar	Professor Phil Scott (posthumus) Mr Alan Rhodes Ms Carys McClure Brown	Mrs Lynne Horton	Liverpool
2011	Professor Steve Jones	Dr Sue Dale Tunnicliffe (The Lady Tunicliffe)	Mr Richard Needham	Reading
2010	Sir Alan Jones	Professor Derek Bell Dr Lyn Haynes Mr Graham Kingsley Dr Roger Lock Ms Lynne Symonds	Mr Manoj Chitnavis	Nottingham
2009	Professor Wynne Harlen	Ms Maggie Hannon Professor Mary Ratcliffe	Ms Carolyn Yates	Reading
2008	Professor Micheal Earwicker	Mr Phil Ramsden Mrs Susan Sharp Mr Keith Ross Mr Mick Revell Dr Jonathan Osborne Mrs Catherine Wilson	Mr Graham Kingsley	Liverpool
2007	Professor Dame Julia Higgins	Mr Duncan Alexander Ms Jane Giffould Mr Roger McCune Mr Malcolm Oakes Mr Ray Vincent	Ms Charlotte Clarke	Birmingham
2006	Sir Gareth Roberts	Dr Martin Hollins Mrs Max de Boo	Mr Bob Kibble	Reading
2005	Sir Mike Tomlinson	Professor Joan Solomon Mr Bob Gallear Mrs Anne Watkinson	Mr David Bevan	Leeds

Year	Presidents	Honorary Members	Association Chair	Conference Venue
2004	Sir Peter Williams	Mr Paul Craig Mrs Caroline McGrath Mr Neil Bonsall Mr John Nellist	Dr Susan Burr	Reading
2003	Dr Gill Samuels	Mr Roy Hawkey Mr Andrew Hunt Dr David Moore OBE Dr Ray Plevey Mrs Betty Preston Mr David Standley	Ms Sue Flanagan	Birmingham
2002	Lord Jenkin of Roding	Mr Andrew Bishop Mr Alan Goodwin	Mr Ian Galloway	Liverpool
2001	Professor Patrick Dowling	Ms Anne Dye Mr Peter Scott	Dr Derek Bell	Surrey
2000	Professor Susan Greenfield	Mr Fred Archenhold Professor Jon Ogborn Mr Maurice Tebbutt Professor Wynne Harlen Dr John Oversby Mr David Archer Mr Alan Welch	Mrs Rebecca Edwards	Leeds
1999	Sir John Horlock	Dr Peter Borrows Dr Neville Evans Mr Jonathan Ling Mr Thomas Scott	Miss Rosemary Feasey	Reading
1998	Mr David Brown	Mr Ken Dobson Mr Christopher Eilliot Mrs Sheila Martin Mr John Slade Mr Joseph Hornsby	Mr Roger McCune	Liverpool

Year	Presidents	Honorary Members	Association Chair	Conference Venue
1997	Sir Brian Follett	Mr Robert Fairbrother Mr Alan Hall Mr Richard Orton Mr Roy Richards	Mrs Mary Ratcliffe	Birmingham
1996	Sir Neil Cossons	Mrs Audrey Randall Mr Ian Robertson Mr Ronald Somerville	Mrs Jane Wheatley	Reading
1995	Dr Bridget Ogilvie	Miss Ruth Schofield Mr David Archer Tawney Professor Richard West	Mr David Standley	Lancaster
1994	Dr David Giachardi	Mr Gerry McKenna Mr Dennis Sutton	Mr Philip Ramsden	Birmingham
1993	Professor Roger Blin-Stoyle	Mrs Norma Broadbridge Miss Joan Fraser Dr Jeff Kirkham Professor Jeff Thompson Dr Martin Brown	Miss Maggie Hannon	Loughborough
1992	Sir John Mason	Mr Vic Green	Dr Boyd Gunnell	Sheffield
1991	Professor Hans Kornberg	Dr Helen Rapson Mr John Carter Mr Carter Dorman Mr Jack Hawkins Professor David Layton	Mrs Elizabeth Preston	Birmingham
1990	Sir Dick Morris CBE	Professor A. Cottenie Mr B.G. Atwood. OBE	Mr E.O. James	Lancaster
1989	Sir Walter Bodmer FRS	Mr J. Jardine Mr A. Garnham	Mr E.O. James (acting)	Birmingham
1988	Baroness Platt of Writtle CBE	Mr J.G. Jones	Mr Graham Hill	Nottingham
1987	Lord Marshall of Goring CBE FRS	-	Miss Angela Dixon	Cardiff
1986	Professor Paul Black CBE KSG	Mr G.E. Foxcroft	Mr John Nellist	York

Year	Presidents	Honorary Members	Association Chair	Conference Venue
1985	Sir George Porter FRS	Mr D.V. Clish Professor H. Halliwell Miss E.W. McCreath MBE	Mr Geoff Barraclough	Keele
1984	Sir James Hamilton KCB MBE	Mr D.W. Harlow Mr J.L.Lewis OBE Professor Harry Messel CBE Mr S.W. Scott	Mr P.J. Scott	Exeter
1983	Sir Robert Clayton CBE FEng	Dr M.M. Collis OBE Mr D.V. Hillier	Miss Ruth Schofield	Manchester
1982	Sir Hermann Bondi KCB FRS	Mr J.S.G. McGeachin	Mr Maurice Savory	Kent
1981	Sir Denis Rooke CBE FRS FEng	-	Mr Jeff Thompson	Warwick
1980	Sir Norman Lindop	Mr D.G. Chisman Mr J. Dawber	Mr John Healey	Hull
1979	Mr Norman Booth	Mr C.W. Othen OBE Mr C.G. Clark Mr J.A. Pool	Mr A.R. Hall	Reading
1978	Mr Norman Booth	Miss Helen Ward Professor H. Lipson FRS		
1977	Sir Alistair Pilkington FRS	Mr Kenneth Pinnock	Mr Dick West	Liverpool
1976	Professor J.F. Kerr	Mr J.C. Siddons	Mr J.L. Lewis	Leicester
1975	Lord Bullock	Dr R.H. Carleton Mr J.J. Bryant	W.J. Kirkham A.A. Bishop	Oxford Durham
1974	Sir Derman Christopherson OBE FRS	Miss F.N. Eastwood Mr R. Thurlow	Mrs J Glover	Leeds
1973	Lord Boyle of Handsworth	Mr N.C. Flower Professor Stacey CBE FRS Mr R.M. Lee	W.F. Archenhold	Birmingham

Year	Presidents	Honorary Members	Association Chair	Conference Venue
1971-2	Mrs M.K. McQuillan	Professor E.H. Coulson OBE Mrs E.W. Tapper Mr E.W. Tapper	E.G. Breeze	Stirling
1970-1	Dr J.L. Cottrell	Mr N. Booth Mr F.C. Brown	B.G. Atwood	Sussex
1969-70	Professor E.R. Laithwaite	Mr I.G. Jones Mr H. Tunley	Helen Ward	Lancaster
1968-9	Mr J.D. Rose FRS	Sir Arthur Vick Mr W.H. Dowland Mr H.P. Ramage	E.H. Coulson	Bristol
1967-8	Professor Sir Ronald Nyholm FRS	Mr H.G. Andrew Dr F.H. Boulind Mr A.J. Mee Professor J.E. Harris Miss C.P. Jones Mr R.W. Stanhope	F.C. Brown	Imperial College, London
1966-7	Professor Sir Ronald Nyholm FRS	Mr M.K. Cassels Dame Kathleen Lonsdale FRS P. Kapitza	J.J Bryant	Nottingham
1965-6	Lord F S Dainton	Sir John Baker OBE FRS Mr R.H. Dyball Sir Nevill Mott FRS	H.F. Broad	Cambridge
1965	Sir John Cockcroft	Professor Dorothy Hodgkin FRS	R.H. Dyball	Imperial College, London
1964	Sir Patrick Linstead	-	Miss F.M. Eastwood	Birmingham
1963	Sir Robert Aitken	-	R. Thurlow	Manchester

Between 1964 and 1972 The Annual Meeting took place over New Year.

References

Chapter 1

Adlam, G.H.J. (1920) 'A Plea for General Science', *School Science Review*, **2**, (5), 197–202

APSSM (1916) *Minute Book*, 22nd May. ASE Archive. University of Leeds, Brotherton Library

AWST (1936) *Report 1935–36*, Association of Women Science Teachers

AWST (1950) *Annual Report 1949–50*, Association of Women Science Teachers

AWST (1962) *Executive Committee Minutes 17th March 1962*, ASE Archive. University of Leeds, Brotherton Library

BAAS (1917) *Report of the Eighty-Sixth Meeting 1916*. London: John Murray

BAAS (1923) *Report of the Meeting 1922*. London: John Murray

Board of Education (1943) *Curriculum and Examinations in Secondary Schools*. London: HMSO Central Advisory Council for Education (England) (1959)

London: HMSO Central Advisory Council for Education (England) (1963) *Half Our Future*. London: HMSO

Jenkins, E.W. (1973) 'The Board of Education and the Reconstruction Committee', *Journal of Educational Administration and History*, **V**, (i), 42–50

Jenkins, E.W. (1979) *From Armstrong to Nuffield; Studies in twentieth century science education in England and Wales*. London: John Murray

Layton, D. (1984) *Interpreters of Science: A History of the Association for Science Education*. London/Hatfield: John Murray/ASE

SMA (1922) *Report for 1922*

SMA (1938) *The Teaching of General Science, Part II*. London: John Murray

SMA (1957) *Minutes of General Committee, 2 March 1957*, ASE Archive. University of Leeds, Brotherton Library

SMA (1961) *Minute Book*. ASE Archive. See also *School Science Review*, **43**, (151), 675–676

SMA/AWST (1961) *Science and Education: A Policy Statement issued by The Science Masters' Association and The Association of Women Science Teachers*. London: John Murray

School Science Review, (1937), **13**, 134–136, London: John Murray

Tilden, Sir W. (1919) *School Science Review* **1**, (1), 12

Chapter 2

ASE (1963–1971) Executive Committee *Minutes*. ASE Archive. University of Leeds, Brotherton Library

Jenkins, E.W. (2009) *75 Years and More: The Association for Science Education in Yorkshire*. Hatfield: ASE (Yorkshire Region)

Layton, D. (1984) *Interpreters of Science: A History of the Association for Science Education*, London/Hatfield: John Murray/ASE

Chapter 3

ASE (1981) *Education through Science: a Policy Statement*. Hatfield: ASE

ASE (1990) *Balanced Science Policy Statement*. Hatfield: ASE

ASE Scottish Region (1991) *The Place of Science in a Balanced Curriculum Policy Statement*. Hatfield: ASE

ASE (2000) *STAR*: Science, technology and reading*. Hatfield: ASE

Bell, D. (2006) 'Editorial', *Education in Science*, (216), 3

Bell, D. (2008) 'Editorial', *Education in Science*, (230), 3

Bell, D. (2009) 'Editorial', *Education in Science*, (231), 3

Bell, D. (2010) *Leading Debate: Twenty-one Years of the National Curriculum for Science*. London: Wellcome Trust

Campbell, P. (Ed) (2000) *Shaping the Future*. Bristol: Institute of Physics Publishing

Central Advisory Council for Education (England) (1963) *Half Our Future*. London: HMSO

Department of Education and Welsh Office (1985) *Science 5–16: A Statement of Policy*. London: HMSO

Donnelly, J.F., Buchan, A., Jenkins, E., Laws, P. and Welford, G. (1996) *Investigations by Order: Policy, curriculum and science teachers' work under the Education Reform Act*. Driffield: Studies in Education Ltd.

Finegold, P. and Wymer, P. (1997) 'Science Education for the Year 2000', *Education in Science*, (172), 10

Goldsworthy, A. (1997) 'Dream On', *Education in Science*, (172), 8

Harrison, C. (2011) 'Assessment for Learning'. In: M. Hollins (Ed) *ASE Guide to Secondary Science Education*. Hatfield: ASE

Holman, J. (2008) 'STEM, Science Learning Centres and the ASE', *Education in Science*, (227), 8

Hull, R. and Adams, H. (1981) *Decisions in the Science Department*. Hatfield: ASE/ Schools Council

Hunt, A. (2011) 'Five Decades of Innovation and Change'. In: M. Hollins, (Ed) *ASE Guide to Secondary Education*. Hatfield: ASE

Jenkins, E.W. (1998) 'The Association for Science Education and the struggle to establish a policy for school science in England and Wales, 1976–81', *History of Education*, **27,** (4) 441-459.

Jenkins, E.W. (2006) 'The Student Voice and School Science Education', *Studies in Science Education*, (42), 49–99

Kibble, B. (2006) 'Just How Does Science work?', *Education in Science*, (216), 13

Layton, D. (1984) *Interpreters of Science: A History of the Association for Science Education*. London/Hatfield: John Murray/ASE

Lewis, J. (1981) *Science in Society*. London: Heinemann

McCune, R. (1998) 'Science Education for the Year 2000 and Beyond', *Education in Science*, (176), 17

Millar, R. and Osborne, J. (1998) *Beyond 2000*. London: King's College London

Munn, J. *et al*. (1977) *The Structure of the Curriculum in the Third and Fourth Years of the Scottish Secondary School*. Edinburgh: HMSO

Osborne, J. and Collins, S. (2000) *Pupils' and Parents' Views of the School Science Curriculum*. London: King's College, London

Osborne, J. and Dillon, J. (2008) *Science Education in Europe: Critical Reflections*. London: Nuffield Foundation

Qualifications and Curriculum Authority (2000a) *Science: A Scheme of Work for Key Stages 1 and 2*. London: QCA

Qualifications and Curriculum Authority (2000b) *Science: A Scheme of Work for Key Stage 3*. London: QCA

Ramsden, P. (1995) 'Science Education for the Year 2000 and Beyond', *Education in Science*, (164), 28

Roberts, G. (2002) *SET for Success: The supply of people with science, technology, engineering and mathematical skills*. London: HM Treasury

Roberts, R. (2009) 'How science works (HSW)', *Education in Science*, (233), 30

Scottish Executive (2004) *A Curriculum for Excellence: Ministerial Response*. Edinburgh: The Scottish Executive

Scottish Office Education Department (1983) *16–18s in Scotland: An Action Plan*. Edinburgh: SOED

Scottish Office Education Department (1993) *Environmental Studies 5-14*. Edinburgh: SOED

Shayer, M. & Adey, P. (1981) *Towards a Science of Science Teaching*. London: Heinemann

Solomon, J. (1983) *SISCON in Schools*. Oxford: Blackwell and Hatfield: ASE

Solomon, J. (1996) *Primary Technology Using Stories from History*. Hatfield: ASE

Waring, M. (1979) *Social Pressures and Curriculum Innovation*. London: Methuen

Watts, M. (2000) *Creative Trespass: Fusing Science and Poetry in the Classroom*. Hatfield: ASE

Westbrook, G. (2010) 'Getting Practical: Improving practical work in science', *Education in Science*, (237), 36

Chapter 4

Alexander, R. (Ed) (2010) *Children, their World, their Education*. London: Routledge

Assessment Reform Group (ARG) (2002) *Testing, Motivation and Learning.* http://www.assessment-reform-group.org/TML%20BOOKLET%20complete.pdf

ASE (1963) *Policy Statement,* prepared by the Primary Schools Science Committee

ASE (1991) *Change in our Future – a Challenge for Science Education.* Hatfield: ASE

ASE (1999) *Science and the Literacy Hour: Executive Summary.* Hatfield: ASE

ASE (2009) 'The Rose Review and the Association for Science Education', *Primary Science Review,* (110), 4–7

Association of Women Science Teachers (AWST) (1959) *Science in the Primary School.* London: John Murray

BAAS (1908) *Report of the Annual Meeting 1908.* London: John Murray

BAAS (1962) *The Place of Science in Primary Education.* London: BAAS

Begg, J. (1993) 'The National Curriculum in primary schools – is it working?', *Primary Science Review,* (28), 4–5

Boyers, P. (1967) *Report to the Department of Education and Science on an Enquiry into the Formation of Scientific Concepts in Children 5–13.* Oxford: University of Oxford Institute of Education

Central Advisory Council for Education (England) (1967) *Children and their Primary Schools.* London: HMSO

Coleman, K. (2001) 'Why SATS are bad for science', *Primary Science Review,* (68), 27

Collis, M. (2001) 'Primary Science in the 1950s and 1960s', in: M. de Boo and A. Randall (Eds) *Celebrating a Century of Primary Science.* Hatfield: ASE

Crossland, R. W. (1967) *Report of an Individual Study of the Nuffield Foundation Primary Science Project.* Manchester: University of Manchester

Department for Education (2011) *Independent Review of KS2 Testing, Assessment and Accountability.* London: DfE

Department of Education and Science and Welsh Office (1982) *Science Education in Schools: A consultative document.* London: DES/WO

Department of Education and Science and Welsh Office (1985) *Science 5–16: A Statement of Policy*. London: DES/WO

de Boo, M. and Randall, A. (Eds) (2001) *Celebrating a Century of Primary Science*. Hatfield: ASE

Evans, P. (1997) *Primary School Technology*. Trent Polytechnic: National Centre for School Technology

Goldsworthy, A., Watson, R. and Wood-Robinson, V. (2000) *Investigations: Targeted Learning*. Hatfield: ASE

Harlen, W. (1975) *Science 5–13: a Formative Evaluation*. London: Macmillan Educational

Harlen, W. (1983) *Science at Age 11. APU Science Report for Teachers: 1*. London: DES/WO

Harlen, W. (1986) 'Technology and science: problems with words', *Primary Science Review*, (1), 26–27

Harlen, W., Palacio, D. and Russell, T. (1984) *Science Assessment Framework Age 11. APU Science Report for Teachers: 4*. London: DES/WO

Harrison, S. (2001) 'SATS and the QCA standards report', *Primary Science Review*, (68), 28

Jenkins, E.W. and Swinnerton, B.J. (1998) *Junior School Science Education in England and Wales since 1900*. London: Woburn Press

Layton, D. (1984) *Interpreters of Science: A History of the Association for Science Education*. London/Hatfield: John Murray/ASE

Murphy, P. (1999) 'Science and literacy – moving forward?', *Primary Science Review*, (59), 2

National Curriculum Council (NCC) (1993) *The National Curriculum at Key Stages 1 and 2, Advice to the Secretary of State for Education*. London: NCC

Peck, S. (1989) 'Implementing the National Curriculum in a first school', *Primary Science Review*, (10), 19

Rapson, H. (2001) 'Changing perspectives', in M. de Boo and A. Randall (Eds) *Celebrating a Century of Primary Science*. Hatfield: ASE

The Royal Society (2010) *Science and Mathematics Education, 5–14. A State of the Nation Report*. London: The Royal Society

Slade, J., Hill, S., Petrie, P., Wilson, J. and the IPSE team (1987) 'What is good primary science?', *Primary Science Review,* (4), 22–23

Sturman, L., Ruddock, G., Burge, B., Styles, B., Lin, Y. and Vappula, H. (2008) *England's Achievement in TIMSS 2007: national report for England.* Slough: NFER

Wright, L., Wiggin, D. and Davis, R. (2001) 'Conversations with Gavin: the Five Year Study', *Primary Science Review,* (67), 26–28

Chapter 5

Department of Education (1985) *Education Observed (3): Good Teachers.* London: DES

Department of Education and Science and Welsh Office (1985) *Science 5–16: A Statement of Policy.* London: DES/WO

Donnelly, J., Buchan, A., Jenkins, E., Laws, P. and Welford, G. (1996) *Investigations by Order: Policy, curriculum and science teachers' work under the Education Reform Act.* Driffield: Studies in Education Ltd.

Jenkins, E.W. (1998) 'The Association for Science Education and the struggle to establish a policy for school science in England and Wales', *History of Education,* **27,** (4), 441–459

McCulloch, G., Jenkins, E. and Layton, D. (1985) *Technological Revolution? The politics of school science and technology in England and Wales since 1945.* Lewes: Falmer Press

Royal Society (1982) *Science Education 11–18 in England and Wales,* London: Royal Society

Chapter 6

ASE (1981,1983) *Technicians' Guides series.* Hatfield: ASE

ASE (1981) *Education through Science.* Hatfield: ASE

ASE (1990) *Technical Support for School Science.* Hatfield: ASE

ASE (1992) *ASE Policy, Present and Future.* Hatfield: ASE

ASE (1994) *School Technicians: An invaluable asset.* Hatfield: ASE

ASE (1997, 2003) *The Prep Room Organiser.* Hatfield: ASE

ASE (1998) *Summary of Policies.* Hatfield: ASE

ASE (2005, 2008) *Working with Glass, Preparation of Gases, Preparing Solutions.* Hatfield: ASE

ASE/ Royal Society/CLEAPSS (2004) *A Career Structure for Science Technicians in Schools and Colleges.* Hatfield: ASE/Royal Society/CLEAPSS

CLEAPSS (2002) *L228 Technicians and their jobs.* Uxbridge: CLEAPSS

Layton, D. (1984) *Interpreters of Science: A History of the Association for Science Education*, London/Hatfield: John Murray/ASE

Ministry of Education (1956) *The White Paper on Technical Education*, In S. Maclure, (Ed) (1965) *Educational Documents, England and Wales 1816–1963.* London: Chapman and Hall

Pearson, C.D. (1999) *School Science Technicians and the Requirements of Science Teachers.* Unpublished MA, University of York

Royal Society/ASE (2001) *Survey of Science Technicians in Schools and Colleges.* London: Royal Society/ASE.

Royal Society/ASE (2002) *Supporting Success: Science technicians in schools and colleges.* London: Royal Society/ASE

Royal Society/ASE/CLEAPSS (2003) *Supporting success: Developing a career structure for science technicians in schools and colleges.* London: Royal Society/ASE/CLEAPSS

SWDB (2009) *Developing People to Support Learning – a skills strategy for the wider school workforce 2006–9.* London: School Workforce Development Board

Chapter 7

ASE (1965, 1972, 1976, 1981, 1988, 1996, 2006) *Safeguards in the School Laboratory.* Hatfield: ASE

ASE (1969, 1974, 1981) *SI Units, Signs, Symbols and Abbreviations.* Hatfield: ASE

ASE (1972, 1982, 1990) *Safety in the Lab.* Hatfield: ASE

ASE (1972, 1979,1985) *Chemical Nomenclature, Symbols and Terminology.* Hatfield: ASE

ASE (1975) *The use of SI units in the early and middle years of schooling.* Hatfield: ASE

ASE (1982, 1988, 2001) *Topics in Safety*, Hatfield: ASE

ASE (1986, 1997, 2001, 2004, 2009) *Education in Science*, (116), 23; (171), 16; (194), 29; (208), 32; (232), 26

ASE (1988, 1990, 2001, 2011) *Be Safe!*. Hatfield: ASE

ASE (1989) *Building for Science, a Laboratory Design Guide*. Hatfield: ASE

ASE (1992, 1994, 2000) *Management of Safety: a course for Heads of Science*. Hatfield: ASE

ASE (1994, 2002) *Safety in Science for Primary Schools, an INSET Pack*. Hatfield: ASE

ASE (1995) *Be Safe! Aspects of Health and Safety in the Scottish Curriculum Environmental Studies 5–14*. Hatfield: ASE

ASE (1995) *Signs, Symbols and Systematics, the ASE companion to 5–16 science*. Hatfield: ASE

ASE (1995, 1999, 2004) *Science Technicians' Health and Safety Course*. Hatfield: ASE

ASE (1996, 1998, 2000, 2005), *Safety Reprints*. Hatfield: ASE

ASE (1997) *Professional Development Pack, based on Be Safe! Aspects of Health and Safety in the Scottish Curriculum Environmental Studies 5–14*. Hatfield: ASE

ASE (1997) *The World of Science. New SATIS 14–16*. London: John Murray for ASE

ASE (1998) *Signs and Symbols in Primary Science*. Hatfield: ASE

ASE (1998, 2006, 2011) *The ASE Guide to Secondary Science Education*. Hatfield: ASE

ASE (1999, 2009) *Safe and Exciting Science, A pack of training activities*. Hatfield: ASE

ASE (2000) *Signs, Symbols and Systematics, the ASE companion to 16–18 science*. Hatfield: ASE

ASE (2010) *The Language of Measurement: Terminology used in school science investigations*. Hatfield: ASE

Borrows, P., Vincent, R.and Cochrane, A. (1998) 'Teaching safety: using mole calculations to teach aspects of safety in post-16 chemistry', *School Science Review*, **79,** (288), 67

DES (1976) *AM7/76 The Use of Asbestos in Educational Establishments*. London: HMSO

DES (1978) *Safety in Science Laboratories,* 3rd edition. London: HMSO

DfEE (1996) *Safety in Science Education*. London: HMSO

Feasey, R. (1998) *Primary Science Equipment*. Hatfield: ASE

Hull, R. (Ed) (1993) *The ASE Science Teachers' Handbook*. Hatfield: ASE

Institute of Biology (1989) *Biological Nomenclature.* London: Institute of Biology

Ministry of Education (1960) *Safety Precautions in Schools, Pamphlet No. 13*, 2nd edition. London: Ministry of Education

McGlashan, M.L. (1968) 'Physico-Chemical Quantities and Units, The Grammar and Spelling of Physical Chemistry', *Royal Institute of Chemistry Monographs for Teachers No. 15*. London: RIC

Nellist, J. and Nicholl, B. (Eds) (1986) *The ASE Science Teachers' Handbook*. Hatfield: ASE

Royal Society (1969, 1971) *Metrication in Secondary Education* (1969), *Metrication in Primary Schools* (1969), *Symbols, Signs and Abbreviations* (1969), *Quantities, Units and Symbols* (1971). London: Royal Society

Royal Society of Chemistry (2005) *Surely that's Banned?* London: Royal Society of Chemistry

Sutcliffe, A. (1950) *School Laboratory Management*, 2nd edition. London: John Murray, Chapter VIII

Whitcher, R. (2011) 'Practical Work using Low-level Radioactive Materials Available to the Public', *School Science Review*, **92**, (341), 65

Chapter 8

ASE (1978) *Electrical Safety for the Users of School Laboratories*, ASE edition of CLEAPSE guide L868 (1976)

ASE (1982, 1988, 2001) *Topics in Safety*. Hatfield: ASE

ASE (2011) *Be Safe! 4th edition* Hatfield: ASE

ASE (1988a) *IPSE Report (Foreword)*. Hatfield: ASE

ASE (1988b) *The School in Focus (Appendices)*. Hatfield: ASE

ASE/CLEAPSS (1991) *Health and Safety Checks on Science Texts: Guidance for publishers, authors, editors and readers*. Hatfield: ASE

ASE (1995) *Be Safe! Some Aspects of Health and Safety in the Scottish Curriculum Environmental Studies 5–14*. Hatfield: ASE

ASE (2011) *Responses from ASE 2011 Membership Survey*

Bell, M. (2007) 'Putting the e in NVQs!', *Education in Science*, (223), 10–11

Broadbridge, N. and Wilkinson, M. (1997) 'Honouring excellence', *Education in Science*, (174), 14–15

Burden, J. (2001) 'Science Year – what's in it for you?', *Education in Science*, (193), 4

Burden, J., Sherborne, T. and Heslop, N. (2001) 'ASE Science Year: bringing science into the classroom', *Education in Science*, (193), 8–9

CfSA (2011) www.subjectassociation.org.uk [Accessed 02.12.11]

CLEAPSS (1996), *L216p / L216s, Inspecting Safety in Science: A guide for Ofsted inspectors in primary/secondary schools*, Uxbridge: CLEAPSS

DES (1965) *Administrative Memorandum AM1/65, The Use of Ionising Radiations in Schools, Establishments of Further Education and Teacher Training Colleges*. London: HMSO

DES (1978) *Safety in Science Laboratories,* 3rd edition. London: HMSO

DES (1987) *AIDS: Some questions and answers, facts for teachers, lecturers and youth workers*. London: HMSO

DES/WO (1984) *DES Circular No. 6/84* and *WO Circular No. 39/84*

DES/WO (1985) *Science 5–16: A statement of Policy*. London: HMSO

DfEE (1996) *Safety in Science Education*, London: HMSO

HSE (1983, 1990), *Guidance Note GS23, Electrical Safety in Schools*, London: HSE

Hull, R. and Adams, H. (1981) *Decisions in the Science Department*. Hatfield: ASE/ Schools Council

Layton, D. (1984) *Interpreters of Science: A History of the Association for Science Education*. London/Hatfield: John Murray/ASE

National Centre for Biotechnology Education (2002) *Plant Tissue Culture*. In www.ncbe.reading.ac.uk/ncbe/protocols/PDF/PTC2002.pdf [Accessed December 2011]

National STEM Centre (2011) www.nationalstemcentre.org.uk/elibrary [Accessed 28.11.11]

SYCD (2001) www.sycd.co.uk [Accessed 26.09.11]

Watts, M. and McGrath, C. (1998) 'SATIS factions: approaches to relevance', *School Science Review,* **79,** (288), 61–65

Wilkinson, M. (1984) *Education in Science*

Index